Kuhlhoff on Guns

KUHLHOFF ON GUNS

by Pete Kuhlhoff

WINCHESTER PRESS

Library of Congress Catalog Card Number: 70-99751

ISBN: 0-87691-009-6

Published by Winchester Press,
460 Park Avenue, New York 10022

PRINTED IN THE UNITED STATES OF AMERICA

Contents

1

What Makes a Gun Buff?

IN AMERICA WE HAVE more dedicated gun enthusiasts than in any other locality in the world. The group includes over 20,000,000 hunters who took to the field this past season, plus target shooters and the many specialized collectors.

Hunters vary from those who own a rifle or shotgun to those who have a complete assortment of sporting arms and are equipped for any kind of hunting or shooting. The one-shotgun individual usually gets out one or more times a year for upland or waterfowl shooting, while the one-rifle man, in most instances, has a deer gun and manages a trek to whitetail country for a day or so, maybe a week, each fall. Both wish they could get out more often.

The chaps who own a battery of guns can be divided into two categories: those who are intrigued by and make an intense study of our latest sporting weapons (they actually are collectors of modern guns who go hunting once in a while) and the real hunters who manage to arrange their lives so that they are in the field regularly, with at least a couple of more or less elaborate trips each year and a lot of off-season shooting on varmints and clay targets.

Collectors range from the odds-and-ends picker-upper, who likes to monkey around with guns of all kinds and learn something about them as mechanical gadgets and a little about their history, to the specialist who makes a definite plan for a collection—say, a certain type of military or sporting weapon, perhaps a certain make, or maybe arms of a period in history; the field is almost unlimited. Members of the latter group are the ones who dig up little-known or forgotten information, assemble it in orderly fashion and make it available to others. These fellows almost always are members of gun collectors' clubs or societies. They arrange and schedule regular meetings for exchange of newly unearthed dope and maybe do a little dickering.

What makes a gun buff and how do they get that way? First, they all have inquiring minds and almost without exception they are fascinated by expert workmanship. Circumstance is nearly always responsible for an individual following any one of the tangents of the gun field. I knew one fellow who became interested in gun collecting after he had retired from business. He was a perfectionist, and in a few years he had assembled one of the finest collections in the country. Another friend found some old guns in the attic of the ancestral home, and started a collection. He became interested in shooting the old ones and finally turned to modern sporting arms. Hunting became a hobby and now he has game trophies from all over the world. Let's take a hypothetical case and see how an individual may start and then develop into a real gun buff.

When a solid citizen—let's call him Joe Gunbuff—goes to a gun or hardware store to buy a gun, perhaps his first rifle or a first rifle for his son or daughter, the chances are that he will take home a bolt-action .22 rimfire single or repeater, and a couple of boxes of ammo. After unwrapping the package, he discovers that the rifle was packed as three separate parts, and his gun education begins. He examines the stock with the trigger guard and butt plate mounted in place, looks over the unit comprising the barrel and receiver, finds that the latter is a housing for the bolt and for the trigger mechanism which is in place, and finally discovers the bolt secured in the package to keep it from rattling around. Eager to get the gun together, he digs out the assembly directions and in a few minutes has a brand-new rifle put together, cleaned of excess oil and all ready to shoot.

Our new gun custodian had little or no gun savvy and he was honest enough to admit the fact at the next meeting of the poker seven. One of the boys gave him a copy of the little "Handbook on Small Bore Rifle Shooting," which was published by the Sporting Arms and Ammunition Manufacturers' Institute, New York, and a couple of other gun books to read. He learned that such simple words as bedding, rib, throat, keyhole, seat and twist, to mention just a few, have somewhat different meanings when applied to firearms. He discovered that a cartridge is the complete assembly of primer, cartridge case, power charge and projectile or bullet, commonly used in conjunction with rifled arms as compared to shell or shot shell for shotguns. At this point, our hero found that he was slightly annoyed when some hard-pressed gunslinger or private eye of the TV or flicker world complained of being just about out of bullets. How stupid can those script writers get? Anyone knows that the word is cartridges, not bullets! Yep, Joe Gunbuff was gradually getting hep to gun parlance.

He dug a bit deeper and found that the Boxer-type primer (developed by Colonel Boxer of the British Ordnance Department) has been standard in the United States since about 1900. This primer, which is pressed into the primer pocket located in the base or head of the cartridge case, is composed of three parts: a primer cup; the primer compound, a mixture that is sensitive to friction or percussion; and the anvil, against which the primer compound is mashed and exploded when the firing pin of the gun

A few of the many elements that contribute to the making of a gun buff.

strikes the primer cup. (The primer compound is mechanically spun into the rim of rimfire cartridges.) The hot flame of the exploded primer flashes into the case to ignite the powder charge. Smokeless powder burns very rapidly when confined, and creates a large volume of gas which exerts great pressure to propel the bullet from the barrel at velocities as high as 4,110 feet per second for the .220 Swift cartridge, or more than 2,800 miles per hour. This is like running head-on into a 2,800-mile-per-hour hurricane—and, brother, that is no gentle breeze for a bullet to overcome on its way to the target! No wonder the shape of a bullet is so important in determining its ability to travel accurately for a great distance.

The pressure developed in the rifle chamber may be as high as 50,000 or 55,000 pounds per square inch, depending on the cartridge. The cartridge case, usually made of brass, is the element that seals the breech, or rear portion of the barrel bore, so that there is no gas leak at that point. It is quite weak, when the pressures developed within it are considered, so that it must be adequately supported by good steel around the chamber and in the breech bolt, and the fit of the supporting parts must be just about perfect. Pressure developed in a gun can raise havoc if it gets out of control.

This brings up a measurement called head space. When this dimension is not correct, the cartridge may not be supported, and the brass of the case may receive gas pressure that it cannot possibly withstand, resulting in possible disaster. Head space is the proper distance from the surface of the chambered cartridge that keeps it from moving forward, back to the face of the bolt or breechblock that supports it in position for firing. If that sounds like double talk to you, read it again, because head space is one dimension, more than any other, that under certain conditions may govern the safety of the arm and the shooter. It is a measurement that is checked and rechecked in arms for high-intensity cartridges when they are being manufactured, and double-checked after proof firing and routine firing before the gun is packed for shipment.

While reading and discussing gun lore for his liberal education in gunology, our now really enthusiastic Joe Gunbuff has added several firearms to his gun cabinet—a deer rifle, a shotgun for a little bird and rabbit shooting, a .22 handgun for target shooting, and an old single-shot centerfire rifle that was made in the 1870s. He bought that single-shot simply because he liked its looks and was fascinated by the fine workmanship. Joe had a slight twinge of conscience over that last deal, because the money he laid out would have bought the little helpmate several new hats. In fact, he sneaked it into the house late one evening, and wondered how in the world he would explain the half-dozen other guns he really needed and intended to get.

When searching for information about the single-shot rifle—this was before James J. Grant's fine books on the subject were in existence—Joe learned that all early cartridges were of the rimmed variety and that most of them had cases with straight sides. And that was when he first ran across the term head space which, with rimmed and semi-rimmed cartridges—be they for rifle, shotgun, or pistol—is the distance from the part of the barrel or chamber against which the cartridge rim abuts to the face of the bolt or breechblock. If the measurement is greater than standard for the particular cartridge, the gun is said to have excess head space, and trouble may begin. Head space with any kind of gun can get out of adjustment by extreme wear, mistreatment, or corrosion.

Excess head space in arms for rimfire cartridges may result in poor ignition and loss of accuracy, misfires or hangfires, bulged cartridge heads or blown rims or heads, with gas and debris under pressure blowing back. Joe learned the hard way about excess head space in rimfire guns when he was shooting an old, rattly .22 that should have been retired. The blowback did no damage—Joe was wearing shooting glasses—but it did encourage him to tell all his acquaintances never to shoot an old gun without first having it checked by a reliable gunsmith. Rather pleased with himself, he further explained that if head-space measurement is less than the thickness of the rim with rimfire cartridges—in effect, this can be caused by dirt and dried grease under the rim—the rim may be squeezed and the cartridge fired when the bolt is slammed forward. This is a surprising and unsettling experience for the shooter and may be dangerous to bystanders. So, cautioned Joe, "Take good care of that twenty-two. Keep it clean and well protected."

Having had the unpleasant experience with excess head space, Joe explained to anyone who would listen, that with rimmed, semi-rimmed, rimless or belted centerfire cartridges, the old bugbear may be responsible for uneven ignition and poor accuracy, hangfires or misfires, protruding or blown primers, and that the head might separate from the case and gas blast to the rear.

A simple question such as, "What is the difference between these different types of cartridges?" gave Joe that heady, satisfied feeling usually associated with a good belt of whiskey, and he shifted into high.

"Well, sir," he would say, "back during the days when repeating rifles having box magazines were first being made—you know, like the Mauser and Springfield—it was found that the rims of the cartridges made it difficult for them to be fed smoothly from the magazine into the chamber. To solve the problem, the rimless type of cartridge with an extracting groove cut into the circumference near the base was developed. As the rim of such a cartridge is no larger in diameter than the body, the rim cannot be used to limit the forward movement of the cartridge as it is seated into the chamber. So head space for bottleneck, rimless cartridges is measured from the face of the breech bolt to a point on the shoulder toward the front end of the chamber.

"The forty-five Automatic is an outstanding example of the rimless cartridge with straight sides. It has the forward edge or mouth of the case left square and not crimped around the bullet as with other pistol, revolver and most rifle cartridges. Here the forward motion of the cartridge is stopped when the mouth of the case makes contact with a square lip or shoulder at the forward end of the chamber." Then he would add with quite some aplomb: "The United States Carbine, caliber .30, M1, which I carried in Korea, is another good example of a gun that fires this type of cartridge where head space is the length of the chamber to the face of the bolt face.

"Belted cartridges are most modern, and they probably are the strongest and safest cartridges we have today. The new Winchester series, the .458, .338 and .264 magnum cartridges, as well as the Weatherby magnums and the older English Holland and Holland magnums all are of belted type. They have a narrow band around the base of the case and are positioned in the chamber on the front ledge of the belt for positive head-spacing."

By now, Joe Gunbuff was a fountain of information for all local shooters. He continued his discourse: "Knowledge of metallurgy, making it possible to use alloys especially compounded to best meet specific requirements, plus up-to-date manufacturing practices where precision is the watchword, have practically eliminated the head-space problem as far as the shooter of modern guns is concerned. However, some of the old, well-worn guns that are floating around the country may not have a clean bill of health. Symptoms of excess head space are easy to spot. First, the case stretches. Then comes the beginning of a crack. The last phase is partial or complete separation at that point. Head space gauges are usually made in sets of three, Go, No-Go and Field, for each caliber. Many gunsmiths have them for checking customers' rifles."

Good old Joe certainly was absorbing a lot of gun information and, being keenly interested, he managed to get to the local range about once a week for practice. So his skill as a shooter gradually improved. After he bought his shotgun, he found that making hits with the scattergun was not as easy as he had imagined.

Fortunately, an experienced shotgun shooter gave him the word without fancy work. "If you really want to learn to shoot a shotgun, you'll have to shoot and shoot—I mean, shoot with regularity. Maybe," the sage continued, "I can tell you what not to do, and what to try to do, but I can't tell you how to do it. You—that is, your mind, eyes, nerves and muscle—are involved in an act of co-ordination. The idea is to make the load of shot and the target arrive at the same place at the same time. Remember, the only thing you have control over is the gun. The shot charge, after it leaves the barrel, and the moving target are free agents. If the target is falling, the gun has to point under it. If the target is rising, the gun has to point above it. For a passing target, the gun has to swing along a certain distance in front of it. No one can tell you how far to swing past it because different people take different lengths of time to pull the trigger. Some guys who lean toward the scientific, call it reaction time. Shooting experience is the only thing that will pay off. With practice, you soon will begin to retain mental images of the target in relation to where the gun is pointing with your shots, and you'll really begin to improve."

With those words in mind, Joe decided to learn to shoot a shotgun. He bought a hand trap, a case of shells and a couple of cartons of clay targets, and headed for a nearby spot where he could shoot safely and by himself. At first, he felt clumsy holding the gun in his left hand while snapping the clay target on its way with the hand trap in his right hand, dropping the trap, recovering his balance, getting the gun to his shoulder and blasting away. Before very long he was regularly powdering those straightaway targets, and he wanted to try some passing shots. Maybe, he thought, he could get his wife interested.

One evening after dinner he broached the subject. Mrs. Joe said yes, she wouldn't mind trying a little shooting. That wasn't exactly what Joe had in mind; he wanted her to throw the targets. But what the hell, he'd work on that angle later.

The next Saturday afternoon they drove to Joe's private little shooting area. Joe explained how the hand trap operated and she quickly learned the knack of snapping the clay target on its way. After throwing a dozen or so clays, Mrs. Joe declared that it was her turn to shoot. Joe decided to pamper her a bit and let her discover that this business of shotgun shooting is no child's play. He gave her a quick run-down on safety and explained how to hold and operate the gun. Then he proceeded to toss a target out in front of her. She centered it. He tossed another, and she powdered it, too. A little shocked, Joe threw out a fast one and she missed. Feeling a bit better, he whanged out another fast one. She hit it. After that, she broke some more targets and missed a few before the sun went down.

To make a long story short, the whole family got into the act. He has two youngsters, and shooting, gun collecting and hunting now are group affairs for Joe's family. At the present time they are giving bench-rest shooting a going over.

2

What Is Accuracy?

HOW MANY TIMES have you patiently listened to a dewy-eyed enthusiast tell about the out-of-this-world qualities of "Surekill," his beat-up hunting rifle? Such an arm, handed down by good old Uncle Deadeye, more often than not has so many alleged deer notches cut into the stock that it looks as though a beaver family had gnawed it in a free-for-all. Always, said rifle is a for-certain tack driver—with stories of feats afield running ad infinitum. The real feat is to stay awake during the mouthings.

One night, when I was in a low, weakened conditioned, I heard a lot of such gabbling. One fellow bragged, with a straight face, about the accuracy of a rustéd and worn-out rifle that I know wouldn't group five shots on a prize-winning watermelon at much over fifty feet.

No one can blame a guy for being enthusiastic about his rifle if it's a good one. But when a fellow raves about a worn-out cluck which, for past performance or sheer age, should long since have been relegated to an honored spot on the wall, I can't help but think what a relevation it would be for him if he bought a new rifle and discovered its accuracy capabilities by shooting it at ranges of 100 and 200 yards, and by using it in the hunting fields.

Accuracy? Just what is shooting accuracy? Actually, in the broad shooting fraternity, it means a number of things.

The hairsplitter of the clan is the bench-rest shooter. Briefly, his all-out effort is directed toward eliminating the human element as much as possible in shooting a series of bullets from a rifle, to give the smallest possible grouping at various distances—all under specified rules and regulations.

At the other end of the shooting scheme is the average big-game hunter. He is interested in accuracy, and in conjunction with big-game sporting rifles, we sometimes hear the expression, "hunting accuracy"—usually when someone is trying to peddle a used piece. I never have been able to find out exactly what "hunting accuracy" means, but I have a hunch that the phrase is a loose way of avoiding commitment, probably indicating that the rifle is accurate enough to hit a deer in the body somewhere at 50 yards when precisely aimed.

Admittedly, the deer rifle, in the eastern woods and brush country, is usually fired at close range, sometimes under 50 yards; but it should be capable of placing the bullet within a couple of inches of the point of aim at 100 yards. In other words, if it will group into four or five inches at 100 yards, there is nothing much to worry about. Such a rifle should be lightweight and short in over-all length, for ease of carrying and for fast handling.

The British "Textbook of Small Arms" for 1909 and 1929 states: "The group of shots made by a good rifle is approximately circular, and at short ranges all the shots should be contained in a circle subtending about three minutes at the muzzle, the bulk of them being well in the middle."

The value of a minute of angle, at 100 yards, is a hair over an inch—1.047 to be exact; at 50 yards, it would be slightly over half an inch; and a bit over two inches at 200 yards. So, three minutes of angle at 100 yards would be 3.14 inches and 6.28 inches at 200 yards—which is good enough for most big-game hunting. Today, almost any ordinary sporting rifle is capable of shooting into three minutes of angle, and many will do better.

The rifleman-hunter in the mountains or on the open plains may, of necessity, have to try shots at really long range or not shoot at all, and he needs a tight shooting rifle of high muzzle and sustained velocity with flat trajectory. This is the reason for some of the recently introduced magnum calibers.

At 400 yards, the "good" rifle of the British textbook might group into about 12½ inches with perfect sighting, holding and trigger letoff. In the field, even with an experienced rifleman from prone position with sling, there very well may be some human error in the shooting cycle to enlarge the probable group of shots. With luck, the bullet from a rifle capable of making a 12-inch, five-shot group at 400 yards might print exactly at the point of aim or in the center of the circle for a perfect shot. But take a bullet from the same rifle that normally would strike at the edge of the circle, add a little error of aim on the negative side to put it further from the average center of impact, and you may have a complete miss or a slightly wounding shot on a deer or antelope. Four hundred yards is one hell of a long distance, and 500 and 600 yards is much more so. I have seen the time when 200 yards seemed like about two miles when I was in a completely pooped condition and vainly trying to hold a rifle steady enough from the kneeling position to keep the cross hairs of the scope on a much stalked, alert and jittery game animal. Yet it certainly is a fact that successful shots are made on big game at 500 and 600 yards—even longer—but everything has to be exactly right, including the goddess of Luck.

This brings up another point. The hunter should always shoot from the steadiest position possible under the conditions. The offhand position is the least steady. Even the most expert shooter can foul up a shot on game

In checking the accuracy of a rifle, any bench rest is better than none.

from this position when under the excitement of the chase, or for any one of a half-dozen other reasons.

Kneeling is a little better, sitting is much better, prone with sling is still better, and shooting from rest is the steadiest of all. In taking advantage of any kind of rest, it is important to pad or insulate the rifle fore-end, especially with a very hard rest, such as a rock or tree. This can be done with the hand, or, if time permits, by use of a folded jacket.

Don't think it is unsporting to use a spur-of-the-moment rest when shooting on game animals. Actually, it is just the reverse, because there is less chance of having a wounded animal on your hands. The more experience a rifleman has behind him, the more he is apt to take advantage of any rest that is handy. Thus, he can utilize the wonderful precision of modern rifles and ammunition. Every veteran hunter I know uses a rest at every opportunity. I feel fairly certain that I would not have the very beautiful record-book reedbuck, as well as a number of other trophies, had it not been for a rest. The reedbuck was shot at 287 of my steps on the plains of East Africa. A thorn tree furnished a little cover and a steady rest for my .264 Winchester caliber rifle.

Our modern high-intensity, flat-trajectory hunting rifles can be termed "very good" in comparison with the "good" of the textbook as mentioned above. Many of them will shoot into half the three minutes of angle or less. I'm talking of factory-production models with no major modifications.

It is a fact, however, that some rifles of a particular model may shoot slightly better than others. The difference usually is so slight that it may not be perceptible under ordinary conditions. This slight variation in accuracy is due to small differences of various dimensions allowed by the narrow tolerances in manufacturing.

Ordinarily, the bolt-action rifle, all things being equal, is conceded to be somewhat more accurate than rifles of other types of action. This does not mean that the faster-to-shoot lever-, pump- and autoloading-action rifles are to be shunned. Their good features more than make up for the slightly lower level of accuracy. However, most of these types of action rifles are not available in the more powerful and more specialized magnum calibers, such as the .264 and .338 Winchester, seven-mm Remington, .300 and .375 H&H, and the Weatherby magnums.

Actually, I have lever-action rifles made by Savage, Winchester and Marlin, pump-action rifles made by Remington, and autoloading rifles made by Remington, Browning and Winchester that are just as accurate as bolt-action rifles of similar calibers.

When Marlin was changing from conventional rifling to micro-groove rifling, I recall that a lot of shooting was done at the plant and accurate records kept. At first, practically every Marlin Model 336 rifle was check-fired. Later, it was the practice to select five rifles at random from the racks as they came from production and shoot them for accuracy with both Remington and Winchester ammunition. Cap Colby did most of the shooting without the aid of scope sights, using the regular open sights. With a vast number of rifles, the .30-30 Winchester cartridge, as made by both Remington and Winchester, averaged slightly under two inches at 100 yards. The .35 Remington cartridge, also as made by Remington and Winchester, averaged slightly under 2¼ inches at 100 yards for five-shot groups.

Cap is one of the best shots with open sights I have known. One afternoon, after shooting all day, he fired a .35-caliber Model 336 rifle. The average for groups with both Winchester and Remington ammunition was 2.78 inches. This was larger than usual. So, the next morning, when he was in a refreshed condition, he refired the rifle with similar ammo and the groups averaged at 1.42 inches. I mention this because it is a fact that rifles sometimes have been condemned as being inaccurate when in reality it was the fault of the shooters and not the rifles.

Talking about Marlin lever-action rifles, perhaps you remember that the Model 336 formerly was made for the .219 Zipper cartridge as a varmint rifle. According to factory records, with a long period of testing, the average for five-shot groups at 100 yards was 1.75 inches, with a majority running about 1½ inches. On one occasion, a series of ten rifles selected at random averaged 1.39 inches using both Remington and Winchester ammunition. That is good varmint accuracy for a lightweight rifle. But the gun didn't catch on because of the general notion that lever-action rifles are not nearly as accurate as bolt-action rifles of similar calibers.

Incidentally, with .30-30-, .35- and .219-caliber rifles, it was found that some, for no obvious reason, would shoot Winchester ammo with slightly better accuracy, while others did slightly better with Remington. This is more proof of the old axiom that, for best accuracy, the ammunition should be mated with the rifle. It is common practice among reloaders to experiment until they find the particular weight and shape bullet and the particular powder charge that gives best accuracy in a particular rifle.

Some riflemen maintain that constant-zero accuracy is more important than precise tack-driving accuracy. Within reason, that is. It certainly is true that a rifle may from time to time change its zero or point of impact in relation to the sight setting. This may be due to slight changes in bedding (relation of wood to metal) caused mostly by movement of the wood induced by atmospheric conditions. For this reason, the smart hunter, before going afield, always checks his rifle by actual firing to make sure it groups exactly where he wants it to group. Some sportsmen want their hunting rifles to group exactly at the point of aim at 100 yards. Others prefer the group to be as much as four inches high at that distance for a longer point-blank range—that is, to take full advantage of the trajectory curve without having to hold over or under on a big-game animal at as long a range as possible with the particular cartridge.

What is the best way to sight in a hunting rifle and check it for ultimate accuracy?

A permanent or portable bench rest furnishes about the steadiest rest. (The National Rifle Association of America, 1600 Rhode Island Avenue, N. W., Washington, D. C. 20036, will send you plans for both for ten cents.) An old ironing board makes a fair substitute for a portable bench rest and I have seen some very excellent shooting done from such an improvised setup. The rifle has to be supported on something; there are pedestals especially made for this purpose on which a bag filled with sand or grain is placed as a rest for the fore end of the rifle. Rifles shoot away from hard, solid supports to give a false point of impact, so whatever the rest may be, it should be well padded. Another filled bag may be placed in position to support the toe of the stock. Two filled bags will do the job without the pedestal, a big one for the fore end and a smaller one for the toe, both resting on the bench. For shooting from the prone position, a firm bedroll or a padded box can give a steady rest.

Before shooting at a longer range, the rifle should be fired on a near mark, say from 15 to 25 yards, to make sure that it will print on a more distant target. Sights should be adjusted so the bullets strike near the center of the target, because any error made at the near distance will be multiplied at the longer one. (A two-inch error at 20 yards would be 10 inches at 100 yards.) Because pest-type game, such as prairie dog, crow and woodchuck are small targets, the long-range varmint shooter usually prefers to have his rifle sighted in to group only about 1½ inches high at 100 yards to take advantage of a longer point-blank range as above.

Serious bench-rest shooters are the accuracy specialists of the shooting sport. They often use special heavy rifles, carefully handloaded ammo and high-magnification scope sights, with the shooting being done from permanent bench rests.

Modern organized bench-rest shooting probably stems from the efforts of a group of hunter-riflemen in the Northwest who organized the Puget Sound Snipers Congress in 1944. In the East, shooting for accuracy was common among isolated groups of skilled and reliable experimenters. At a bench-rest match held on the range of the Pine Tree Rifle Club, near Jamestown, New York, in 1947, the Eastern Bench Rest Shooters Association was formed and the very remarkable shooting done during that year caused nation-wide interest. In 1951, the Nation Bench Rest Shooters Association was organized, with the understanding that any rifle could be used, no weight limit, with safe ammunition; any sights, with detonation set off by mechanism on the rifle which shall be actuated by finger and fired from rest. Many astounding one-hole groups have been fired.

Gradually, lighter-weight rifles, suitable and convenient for field use, got into the act, and in 1960, the first Annual National Championship Varmint and Sporter Matches of the NBRSA were held. Rifles allowed in this event are of three classes: Sporter Rifle; Light Varmint Rifle, and Heavy Varmint Rifle. All must have stocks of conventional design, must not be more than three inches wide, and must meet certain other requirements. Six five-shot matches are fired in each class at both 100 and 200 yards, with the first match at each range fired for warm-up and not counted in the aggregate. Winning scores of a recent shoot, 100-yard aggregate of five matches, were .4120 of an inch for Sporter Rifle, .3046 of an inch for Light Varmint Rifle and .2742 of an inch for Heavy Varmint Rifle. My friend, that is accuracy!

Regardless of the kind of shooting—be it plinking, small-game hunting, varmint hunting, big-game hunting or target shooting—the scope sight is of tremendous help in accurate aiming.

Once in a while, a person who is not familiar with scope sights comes up with the idea that if a 2½-, 3- or 4-power scope is fine for big-game and small-game hunting, why not a 10- or even 30-power for greater magnification and a more detailed view of the target when aiming? Unfortunately, it is a fact that, with any gain in magnification, other elements being equal, we lose in illumination and in extent of field of view.

In a hunting scope, we want good illumination for seeing the image of the target in dull light and we need a large field of view so we can quickly pick up the target, especially if the target is running. Good 2½-power scopes have a field of 40 feet or slightly more at 100 yards. This means a field of 20 feet at 50 yards and only 10 feet at 25 yards. A 4X scope has a field of around 30 feet at 100 yards and a 6X scope about 20 feet. A 10X scope has a field of about 14 feet at 100 yards and a 25X scope around four feet at 100 yards. For big-game hunting, a field of much less than 30 feet at 100 yards is slicing it pretty thin. Can you imagine picking up a running animal in a 4-foot field? It is impossible. With target shooting, where there is plenty of time for aiming, the field makes little difference as long as it covers the aiming point.

Also, with a hunting scope, we need what is loosely termed a non-critical eye relief (eye relief is the distance from the eye to the eyepiece of the scope)—that is, a usable field of view with the eye placed at any point from about 2½ to about 4 inches, or a bit more, back of the scope.

The reason for so-called non-critical eye relief is to make it possible for the shooter to get on the target quickly without fooling around positioning the eye at the exact point where the full field can be seen. With critical eye relief, the field grows rapidly smaller if the eye is moved much from that point and completely blacks out if the eye is too far away or too close to the eyepiece. Also, the eye has to be far enough back of the scope to avoid being clipped due to recoil of the rifle.

The scope sight has a few disadvantages: it costs more and is a bit more fragile than the best of iron sights, and it is more liable to be put temporarily out of use by wet brush, rain or snow. In some instances, a scope raises the line of sight enough to make it desirable to raise the comb of the stock. However, the majority of modern rifles are stocked with the scope in mind, and the stock rarely has to be modified to fit the shooter.

All in all, the advantages of the scope sight far outweigh the disadvantages. The most important and overwhelming advantage of the scope, besides magnification, is that it puts the cross hair and the target in the same optical plane. With the open sights found on most rifles as they come from the factory, three points have to be lined up—the rear sight, the front bead or blade and the aiming point on the target. No eye can focus at three distances at the same time. What actually happens is that the eye shifts its focus rapidly from one to the other, and this muscular feat becomes increasingly difficult as a person grows older. With peep or aperture rear sights, the eye automatically centers itself, and only the front sight and the aiming point require the fast shift.

With the scope sight, the shooter has only to see the target in the enlarged field of view, put the sharp and clear reticle on it, and he is in business. Another important advantage of the scope sight is that, by adjustment of the eyepiece, the shooter can correct for nearsightedness or farsightedness. Thus the image seen in the scope is sharper and clearer than any image observed with the unaided eye. The scope certainly is the great equalizer. With a good one on the rifle, properly adjusted, every shooter, regardless of age, has an equal chance as far as sighting is concerned.

Practically everyone the least bit familiar with rifle shooting knows that there are a number of very excellent lines of scope sights on the market. Names such as Weaver, Lyman, Bausch & Lomb, Redfield, Leupold and others are household words to the rifleman.

The Browning Arms Company, world-famous for Browning shotguns, rifles, and pistols, also has a full line of quality rifle scopes in 4X for .22s, 5X, 2X to 7X and 3X to 9X variable power for high power rifles. Factory specifications indicate that the Browning scopes are of high quality in every respect.

Relative brightness is high. (Relative brightness is a number which refers to the area of the exit pupil of the instrument and actually is the square of the exit pupil expressed in millimeters. The exit pupil is the quotient of the entrance pupil, which is the free aperture of the objective lens, and the power of magnification of the scope.)

The tubes of the Browning scopes are in the popular one-inch diameter and are formed of a tough alloy which is anodized to a rich blue-black mar-resistant finish to match the fine finish of the Browning rifles. Finest coated lenses are used, and the scopes are carefully sealed under electronically controlled atmospheric conditions to insure against fogging and dust. Reticles always appear perfectly centered to the eye and internal adjustments are made by turning coin-slotted screws. Calibrated dials are easy to read and may be reset to zero after sighting in, so that temporary corrections may be made from the zero readings.

Browning also has a line of scope-mount rings and a streamlined one-piece mounting base designed for the Browning High-Power rifles. Both are matched to the contours and finish of the scope and are designed not to shoot loose. The base mount is built so that course horizontal adjustments can be made in the base itself and allows for quick removal and replacement of the scope without affecting zero.

3

Bringing Home the Buck

THE FRESH TRACKS of the two whitetail deer stood out sharply in the three inches of newly fallen snow. A light wind was in my face and all conditions were ideal for still-hunting. I had picked up the tracks at the swampy edge of a small lake and had followed them up the little valley for about two miles before they separated. At this point it was obvious that I was following a doe and a buck. One set of tracks was smaller and without the drag of the hind feet, characteristic of the buck during rutting season.

My little trek took place one fall during the early days of the Winchester Model 70 rifle. I was carrying one, of .30-'06 caliber, equipped with a little four-power scope sight. At that time two- or two-and-one-half-power was considered the highest magnification that could be used successfully at comparatively close range on big game in motion. The rifle-scope combination had worked out well on the running-deer target and I wanted to find out if I could quickly pick up and aim at a real live deer in heavy cover with that four-power scope.

According to the general idea of what constituted a deer rifle, I was over-armed, or at least heavily armed for hunting in the thick brush of this cut-over area where it was impossible to see in any direction for more than fifty yards. Actually, visibility was down to about twenty-five yards most of the time. To complicate matters, the shadows were lengthening.

In those days I had confidence in my ability for still-hunting and figured that I had a good chance to spot the pair before they were aware of my presence. However, on rounding a big bramble patch I saw that both deer had stopped to listen and look over their back trail. At this point the doe continued straight ahead, while the buck veered slightly to the right.

It seemed logical that he was going to meander back to the small lake where I had picked up the tracks. So, in an effort to cut him off, I turned to the right, crossed the valley and climbed a small bluff which gave me a fair view.

Within twenty minutes I spotted that buck. Apparently he had picked up my scent, for he was skulking, and believe me, he was doing the neatest sneak act I've ever seen. It was a miracle that I saw him at all in that light for he was at least 300 yards away. My rifle was loaded with cartridges having 180-grain, open-point bullets, and sighted in for 100 yards. After finding the buck in the scope I held at what I judged to be a foot above his back and in line with the center of his front legs—hoping for a hit at the junction of the neck spine and backbone to put him down. I was lucky all the way. The bullet dropped more than I had expected, hit the shoulder bone, churning slightly downward, and mangled his heart. That was one time a deer did not run the customary 100 yards after a heart shot. He folded in his tracks.

As I said before, according to popular conception, especially at that time, I was improperly armed and my sighting equipment was poor for hunting in that area. But as luck would have it, I got a fairly long shot under poor lighting conditions—and the combo paid off. With iron sights and a less powerful rifle, I probably would have missed that buck—or worse yet, only wounded him. Actually, I doubt if I would have chanced the shot with iron sights, for it would have been difficult to see the sights clearly in relation to the target. This experience, and several others, have sold me on the idea of using a slightly more powerful rifle than is usually recommended.

But I certainly do not want to give you the impression that I condemn any rifle less powerful than the .30-'06 for whitetails. Actually, they are not too difficult to kill. A perfectly placed shot from almost any caliber rifle will do the job at reasonable ranges. Carloads of them have been taken in the past with such weak sisters as the .38-40 and .44-40. However, because too many animals have been wounded and lost with such cartridges, they are gradually being outlawed from the game fields.

When you select a rifle, here's a point to remember: The black bear is usually found where whitetails range, with the exception of thickly populated areas. Usually he will carry more lead than a whitetail, and some of the less powerful of the so-called deer rifles may be on the light side for him.

While we're on the subject I'd like to point out that the most successful way to hunt black bear is with dogs. Still-hunting is mostly luck, even with the most experienced woodsman, because a black bear makes it his business to stay out of man's way. He has a keen sense of smell and can pick up human scent at twice the distance that a whitetail can. Yet, strange as it may seem, the majority of bears in the East and Northeast are surprised by deer hunters.

Any rifle and cartridge (with sporting bullet weighing 90 grains or more) that delivers in the neighborhood of 1,200 foot pounds of catalogue energy at 100 yards will nail a whitetail or black bear when shot at ordinary ranges and the bullet placed in a vital area. However, the heavier and more powerful cartridges in the deer-rifle category are best for black bear.

I receive hundreds of letters from readers seeking information about deer

Hunting exotic game—8-point Sika deer in Japan—adds spice to the chase.

and bear rifles. They usually start out something like this, "Tell me the honest truth. Which is the very best rifle for whitetail deer? I will keep the information confidential."

Well, sir, there is no mystery surrounding deer rifles. The honest truth is there is no such thing as a "very best" deer rifle. It all depends on the individual and conditions in his hunting area. Which type rifle—the lever-action, the pump-action, the semi-automatic, or the bolt-action—can he handle best? Does fairly heavy recoil bother him? Does he do his most accurate shooting with a rifle of light recoil?

Winchester produces semi-automatic, lever and bolt action rifles, Marlin and Savage makes lever and bolt action rifles and Remington makes semi-automatic, pump and bolt action rifles in calibers suitable for deer and black bear. Somewhere among these rifles and calibers is the combination to fit the needs of almost any shooter.

The real secret of putting meat on the table—which we all know, but sometimes ignore—is developing our marksmanship to a point where we can place the shot accurately, in a vital area of a game animal. This, of course, is the fundamental problem that is up to the individual. In order to hit a running animal we need plenty of practice shooting on a moving target, for that is the only way we can learn proper lead. A running deer target is ideal for this purpose.

The vital areas of a deer (and practically all game animals) are the neck spine (well centered in the neck), the backbone (located within the top quarter of the deer's body), the shoulderblade (beginning at the backbone directly above the front legs and running downward and forward to the shoulder joint), the shoulder joint (slightly upward and forward of the elbow), the elbow (located at the point where the front leg joins the body), the heart (low in chest cavity, directly above the front leg), the lungs (within rib cage or chest cavity). A shot put back of the diaphragm, which separates the chest cavity and abdomen, is a messy paunch shot and should be avoided if possible.

Many hunters have the idea that a deer's heart is located somewhere in the center of his body, and as a result put the shot too high and too far back, which means a long chase to come up with it and kill it, or a lost deer.

The heart is much lower in the chest cavity than most people realize. It is well in the lower half of the body and directly in line with the front leg as seen from the side. The heart shot is always fatal, although the animal may run a hundred yards or so before collapsing.

Actually, a shot in any of the vital areas will prove fatal, or do a knockdown job, making it possible for the *coup de grâce*.

The instant-death spots are the brain, the neck spine and the backbone. It is the objective of all sportsmen to make quick, clean, one-shot kills. So, why not always try to place the shot in one of these quick-kill areas? Sometimes such a shot is impractical or impossible. The brain offers a very small target, especially difficult when the animal is in motion. And a high-speed bullet at that point certainly is a trophy destroyer. On game that may prove dangerous, a near miss of the brain area may mean a wounding shot that can spell trouble.

When possible, the neck shot is a good one. It kills instantly and destroys very little good eatin' meat. Knowledge of the exact location of the well-centered neck spine is necessary. A high shot that misses the spine is only a wounding shot, usually necessitating a long chase and possibly a lost deer. A bullet placed slightly on the low side can cut the jugular vein and windpipe, in which case the deer quickly bleeds to death.

Unfortunately, all shots at whitetails are not broadside. Quartering-away shots are perhaps in the majority. Here an expanding bullet angling into the lung area, toward the opposite shoulder, invariably does a lot of damage for a sure kill. Quartering on shots should be taken high on the near shoulder. Luckily the soft, lightweight whitetail does not offer the penetration problem of larger members of the family.

Practically every American-made center-fire cartridge, from the .243 Winchester to the .45-70, has been used successfully at one time or another on whitetails. However, authorities usually agree that any cartridge with a bullet weighing less than 90 grains, or developing less than 1,200 foot pounds of energy at 100 yards, is not powerful enough for quick kills on whitetails. This eliminates practically all cartridges of black-powder days and those designed especially for varmint shooting.

The most important element for a hunter, in addition to shooting skill and being adequately armed, is to know the trajectory of his rifle. He should sight in carefully for a known range and, by actual shooting, determine the exact rise and fall of the bullet above and below the line of sight at ranges where game might be taken.

For instance, 180 yards is an effective range to sight in a scope-sighted .30-'30 rifle. With most rifles this will put the 170-grain bullet about 2¾ inches high at 100 yards, and about 2½ inches low at 200 yards. Any rifle with iron sights does not have the apparent flat trajectory of a scope-sighted rifle because the scope is higher above the bore axis. So, an iron-sighted .30-'30 rifle is best sighted in to hit the point of aim at 100 yards. This puts the 170-grain bullet an inch high at fifty yards and about three inches low at 150 yards.

Cartridges of flatter trajectory have the advantage of greater point-blank range. This means that shots may be taken at various ranges without the necessity of aiming above or below the target. The scope sight of a .270-caliber rifle may be adjusted so that the 130-grain bullet strikes the point of aim at 235 yards. With this setting, all shots up to about 260 yards may be taken at the point of aim without the bullet striking more than 2½ inches above or below that point at any range from muzzle to 260 yards. Individual rifle characteristics and other variables can change performance. So check-fire your rifle.

The shooter who really knows his rifle and the game he is hunting is the fellow who puts meat on the table.

4

The Shooter's Secret Weapon

"THAT GUY HAS a secret weapon!"

Three of us were lolling in front of the lean-to we had pitched the day before. Our bellies were full of sliced moose heart cooked with onions, a delicious dish, washed down with strong tea, so black that I'm sure it could have been used for writing if we'd had a pen handy. It was well below freezing, but the flickering campfire was toasting us on one side, while the reflected heat from the lean-to canvas was warming us on the other. Outside the range of our gas lantern, the stars seemed to quiver in the cold as they sparkled and winked at us through the crystal-clear air of Western Ontario.

We were tired from a long day of moose hunting, but contented and just about ready to hit the sack, when my friend, talking about the third member of our party who had downed the big moose we were enjoying for supper, continued, "Yep, there is no question about it, Harry certainly has a secret weapon. He almost always is first to bring in meat. And when the rest of us are skunked, he usually is the one with something to take home for the freezer."

That's the way our gag about the "secret weapon" began. Most of us know fellows like Harry. Perhaps you are in this category. If so, the chances are that you too have the secret weapon.

Harry is a careful, patient hunter, and his secret weapon is nothing more than lots of practice with his favorite hunting rifle. He loves shooting, and conditions are such that he can practice a couple of times a week at distances up to several hundred yards. With this regular practice he has developed into an excellent off-hand shot. His favorite caliber is the .30-06, probably because he has done a lot of military-type target shooting with his National Match Springfield, as well as with the M1. Also, there is a greater variety of American factory-loaded ammunition in .30-06 than for any other caliber: 110-grain bullet loading (3300-3400-feet-per-second muzzle velocity) for varmint hunting; several 150-grain bullet loadings (2970-fps muzzle velocity); more than half a dozen with 180-grain bullet loadings (2700-fps muzzle velocity); four 220-grain bullet loadings (2410-

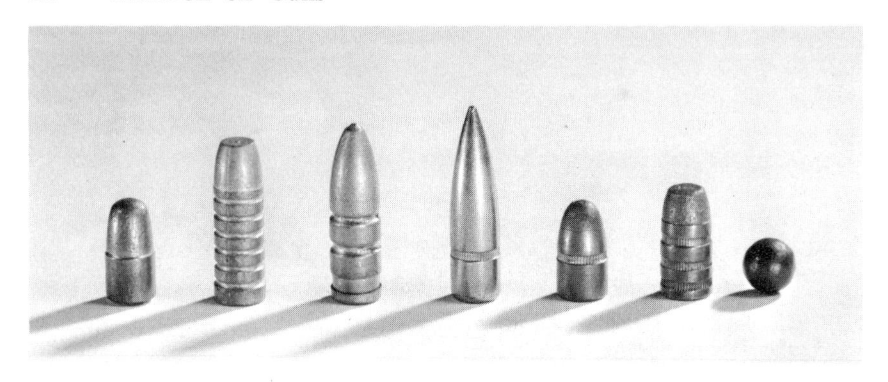

A few bullets—Speer Plinker, 100-grain; Lyman-Pope, 172-grain; Lyman-Squibb, gas-check, 169-grain; Service bullet, 150-grain; .30 caliber Luger, 93-grain; .32-20 bullet, 115-grain; No. 0 buckshot, about 48.2-grain—for making inexpensive practice loads with most any .30 caliber rifle.

fps muzzle velocity); the 150-, 180- and 220-grain loadings for various kinds of big-game hunting.

This makes the .30-06 pretty much of an all-round proposition, especially for the sportsman who wants to become completely familiar with one gun and use it for all types of shooting. Other modern calibers with similar characteristics include the .270 Winchester, .280 Remington and .308 Winchester. For really long-range shooting on varmint and big game up to about the size of elk, the .264 and 7mm magnum works out well in the hands of a good marksman. And for a combo to use on varmint and big game, such as whitetail and mule deer and black bear, the .243 Winchester, 6-mm Remington, .250 Savage and .257 Roberts will do the job.

Not many shooters have established range facilities readily available like my friend Harry, but this problem can be solved in a number of ways and one will surely meet the conditions of almost anyone who wants to get in year-round practice.

Our little group of "secret weaponers" has developed a number of inexpensive loads for various caliber rifles that can be conveniently fired at from thirty to fifty feet in the basement or outdoors with a good backstop, up to about 200 yards, depending, of course, on the load. Some of these loads date back to the days when I had but one centerfire rifle and used it on everything from woodchuck up, including target shooting.

Now it is not unusual for one of the boys to call on the phone and say, "How about a workout with the old secret weapon this Saturday afternoon?" This may mean some 200-yard practice at the nearby Blue Trail Range, or a session of short-range plinking in our back yard where we have a good safe backstop. We get in a fair amount of practice shooting our favorite rifles.

Quite a number of deer hunters manage to get out to a range just before the season and fire a few rounds to check the sight-setting of their rifles. Some labor under the delusion that this is practice. It is actually the beginning of practice.

Ten or twelve years ago, at a sportsmen's meeting, I met a fellow who lives a few miles from our place and I see him now and then. He has been going deer hunting in Maine just about every year since I have known him. Until last fall, he always came home empty-handed.

It was his habit to follow the old line and check-fire his .30-30 with a few rounds just before hitting the highway north. Season before last, he returned from the woodsy country with a long face and a sad tale. He had an easy chance at a whitetail and never turned a hair. "How come?" he wanted to know. "I could practically see his eyelashes. Got off two shots before he took off. He had a nice set of hatracks, too."

"You probably had buck fever," I said. "Maybe you need a little practice so you can line up the sights and shoot almost automatically—fast and accurate. By the way, what did the sight picture look like when you touched off your first shot?"

With a puzzled look on his pan, he answered, "I'll be damned if I know. Guess I do need some shooting practice."

So he started shooting from the off-hand position at seventy-five yards and was amazed to find that with deliberate aim he couldn't keep his shots on the fourteen-by-sixteen-inch paper of the 100-yard target. He moved in to about thirty yards and fired about twenty shots. I noticed that he was yanking the trigger and suggested that he put up a small bull's-eye in his den and do some dry firing—that is, line up the sights on the target and squeeze the trigger, while trying to retain a mental picture of the sights and target as the hammer of his rifle snapped home.

I didn't see him for several months. Then, just before the hunting season, he appeared and wanted to do a little shooting at 100 yards. He said he had practiced dry firing several times a week. In the meantime, he had mounted a 2½-power scope sight on his rifle and wanted the gun sighted in for 100 yards. I did a bore sighting job, fired a couple of rounds at 20 yards as a check and zeroed at 100 yards from bench rest. He fired a couple of shots from the bench and then proceeded to touch off five from the standing position. In shooting, he quickly raised the rifle to his shoulder and fired almost instantly. It was easy to see that he had been following this routine in his dry-firing practice. He called one shot high and to the right. I was watching the target with a spotting scope. Four shots were well within the six-inch black of the target and one was out an inch or so at one o'clock. Not bad shooting.

Off-season hunting with the camera is excellent practice, requiring as much or more snooping skill than with the rifle for meat in the pot.

My friend took to the road to make the opening day of the deer season in Maine. About ten days later, he showed up at the house with a hunk of venison. By his expression, one would think he had located the gold pot at the end of the rainbow. He had killed the big buck with one shot, at a range of about eighty yards.

"I certainly am glad I got in that practice," observed our deer slayer. "I doubt I'd have got off that shot at all if I hadn't been so used to handling that rifle!"

Some fellows hesitate, or figure they can't afford to spend from five to fifteen dollars for full-power factory ammo burned in a session of shooting practice. In training muscles for steady holding of the gun, trigger control, co-ordination and learning to sight properly, a number of inexpensive low-power, short-range loads in the various big-game-hunting calibers will work out just as well as full-power cartridges. Such shooting is much more satisfying than the snapping or dry-firing exercises mentioned above. However, I do believe that a sportsman should get in some practice just before the hunting season with the load he intends using on game.

My first centerfire bolt-action, repeating rifle was an old .30-40 caliber Krag-Jorgesen, Model 1898, remodeled to sporter form in the simplest way. The Krag was adopted by the U. S. Army in 1892 to replace the .45-70 Springfield single-shot rifle and was the first U. S. Service rifle designed for smokeless powder. Colonel Townsend Whelen, the dean of America's gun writers, hunted with an "as issued" Krag while stationed in the Philippines and gave it quite some publicity. The first Krag sporter was concocted for Dr. Paul B. Jenkins, long-time curator of the gigantic Nunnemacher gun collection of the Milwaukee Public Museum.

For ten or fifteen years after World War I, the Director of Civilian Marksmanship sold good, serviceable Krags to members of the National Rifle Association. The price of the Krag was a dollar and a half, plus packing and shipping charges. Also, there was a sporter type "arsenal conversion" which had the barrel cut to twenty-four inches and a Springfield front sight installed. The service stock fore end was cut off two and three-quarters inches forward of the sling-swivel band and nicely rounded. If I remember correctly, this sporter sold for five dollars. With nothing more than the installation of a receiver sight, it made an excellent hunting rifle. Actually, there are plenty of Krags still seeing service among hunters. And, I might add, they have the smoothest action of any turn-bolt arm ever produced.

Service ammunition was readily available and I shot quite a lot of it in my first Krag. But the 220-grain bullet of that cartridge was jacketed with cupro-nickel which often caused a lumpy bore fouling that was difficult to remove. So I began reloading the fired brass.

The old Lyman bullet, cast in mould Number 311403, was designed by Harry Pope, the famous old-time barrel maker and off-hand shooter, for extreme accuracy up to 200 yards in the .30-06 rifle. It gave excellent accuracy in the .30-40 Krag, as well as the .30-06, when propelled by thirteen grains of Du Pont powder Number 4759. This almost forgotten reload is easy to produce with fired and reprimed cartridge cases. A primer is seated, the powder charge, weighed or measured, is dumped into the case and the bullet seated into the mouth of the case with the fingers. Owing to the shallow seating depth of this bullet, the loaded cartridges are not practical for handling except on the target range. By being very careful, I have used them for woodchuck hunting.

An excellent short-range practice load is made with the bullet cast with Lyman mould Number 311245 and 3.5 grains of Bullseye or four grains of Unique powder in the .30-40 or .30-06 cartridge case. This bullet was especially designed for the U. S. Marine Corps for twenty-five-yard practice with the Krag.

Before examining a couple of other practice loads, let's take a quick look at smokeless powders for rifles. There are fast- and slow-burning powders. Fast-burning powders were designed for small-capacity cartridge cases with lightweight bullets, such as the .22 Hornet. Slow-burning powders were developed for medium and large cases with heavier bullets. Each powder has a definite place in the scheme of cartridges where they work best. The fast powders are sometimes used by reloaders in large cases, such as the .30-06, with lightweight bullets and relatively light charges. Heavy charges of a fast powder or heavy bullets, under these conditions, will blow up rifles and perhaps shooters. Also, light charges of the quick-burning powders leave room in medium and large cartridge cases for accidental overloads of two or even three charges, which will take a rifle apart. For instance, a double charge of an old recommended charge of Number 2400 powder in the .30-06 cartridge produces a bomb.

So, before doing any reloading of ammunition, the shooter should study some of the books and manuals on the subject. *Lyman Handbook* No. 45, *Hornady Handbook of Cartridges, The N.R.A. Handloader's Guide, Pocket Manual for Shooters and Reloaders,* by P. O. Ackley, *Shooter's Bible, Reloader's Guide, Speer Manual for Reloading Ammunition, The Winchester-Western Ammunition Handbook.* When recommended practices, listed in these books, are followed, handloading is a safe and fascinating addition to the shooting sport. In fact, every shooter and hunter, whether he handloads or not, should read these manuals for a better understanding of the ammunition he shoots.

We have fired a great many easy-to-make reloads for .30-caliber rifles, which I shot in my old Krag at short ranges up to twenty or twenty-five yards. One is particularly easy to put together. Reprimed cases—.30-30, .30-40, .308, .300 Savage, .30-06—that have been form-fired in the rifle they are to be used in, are charged with a fired .22 Long Rifle cartridge case level-full of Bullseye powder and a beeswax-dipped Number 0 buckshot, firmly thumb-seated in the mouth of the case. I solder a finishing nail to the fired .22 Long Rifle case to form a dipper. A charge by my way of dipping is 2.7 grains of Bullseye. Remember, in weighing smokeless powder, the avoirdupois-weight system is used, in which there are 7,000 grains to the pound. (Bullseye is a very fast-burning pistol powder that ordinarily is not used in rifle cartridges, so great care should be employed to make sure that the cases are not charged with double or triple loads of powder.) Powder, ball, beeswax and primer for this load cost less than one and a half cents. It is accurate enough in most .30-caliber rifles to print within the ten ring of the standard 100-yard target when fired on at a range of twenty or twenty-five yards. The ball of this load zips through two seven-eighth-inch pine boards, and the ricochet and danger range is considerable—say, about like that of the .22 rimfire cartridges.

Lately I have been experimenting with the 100-grain Speer .30-caliber

"Plinker" half-jacket bullets introduced by Speer Products Company of Lewiston, Idaho, the well known makers of bullets for reloaders. Plinkers are intended for informal practice and varmint shooting. Loading data for fourteen .30-caliber rifles, including such popular sporting arms as the .30-30 Winchester, .30 Remington, .308 Winchester, .300 Savage, .30-40, .30-06, .300 Weatherby Magnum, .303 British, and so on, are included with each package of 100 bullets.

Having only a limited supply of the .30 Plinkers, I tried them in the .30-30 and a couple of .30-06-caliber rifles. For a trial run, I loaded twenty unfired Remington .30-06 cases, each with fifty-four grains of I.M.R. 4895 powder, lot Number 27278 and Cascade Number 200 rifle primers behind the Plinker bullet seated .2-inch into-the-case neck. With this lot of 4895 powder, velocity probably is more than 3200 feet per second at the muzzle. Shooting at fifty yards in series of five shots each from two rifles, a Winchester Model 70 and a Husqvarna, both with one-shot fouled barrels, the groups were very tight. Clusters measured from ¾-inch (center to center) on down to a one-hole group measuring 1⁷⁄₃₂-inch vertical by 1³⁄₃₂-inch horizontal, not center to center of bullet holes farthest apart, but over-all measurement!

Then I loaded forty neck-sized cases with the same load and ran into trouble. The first 100-yard, five-shot group measured slightly over five inches, the second even larger. Something certainly had gone haywire. Then I remembered a warning given in the data sheet to the effect that the shooter should make sure that the bullets were not tipped slightly as they were seated in the cartridge-case neck. Several of the bullets in my loads seemed to be very slightly tipped, hardly discernible, but showing a slight wobble when the cartridges were spun rather slowly. Upon firing in groups of five, the cartridges with bullets showing the most wobble gave the greatest dispersion at the target. By not doing a thorough checking job after the cartridges were assembled, I had evidently made a booboo.

In the meantime, I had loaded twenty .30-30 cases with 36.2 grains of the same lot of 4895 powder and the Plinker bullets. Five-shot groups at fifty yards measured from an inch to 1⅛ inches. The particular Marlin Model 336 Carbine ordinarily groups five shots with selected lots of factory 170-grain ammo into less than two inches at 100 yards, so the Plinkers worked well in the .30-30.

At this point, I was just about out of Plinker bullets. So, after chamfering the mouths and full-length sizing some once-fired .30-06 cases, I expanded the necks for .3085-diameter bullets and weighed a charge of fifty-four grains of 4895 powder for each case. Then the Plinkers were carefully seated straight into the primed and charged cases. Three five-shot groups at 100 yards measured right around two inches, with the largest at 2⅛. Inasmuch as these new bullets are mainly intended for inexpensive plinking, this seems to me to be good accuracy.

There are moulds available which cast bullets that are suitable for loading in practically all hunting calibers for inexpensive practice.

If a shooter does not want to reload ammo for his hunting rifle, there are other ways of getting in odd-time practice. With a bullet trap, the .22 works well for basement shooting at thirty to forty feet. We have fired a Mossberg Model 320 single-shot rifle with Elly .22 CB Caps, imported by S. E. Lazzlo, 25 Lafayette Street, Brooklyn, New York, and .22 BB Caps, imported by Stoeger Arms Corporation, 55 Ruta Court, South Hackensack, N. J., for this purpose. These little cartridges give good accuracy and muzzle report is low.

Good practical practice also can be had indoors with the CO_2-powered rifles and the so-called air rifles. A favorite is the Crosman Model 160 Pellgun in .22 caliber. Our 160 Pellgun has the Crosman S331 micrometer receiver sight which makes sighting-in easy and aiming more accurate.

Any kind of practice, as long as the sights are properly lined up with the target, and the trigger squeezed, is good. This includes everything from dry-snapping with any rifle on through shooting CO_2 Pellguns and air rifles and .22s, on to reduced loads and factory ammo fired in the trusty hunting rifle. Every shooter knows that shooting practice pays off, but comparatively few get around to doing it!

Why don't you get into the "secret weapon" club?

5

The First Shot Goes Wild

MORE THAN A HALF-DOZEN shooters and hunters were enjoying a heated bull session having mostly to do with sporting rifles. One guy, a pessimistic type, spouted off.

"In my opinion," he said, "these de luxe rifles being produced today—and most of the gun companies are making them—are spit-and-polish dressed up just to take a few more bucks from the shooting sportsmen."

"Oh, I don't know about that," another fellow chimed in. "I have a couple of very fancy rifles. And they're pleasant to look at, much more attractive than the ordinary field or standard grade."

"That's just the point," the first guy came back. He licked his chops as if preparing to devour a tasty morsel. "Those de luxe guns are made for flashy looks, with most of the work on the outside. I think the chuckle-heads who buy them are mostly not real shooters and hang them on the wall just to show off. And I'll bet dollars to fired shotshells that most of those fancy rifles are not really accurate."

That pulled the plug.

What had been a pleasant, conversational, beer-sipping conclave, turned immediately into a couple of almost hostile camps. Members of one group maintained that they preferred the custom appearance of the de luxe guns and did not expect them to shoot better than those of standard grade. After all, the gun makers do the best job they can with all their products. The other side had no particular interest in the looks of a rifle, being interested only in accuracy and field performance.

When the repartee started getting personal and somewhat barbed, I broke it up with what seemed a sensible idea.

"Between us," I said, trying to imitate a Brownie den mother soothing an out-of-hand brood, "we have some handsome de luxe rifles in various practical calibers. Let's shoot them and see what happens."

Having their attention, I continued. "I'll furnish the ammo and do the shooting under as near ideal conditions as possible. After all, in the final analysis, accuracy is a most important element of a rifle—that is, unless it is a rare piece that belonged to Napoleon or maybe a real masterpiece from the artistic angle."

After a lot of argy-bargy, which we called sophisticated reasoning, it was finally decided that the shooting should consist of one five-shot group fired with each rifle, with the first shot in each instance fired from an unfouled, well cleaned bore. That is, the bores were to be thoroughly cleaned with solvent and light oil, then dried by running a clean patch through. The idea behind the clean-bore procedure was logical. It is a fact that the first shot from a barrel that has not been fouled by firing usually will print at a different point on the target from succeeding shots. It is the habit of many hunters in the field to fire the first shot on game from an unfouled or clean bore. We wanted to see how far out of the normal grouping area this first shot would print, if at all, with a number of different rifles. If the first shot really is what could be called a wild one, would it be far enough away from the normal group to cause a miss on game being fired at?

As our plans progressed, the idea of accuracy with de luxe rifles faded a little, with more interest in where that first shot from the clean barrel would land at the target. It was agreed that the program would not be a contest between de luxe rifles, and a couple of standard grade rifles got into the act. The final objective simmered down into a sort of premise: What sort of accuracy can a hunter expect with a modern rifle and modern ammunition as they come from the dealer's shelves, with, of course, attention given the first shot from the unfouled barrel? There was to be no experimenting, such as mating ammo to a rifle, checking bedding of metal to wood, etc. A total of fifteen rifles, all bolt-action, were fired during the testing—eleven of the big-game type and four varmint rifles. There were some real beauties in the group.

Weather conditions during the shooting varied from cloudy to bright sunshine. There was a little breeze at all times, but only once was the wind strong enough to be really bothersome. For more precise aiming, scope sights were mounted on all rifles but one, and there was quite a variety of them. The shooting was from benchrest.

The .30-06 Springfield is a most popular cartridge among hunters, so the majority—five, to be exact—of our rifles were of this caliber. The ammo was Winchester Super-Speed with 180-grain Silvertip bullet. The first sporter fired was a very good-looking example of the BSA Monarch Deluxe, Featherweight, imported from England by J. L. Galef and Sons, Incorporated, 85 Chambers Street, New York City. This particular rifle has a blond walnut stock with rosewood forearm tip and grip cap having white-line spacers. Hand checkering is fine-line. The stock has a Monte Carlo comb with comfortable cheek piece. A recoil pad and one-inch sling swivels are installed. The bolt body is polished bright, while the bolt handle and sleeve, as well as the receiver and barrel, are highly polished and blued. The fore-and-aft operating safety has a red fire indicator, and a red pin, convenient to the thumb, protrudes from the top of the bolt sleeve

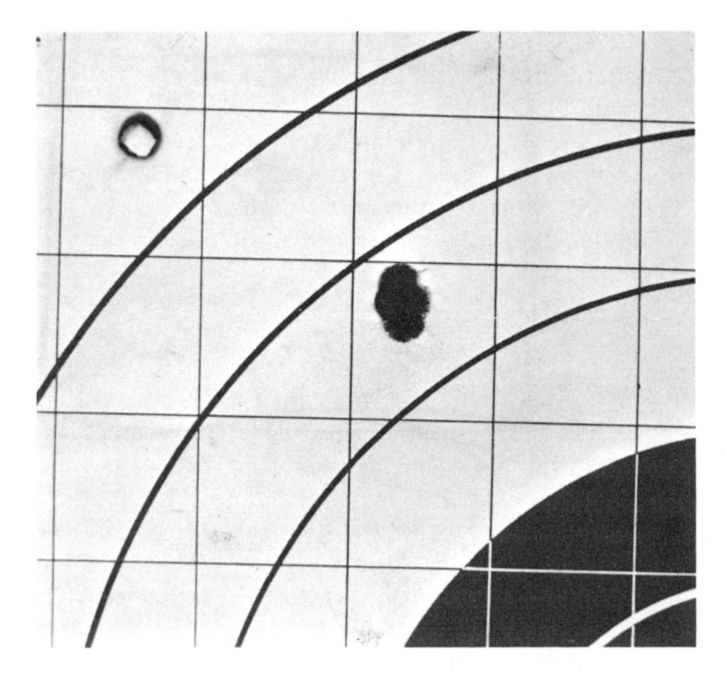

Five-shot group fired at 100 yards with .30-06 caliber target rifle. First shot, from unfouled barrel, printed over 1½ inches from grouping point.

when the rifle is cocked. Sights are hooded bead on ramp front and an adjustable open rear, which adapts to U or V sighting notch. Trigger is fully adjustable for length of pull and weight of let-off; the floor plate is hinged and dovetail scope bases are integral with the receiver ring and bridge.

I shot this rifle first, because no Parker-Hale scope mounts for the dovetail bases were at hand and I wanted my eyes fresh for sighting with the open sights. The first shot, from the unfouled barrel, printed high and to the left, about two inches from the group of the succeeding four which grouped into 1.64 inches. This is very tight and actually better than I usually can do when aiming with open iron sights.

The second .30-06-caliber rifle to be fired was a de luxe Kodiak Imperial. This sporter was available in seventeen popular calibers, ranging from .22-250 to .358 Norma Magnum and was made up around the 98 Mauser action. Standard sights are hooded bead on ramp front and Williams Guide open rear, which is adjustable for windage and elevation by loosening one screw. The bolt body and handle are polished bright; the remaining metal parts are blue. The custom-type stock has a forearm tip and grip cap of rosewood. The modern, forward-slanting Monte Carlo comb (to minimize recoil effect at the shooter's cheek) is of roll-over design with full cheek piece.

I mounted a new Weaver V9, 3- to 9-power variable scope on the Kodiak rifle and set the power at 9x. (In each instance, with variable power scopes used in the experiment, the highest power was used.) The first shot, from the unfouled bore, printed slightly to the right, about one inch from the vertical center of the succeeding four shots. The four shots measured 1.78 inches, center to center of holes farthest apart, with all five shots in two inches.

The third rifle is .30-06, the Winchester Model 70 Standard, which has a number of custom-type features. For instance, the Monte Carlo comb, with full cheek piece, is high to support the shooter's cheek so that the eye is in line with the high-standard open sight, or in line with the axis of a low-mounted scope for fast aiming. The iron sights are easily removed for non-interference with a scope. Here again, the comb and cheek piece are designed to minimize recoil effect. Incidentally, the Monte Carlo comb stock is standard on all Model 70s, excepting the target version, and sling swivels are standard on all six versions. New decorative checkering further dresses up the new Model 70 Standard.

Group fired at 100 yards with my Winchester Model 70 hunting rifle, .264 Win. Magnum caliber, 100-grain bullet, shows first shot, from unfouled barrel, well outside main cluster, which measures .70".

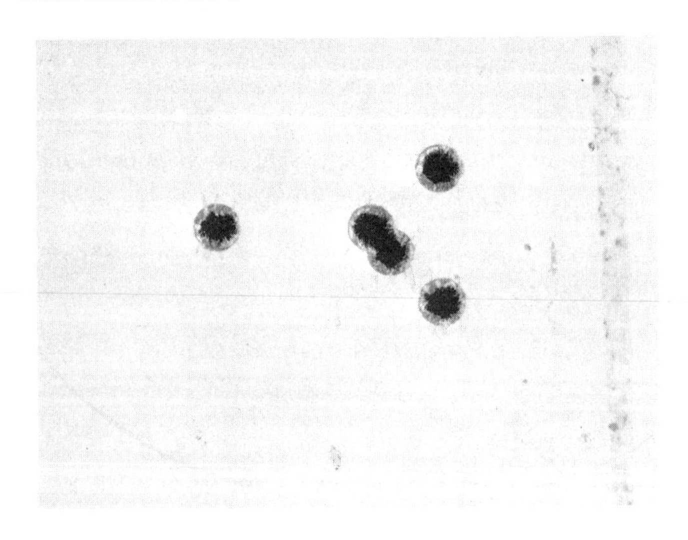

This rifle was mounted with a Bausch and Lomb Balvar 8A, 2- to 8-power variable scope. The first shot from the freshly cleaned barrel struck the target almost four inches from the center of the group formed by the next four shots, which measured 1.73 inches. Just for the hell of it, I deviated from the routine and fired two more shots. They centered in the four-shot group.

The next rifle fired was an example of the Remington Model 700 Custom. This is a real custom rifle, listed in the Remington consumer catalogue and made only on special order. To my way of thinking, this is the handsomest of the big-game rifles used in our experiment. The stock is of fancy American walnut with rosewood forearm tip and grip cap and with excellent hand-checkering. The butt plate, of finely checkered steel, and quick-detachable swivel are standard. This particular rifle is without iron sight and the Monte Carlo comb and cheek piece are especially shaped for use with a low-mounted Redfield Master 4x scope.

The first shot printed high and to the right, about 2.25 inches from the group formed by the next four shots, which measured 1.68 inches.

The fifth rifle of .30-06 caliber to be fired was the brand-new Winchester Model 670, also available in .243 and .270 Winchester calibers.

The Model 670 looks somewhat similar to the Winchester Model 70. It has a Monte Carlo comb, but without cheek piece. The bolt does not have the three-position safety on the sleeve, as with the 70, but has a two-position safety located at the right side of the receiver tang. In the forward position, the arm is ready to fire by a pull of the trigger. When in the rear position, the firing pin is locked and the rifle cannot be fired. However, the bolt may be operated. This means that the chamber can be unloaded and any cartridges in the magazine can be removed, all with the arm safe.

My feelings are that the Model 670 is an excellent sporting arm at a low price. Before firing, I installed bases and transferred the Weaver V9 variable to it and sighted-in at 100 yards. After the bore was thoroughly cleaned, the first of five shots proved to be centered in the group made by the next four; the five-shot group measured 1.82 inches.

The next step in our program was to fire three very fine rifles of 7-mm Remington Magnum caliber. Our ammunition, with 150-grain Hi-Shok bullet, was made by Federal Cartridge Corporation. The first was the Remington Model 700 ADL Deluxe, mounted with a Leupold Vari-X 11, 3- to 9-power variable scope. The first shot, from the unfouled barrel, printed high and a bit to the left on the 100-yard target, about 1.5 inches from the center of the subsequent four-shot group, which measured 1.65 inches.

Incidentally, the Remington Model 700 rifle is made in ten popular calibers in ADL Deluxe Grade and in fifteen calibers in BDL Custom Deluxe Grade—from .22-250 Remington to .458 Winchester Magnum, a caliber for every kind of hunting found in the world.

The second rifle in 7-mm Remington Magnum caliber was the Harrington and Richardson Ultra Model 300. Made on the F. N. Mauser action, this rifle is refined with an adjustable trigger and it features an American-walnut, hand-finished and hand-checkered stock having roll-over, Monte-Carlo comb and cheek piece. Contrasting wood is used in the forearm tip and grip cap. Sling swivels are standard. The Ultra is available in six other calibers—.22-250 Remington—.243, .270 and .308 Winchester, as well as .30-06 and .300 Winchester Magnum.

Mounted on the Ultra was a Bushnell Scopechief 11, 3- to 9-power variable scope with Command Post—a slight turn of a knurled ring snaps up a post at the cross-hair for quick aiming in close cover or shooting in dim light.

The first shot struck the target a little over 2.5 inches above the subsequent four shots, which grouped into 1.64 inches.

The third 7-mm Magnum-caliber rifle was the Savage 110 Premier Grade, available in left-hand action at the same price. This very handsome rifle was mounted with a Savage Model 3833, 3- to 8-power variable scope. The 110 Premier has a fine French walnut stock, hand-checkered in skip-line design and hand-finished, with Monte Carlo comb and cheek piece. The forearm tip and grip cap are of rosewood with white line spacer. Studs for quick-detachable swivels are installed. The 110-P also is made in .243 Winchester and .30-06 calibers, right or left hand action and stock.

The first shot, from the unfouled bore, printed about an inch above the succeeding four, which grouped into 1.25 inches.

The next two rifles were Winchester Model Magnums. The first one fired was of .300 Winchester Magnum caliber and mounted with a Weaver V8, 2.5- to 8-power variable scope. Ammunition was Western Super-X with 150-grain Power Point bullet. The bullet from the unfouled bore printed high and slightly to the right, about 1.75 inches from the center of the succeeding four-shot group, which measured 1.28 inches.

The second rifle, of .264 Winchester Magnum caliber, is one that I used in Africa. It was mounted with a Redfield 2- to 7-power scope with Accu-Range (a range-finding element). Ammunition was Winchester Super-Speed with 140-grain Power Point bullet. The first shot printed five inches to the right of the second one. The succeeding shots move on across the target. Now, this rifle has always grouped into a bit over a minute of angle and I was bewildered. Just now, I had sense enough to make a check. The two guard bow screws and the magazine-cover hinge-plate screw (they hold the metal parts to the stock) were all loose by a good half-turn or more. I have no idea how the three screws became loose, other than by wood shrinkage.

As I said, this rifle has always shot very well indeed and it had been sighted-in to shoot three inches high at 100 yards, which puts the 140-grain

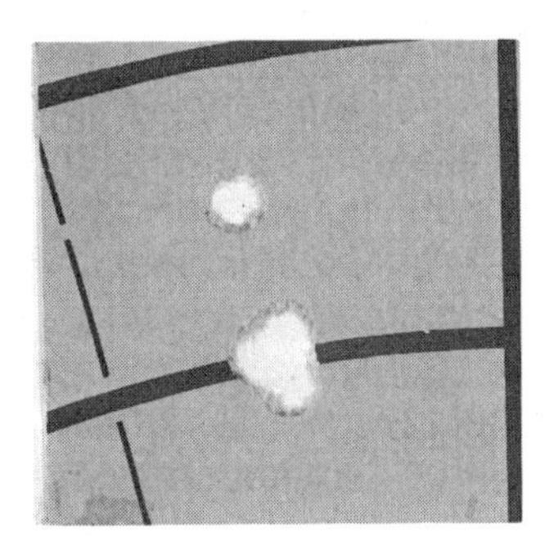

Unfouled barrel first shot printed high to spoil an otherwise excellent group from my .22 centerfire varmint rifle.

bullet at the point of aim at a little over 250 yards. If I had taken it hunting without resighting and had a shot at around 300 yards, I could well have been in a very unhappy situation with a miss or—worse yet—with a wounded animal to try to track down and maybe never find.

The last big game rifle fired in the experiment was a Mannlicher-Schoenauer Carbine, imported by Stoeger Arms Corporation, South Hackensack, New Jersey. It was mounted with a Redfield 3- to 9-power variable scope. This slick-looking little carbine is of .270 Winchester caliber, and ammunition used was Federal with 130-grain, soft-point bullet. The first fired bullet hit the target high and right, about three inches from the center of the group made with the next four shots, which measured 1.49 inches center to center of holes farthest apart.

The next day, I fired four high-grade varmint rifles, also at 100 yards on the Blue Trail Range. The first to see action was a Remington Model 700 BDL Custom Deluxe in .22-250 Remington caliber, with the new Weaver K8 (8-power) scope installed. Ammunition was Remington Power-Lokt with 55-grain, hollow-point bullet. The shot from the unfouled bore printed almost 1.13 inches to the right of the next four shots, which grouped into .70-inch.

The next rifle was the Winchester Model 70 Varmint, with heavy barrel, in .225 Winchester caliber. A Lyman Super-Targetspot scope of 25-power was installed. Ammunition was Western Super-X with 55-grain Pointed Soft Point bullet. The shot from the unfouled bore was only about .75-inch from the next four shots, which grouped in .69-inch.

Then we went back to the .22-250 Remington cartridge in the Browning High-Power Rifle, with heavy barrel. This varmint rifle was mounted with a Bausch and Lomb Balvar 24 variable, 6- to 24-power target-type scope. I didn't dry-swab the bore of this rifle as much as the others, leaving a thin layer of light oil just to see what would happen. This biz is not to be recommended, as too much light oil or a bit of grease can very well result in a blown-up gun. The first shot hit the target almost three inches to the right of the group formed by the next four, which measured .84-inch. The last three shots were to the left of the second and printed into a little over a half-inch. Then I fired a sixth shot to see what would happen. It grouped with the last three.

The last rifle to be fired and end our program was a very beautiful Weatherby Mark V Varmintmaster, of .224 Weatherby Magnum caliber. The first shot, 55-grain bullet, landed to the right and slightly below the group made with the next four. It was late in the afternoon and this was the only rifle we fired with lousy wind conditions. I tried to let off shots during lulls and did fairly well. The four shots went into .94-inch, mostly strung out horizontally. At this point, I ran out of time for this experiment.

As I said, the program was no contest between rifles or cartridges. For one thing, the scopes varied quite a lot in power and in crosshair width. And light conditions were from bright to overcast. However, the groups fired were excellent and, within caliber, they varied but little in measurement.

Why the first shot from an unfouled barrel is often slightly wild is problematical. As near as I can determine, from years of observation, there is no way of predicting where it will land. A number of variables enter the picture. That first shot evidentally cleans any slight amount of solvent or light oil residue from the bore and tends to settle the component parts of the rifle.

This experiment indicated to us that we have some very accurate rifles. And I might point out that a hunter, in an area where he may have to take a really long-range shot, should have precisely sighted-in his rifle and should know its grouping capabilities. He should know the trajectory of the bullet of the ammunition he is using and he should have fire-fouled the bore by firing a couple of shots before getting into the position of having to make a long-distance shot. If his rifle throws that first shot three or four inches from the point of aim at 100 yards, it would be out a foot or more at 300 yards. That's enough for a miss or not immediately fatal wound on whitetail deer or antelope, without even considering error in sighting or holding.

Why not experiment with your rifle before the next big season opens? It's a lot of fun, you'll know your rifle better and I'm sure you'll obtain some valuable information. And I say, more power to the sportsman who prefers a dressed-up or fancy custom rifle!

6

Dangerous Game

WE WERE SEARCHING for African lion, a strikingly large one—we hoped—a rare one with a long, thick and bushy black mane. Leaving our Land Rover, we walked about a mile, keeping well under cover. Then we moved with greater caution, crawling and creeping through waist- to shoulder-high, noisy grass that was sun-cured dry and brittle. After snaking for a quarter of a mile, we finally came to the edge of a thirty-foot-deep gully, actually part of a sand river. This was our objective. Carefully, we peered through what amounted to a thorn bush and reed hedge that seemed to guard the wide gully.

At this point, we had been in the bush for about a month and had meanderingly hunted our way across Uganda—350 miles wide—from the east in primitive Karamoja, through more than half a dozen districts. We were now in the Simliki Valley in the Toro District. To the west, we had seen the beginning of the vast stretches of the Congo. To the south was the high rise of the Ruwenzori range, the famous "Mountains of the Moon," with peaks climbing to almost 17,000 feet—some of the most beautiful and breathtaking scenery in the world.

A couple of days earlier, in this sparsely settled, wild country, we had talked with an African and had examined the mangled remains of a donkey that had been killed by a lion. In his native upcountry Swahili, he told us the lion was killing off his small herd of cattle.

We found a likely spot and put out bait. The next afternoon, we returned for a look-see. It was almost dusk, nearing the time to quit hunting for the day. Carelessness does *not* pay off. After driving to within a quarter-mile of the bait, we walked openly the rest of the way. I got a flashing glimpse of a lion taking off, with no chance for a shot.

Before that experience, I had been lucky enough to observe twelve members of the species *Panthera Leo* in their wild habitat, including lions, a lioness and her cubs.

Experienced hunters in Africa distinguish five kinds of dangerous game—lion, elephant, buffalo, leopard and rhino—usually called "the big five." In some instances, the hippo is included. He can be cantankerous, and when he is, he can bite a man in two with his huge teeth.

Leopard, a comparatively small cat, pound for pound is the most dangerous animal in the world.

Lions have always been common in East Africa—Kenya, Tanzania and Uganda—as well as in Mozambique, Somalia, Botswana, Angola and other areas. For years, lions were considered vermin, and a sportsman could take as many as he could find. Now, in most places, one is the limit.

The male lion, of all the cat family, is maned, and the mane is regarded very highly as a trophy, just as antlers are by the deer hunter. The thicker the mane, the better, and the finest of trophies is a big, black-maned lion. The lion in the wild, I might add, usually does not have the thick, elegant mane of his brothers who have been raised in captivity.

On the third day after putting out our bait, we were peeping through the scrub that edged the sand-river gully. Although it was about five o'clock in the afternoon, the very bright light on the sun-bleached grass and bush made the shadows in the depression seem almost midnight-black, and it was difficult to distinguish details. Finally, I made out a lump on a slight mound across the gully to my right, at a distance of around eighty-five yards. The lump stirred and, in silhouette, a lion stood up, suspiciously alert. As I watched him for a couple of seconds, a vivid picture of the row of little white crosses in the Nairobi graveyard flashed across my mind—each marking a victim of a mishap with wounded African dangerous game. I had plenty of confidence in my scope-sighted, .375 H&H Magnum caliber rifle (300-grain Silvertip Expanding bullet), and I hoped I could place a shot fairly accurately.

Glen Cottar, my companion and a professional hunter, whispered, "That's a good lion. Take him!"

Old Simba stood facing the right and slightly away from me. He seemed ready to spring into the dense, junglelike growth back of him, so I eased the rifle into shooting position, put the cross hair on a spot back of his front leg and not quite halfway up the body and touched off a shot. Remember, the beast was slightly below me, and I wanted a bullet through the boiler room and a busted shoulder to break down locomotion, if possible.

To quote my diary: *"Stalked lion about 5 p.m. Shot him in top heart, broke left shoulder with .375."*

He went down and didn't move. We approached him with caution. That shot actually did the job, but we were unaware of the fact at the time. He was a big, black-maned fellow. A lion can weigh 400 to 500 pounds, and we had to have help getting him into the Land Rover. In fact, it took five of us to do the job.

The majority of lions, as well as other game, are taken in just about that way. It amounts to finding the game animal wanted, making the stalk and doing the shooting.

That doesn't sound very exciting when coldly told, but I can assure you that it is highly electric, almost agonizing, for the guys who are there.

Someone once said that a person is scared three times by lions: first, when he hears one roar; second, when he sees one for the first time in the wild, and third, when he shoots one. If the beast is not killed almost instantly, the shooter can be in for a lot of trouble.

Speaking of adequate rifles, I met a fellow in Nairobi who had just returned from the bush in an area where there were no laws on minimum calibers for various game animals. This lad's favorite rifle was a .243 Winchester caliber, a great one within its limitations. I asked him if he had trouble using such a light rifle on African animals. He said yes. A real understatement!

Later, I talked with his hunter. In some disgust, he said that most of the time on that safari was spent in chasing wounded animals. Such activity

Due to his 5- or 6-ton weight and his brute strength, the elephant can do more damage under adverse conditions than any other game animal in the world.

certainly is on the stupid side and can be very dangerous for everyone involved. I can't imagine why the professional hunter allowed it. He told me that this fellow was very headstrong and the only thing the hunter could do was to terminate the safari as soon as possible.

A hunter who follows almost any African game, especially the dangerous kind, does so at a certain risk. But this risk is minimized almost to zero by explicitly following the advice of his professional hunter. Practically all these chaps are cool, cautious, of good judgment and with a lot of field experience in the background.

Just about every American hunter has a keen desire to give Africa a try. For most, it's a dream come true. Plans for such a trip should be under way six to eight months ahead of take-off time. And equipment needed in the field, such as arms, ammunition and other heavy or bulky items, should be shipped by sea freight at least four months before the starting date of the safari. It is probably best to carry cameras, film and binoculars along with you on the aircraft.

If the landing spot in Africa is Nairobi I know for a fact that hunting clothing and footwear can be had, made to measure, very quickly and at a reasonable cost.

My gear didn't show up in Nairobi when I did. We planned to head for Karamoja in a couple of days to try to retrace some of the steps of W. D. M. Bell, the great elephant hunter, and I had to have the bare necessities in hunting clothes. Two bush jackets, two pairs of slacks and three shirts as well as a pair of shoes, somewhat similar in design to the well-known Clark's desert boots, were all made to my measure overnight, in less than fifteen hours.

Other items needed for the bush included three changes of underwear, about a half dozen pairs of lightweight wool socks, two pairs of pajamas, an extra pair of ankle length walking boots, a pair of sneakers and some lightweight rain gear. It can be chilly to downright cold in the morning and evening, so a neutral-colored pullover will come in handy. Your professional hunter can steer you right regarding any special clothing that may be needed for the area to be hunted. Our hunters usually wore only shorts, sneakers and a hat.

A pair of high-magnification binoculars or perhaps a spotting scope, carried in the hunting car, helps a great deal for close examination of distant game. I had a big pair of Bausch & Lomb glasses for this purpose. Also, I had a pair of the little Bushnell Broadfield binoculars which can be carried out of the way in the shirt or bush jacket breast pocket. A pair of shooting glasses, in my estimation, is a must. Maybe I'm a sissy, but I will not shoot a gun of any kind without wearing a good pair of shooting glasses. I had two pairs, both Bausch & Lomb, one in light yellow (Kalichrome) which amazingly brightens and gives things more contrast on dull, overcast days, and a pair of medium green ones (Ray-Ban Green) for bright days.

The best time to hunt and the seasons vary quite a bit in great hunting areas. Naturally, the time to be there is when it is not raining. In East Africa—in Kenya, Tanzania and Uganda—the long rains usually begin about the end of March or the beginning of April and taper off in June, with May usually seeing the real downpours. The short rains generally start during the latter part of October and end about the first of the year. Probably January, February and March would be most satisfactory from the standpoint of fine weather and successful hunting.

In Angola (Mucusso Concession), the hunting season is from June first through December; in Botswana, one of Africa's newest safari countries, it is from April through October; in Mozambique, along the eastern coast south of Tanzania, it goes from April through December fifteenth; Somalia, bordering northern Kenya and Ethiopia, has two hunting seasons—July first to October fifteenth and from December first through March thirty-first; in Zambia (Northern Rhodesia), it lasts from May twenty-fifth through November third.

7

Secrets of Long-range Shooting

JUST WHAT IS A long-range rifle?

Well, my friend, it's all relative. A long-range rifle for an eastern deer hunter may be one that will shoot well enough to clobber a whitetail at 150 yards. That's a long shot in many parts of the East, where the majority of deer are taken at 150 yards and less, and calls for a rifle that will group 5 shots into a cluster measuring about 4 to 6 inches at that distance.

While speaking of that kind of shooting, it is pertinent to mention that a great many deer hunters using rifles for the famous .30-30 Winchester and .35 Remington class cartridges (as well as a great many other calibers) handicap themselves by not sighting-in their rifles properly for the longest point-blank range possible for the particular cartridge. With such zeroing, a shooter is better equipped for success when a longer shot than usual is necessary.

Probably the best way to sight-in a big-game rifle is to adjust the sights so that the bullets strike about 3 inches above the aiming point at 100 yards. The .30-30, with 170-grain bullet from a carbine with open sights, sighted-in to group at the point of aim at 100 yards, will group 8 or 9 inches below the point of aim at 200 yards and around 28 to 30 inches low at 300 yards. Sighting-in for grouping 3 inches high at 100 yards gives a longer point-blank range without having to hold over or under at distances up to about 200 yards on deer-size game.

The open plains or mountain rifle definitely should be scope sighted-in for the longest distance that will not cause midrange misses by overshooting. Here again, the rule of thumb is for grouping 3 inches above the sighting line of the scope at 100 yards. This gives a more favorable point-blank range than the conventional sighting-in at 200 yards, where, with most high-velocity cartridges, the group will print from slightly over an inch high (for the really fast ones) to nearly 2½ inches high (for those in the 2,700-feet-per-second bracket) at 100 yards and from around 5½ to about 10 inches low or below the aiming point at 300 yards.

Two highly popular calibers in North America are the .30-06 Springfield and .270 Winchester. Ballistics figures for the .308 Winchester are very similar to those of the .30-06, and those for the .280 Remington (a 7-mm with .284-inch-diameter bullet) are about the same as for the .270. These cartridges have proven adequate for any species of American game animals. The .284 Winchester (also a 7-mm) was designed and developed to give .270 performance in the short-action Winchester Model 88 lever-action and Model 100 autoloading rifles. (These rifles also are made in .243 and .308 Winchester calibers.)

When sighted-in to group 3 inches high at 100 yards, such cartridges as the .264 Winchester Magnum with a 140-grain bullet, the 7-mm Remington Magnum with a 150-grain bullet, the .270 Winchester with a 130-grain bullet, the .280 Remington with a 125-grain bullet, the .300 Winchester Magnum and .300 Weatherby Magnum with 150- or 180-grain bullets will shoot just about at the point of aim at 275 yards, a little low at 300 yards, about 5 inches low at 325 yards. The .30-06, with a 150-grain bullet, will print about on the nose at 250 yards and 5 or 6 inches low at 300; the 180-grain bullet shortens the range by about 25 yards. These figures are approximate and the rifleman should check his rifle by shooting at the various distances.

The objective in using the magnums is that, in many instances, besides flatter trajectory, the striking energy is greater at the longer distances. However, higher velocity, flatter trajectory and higher striking energy of a given weight bullet of a caliber mean higher foot pounds of recoil and more whack at the shoulder.

Also, long-distance shots on game can introduce other problems; accurate estimation of distance to the target is one. If you ever have been involved with range-determination exercises of the Army and Air Force, you know how difficult this problem is for the inexperienced with the average error in estimation at distances beyond 200 yards being about 30 percent. Let's say a sportsman has spent a lot of time and money in obtaining a new long-range rifle in .264 or .300 Winchester Magnum, 7-mm Remington Magnum, or one of the Weatherby magnums, and has sighted it in to group at the point of aim at the conventional 200 yards. He has little or no experience in judging distance and, in western mountain country, he spots a game animal—it could be a sheep, goat, antelope or deer—at a range of 350 yards.

With his inexperience, and in the crystal air, the target seems to be much nearer than it actually is. He misjudges the distance by 30 percent. Believing the range to be a bit under 250 yards, and with his rifle accurately sighted-in to group on the point of aim at 200 yards, he figures that he should aim (from a steady rest) dead center on the lung-heart area, maybe a couple of inches high. He really bears down, carefully squeezes the trigger, and the rifle fires with the cross hairs of his scope exactly in the specified place. Whups, what happened? The bullet hit about a foot low

Game often must be taken at great distance or not at all. This roan antelope, world's record for Uganda, was collected with the long-range .264 Win. Magnum.

for a miss or a nonfatal crease at the lower chest, depending on the size of the animal. Off takes the trophy in high gear!

If our hypothetical hunter had overestimated the distance by 30 percent and figured the range to be more than 500 yards, he knows, from actual shooting, that the center of bullet-group impact is about a yard and a half low at that distance. So, he aims that far above the target and, sure enough, shoots over it.

Long-range shooting on game animals involves too many variables. Actually, I am a nonbeliever in really long-distance shots. A complete miss is a no-damage proposition, but there is always the chance of sorely wounding a fine game animal and having it get away to suffer needlessly.

However, in all honesty, I must admit that I have made several long shots that were mostly luck—maybe I should say slightly educated luck. And I missed one important shot that certainly will be remembered as long as I live. It was in East Africa. Glen Cottar and I had followed a really great Lesser Kudu for two days. From glassing him, we judged his spiral horns to be over 30 inches in length—big for a Lesser Kudu, maybe a record—and he was a beauty. Late in the afternoon of the second day, while crawling through high grass, I got nearer to him than at any time before. I tried to figure out what to do. My .264 Magnum caliber Winchester Model 70, with Weaver variable-power scope set at 7x, was sighted-in at 250 yards with the 140-grain bullet. It was make a try or give up. I decided that a base-of-the-spine shot would be the best bet. The grass was too high for the sitting or kneeling shooting position and there wasn't anything handy for a rest shot.

The animal, standing under a tamarind tree, stayed put as I slowly raised my head above the thick grass. Trying to hold the horizontal cross hair about a foot and a half above the Kudu's back (I was pretty well pooped), I increased the trigger squeeze as the cross hairs appeared in proper alignment. Finally the rifle fired, but at the instant, the reticle wavered slightly to the right. My elevation apparently was about right. The bullet evidently creased the right hip, enough to cause the animal to jump sideways, almost down. He jumped and disappeared before I could extract the fired case and reload the chamber of my rifle. We followed the tracks until dark, but never saw that Kudu again.

Many of the high-velocity, flat-trajectory big-game rifles are excellent for varmint hunting when used with lighter-weight bullets that are factory-loaded for that purpose. Or it is easy to handload almost any cartridge as a special-purpose load. High-velocity rifles will prove handier, especially if used for hunting small varmint, if they are sighted-in to group 1½ inches high at 100 yards.

It may be pertinent to mention that extremely high velocity results in shorter barrel life for a rifle. This can be quite serious for the rifleman who touches off several hundred shots during a season of varmint hunting.

Speaking of high velocity and flat trajectory, the .240 Weatherby Magnum cartridge in three bullet weights—70-, 90- and 100-grain—is the fastest of the factory cartridges using .243-inch-diameter (usually called 6-mm) bullets. Ballistics data for the three bullets is impressive. Muzzle velocity of the 70-grain bullet is 3,850 feet per second, with muzzle energy of 2,304 foot-pounds. Remaining velocity at 300 yards is 2,585 feet per second, with 1,038 foot-pounds of energy. Midrange trajectory for 200 yards is 1.5 inches and under 4 inches for 300 yards. The 90-grain bullet, with initial velocity of 3,500 feet per second, has a midrange trajectory of under 2 inches for 200 yards and 4.5 inches for 300 yards. The 100-

grain bullet starts out at 3,395 feet per second and has trajectory figures almost exactly the same as for the 90-grain bullet. Its remaining energy at 300 yards is a high 1,495 foot-pounds. This indicates that the Weatherby Mark V rifle for this cartridge could be sighted-in to group at the point of aim at 250 yards and have a point-blank range of around 300 yards, with the necessity of having to hold only about 6 inches high at 350 yards. I haven't given this a try, since I have shot only the 90-grain bullet.

In shooting the Weatherby Mark V with the 90-grain bulleted .240 Magnum cartridge, I fired a series of 3-shot groups over a period of several months, including warm, humid weather, on through various changes to subzero conditions. The idea behind this procedure is that in the field, on game animals, the first shots are the really important ones, and I also wanted to determine if the rifle had any tendency to change its point of group impact under seasonal changes. The targets I used were green, printed on a very light buff paper, with seven targets on each 24-by-18-inch sheet. The central target is 12 inches in diameter, divided into 12 pie-piece segments numbered like a clock face. It has a 1-inch wide outer ring of solid green, then two 1-inch rings in white and a 6-inch green bull with a 2-inch white center and 1-inch dotted X-ring. Four white channels extend from the white center to the outside edge of the 6-inch bull for scope cross-hair alignment. Four of the 6-inch bulls, as well as two 2-inch green squares with 1-inch square white centers, are included on each sheet. These targets, made by Texas Riflesmith Supply, 214 Regent Street, San Antonio, Texas, are excellent, especially for sighting in scoped sporting rifles.

The first of the 3-shot groups, 100 yards, measured 1.26 inches; the second one, about 2 inches (by far the largest one fired), but with two shots in one hole. These groups were fired by sighting with a Weatherby 4-power Imperial scope. I wanted more magnification and replaced it with one of Weatherby's Imperial variable-power scopes, 2 to 7x. The third group measured a hair over an inch; the fourth, .70-inch, and the fifth, .80-inch. That's about the way it went through the rest of the series. Practically all of the shooting was done with a wind blowing from left to right. There was but little indication of wind drift.

During the several months—four to be exact—there was no change in point of group impact on the targets. The accuracy has been near or less than a minute of angle, except for the first couple of groups. This .240 Weatherby Magnum should prove excellent for longer-than-average shots on deer-size game, especially antelope.

And remember, the less a hunter has to be concerned with trajectory when in long-range country, the better off he is; the farther he can hit with a center-of-the-chest hold, the more game he'll take!

8

Varmint Hunter's Guide

"NOW, YOU TAKE little *tamias striatus;* he is one varmint that takes but little in cartridge-rifle combo to bag. On the other hand, *felis concolor* most often requires more ordnance, unless he is hunted with dogs. And old *panthera leo* really takes a lot of killing. *Marmota monax* often can be, and is, taken at ranges of from a few yards to several hundred, and more often than not, the enthusiast needs a small-caliber cartridge that delivers very flat trajectory in a very accurate rifle. So, it's easy to understand that a real all-around varmint hunter may need quite a battery of rifles."

That was Aak speaking. He is a prominent member of our hot-stove league and a treasury of obscure facts and odd bits of information. He also loves to use the scientific names of various game animals when he can think of them, which can be rather confusing. However, Aak is an experienced hunter, is well liked by the fraternity and is generally considered an authority on outdoor subjects. Some years ago, someone called our talkative friend "Accurate Angus," affectionately shortened, in time, to "Aak."

Aak was speaking of the common eastern chipmunk, the mountain lion, the African lion and the woodchuck, in that order. He took in a lot of territory when considering the pest and varmint class of animals and was a little haywire in respect to the lion. In the past, the "King of Beasts" has been considered in thc varmint category, with no limit to the number taken by a hunter. But now, he is considered a game animal in some areas of Africa, with but one kill permitted per hunting license. However, marauding lions are classified as dangerous varmints and are relentlessly hunted.

Turning to me, Aak continued, "Pete, you have killed at least one example of the *panthera-leo* family. What would you say is the best rifle for this varmint?"

Now, killing an African lion certainly does not make one an expert on the subject, but I do know that in Africa, Persia and India, lions have been taken with many different caliber rifles. Let's take a look at this creature.

The lion is a large and powerful carnivore, measuring from nine feet to eleven feet in length and standing to about three feet, nine inches at the shoulder. He weighs from 400 to 500 pounds and can crush the skull of an ox or break the back of a horse with a single blow of his massive forepaw, and carry off a bullock in his jaws. He can cover thirty feet at a single bound, and few animals, except the antelopes, can outrun him. Maneating lions are rare, but they have been known to enter native villages and carry off a man or a woman in their jaws.

That, my friend, is big varmint. Maybe I'm a member of the chicken patrol, but for my money, I want something powerful enough to knock him down and keep him there. The .375 will do that, with some to spare.

Actually, most every caliber rifle in the .30-06 and 8-mm Mauser class, as well as heavier and lighter calibers, have been used on lion for years. The .256 Mannlicher-Schoenauer once was a popular caliber for practically all African game (now considered adequate only for normal plains game) and even the old .22 Hi-Power was touted by some individuals as the ideal weapon for all African animals, with the possible exception of the very largest pachyderms. There is no question but that lesser-caliber

The lion was formerly the world's largest no-limit varmint, and is now considered a game animal in most areas.

rifles have taken thousands of head of dangerous African game, including elephant. However, there are many victims of misplaced confidence in inadequate-caliber rifles for lion, rhino, buffalo and elephant.

Most hunters who have experience with African hunting suggest that rifles chambered for such cartridges as the .300 and .375 Holland & Holland Magnum and Weatherby .300 and .375 Magnums are good medicine for lions. Rifles of these calibers are regularly produced by American manufacturers. The game departments of East Africa insist that the minimum caliber for lion, buffalo, rhino and elephant is the .375, and they prefer something bigger for elephant.

The .375 H & H Magnum is not a controversial cartridge. Introduced in 1912, it has long been considered by many experienced hunters as the most nearly all-around proposition for world-wide dangerous game. It perhaps is overly powerful for American game, but it really will do a job on elk, moose, grizzly and Kodiak brown bear. Many Alaskan guides regularly tote the .375 as a lifesaver, in case of trouble with a big brownie.

Before the advent of the heavier Weatherby Magnums and the .458 Winchester Magnum, the .375 was the most powerful cartridge commercially produced in the United States—with the Winchester Model 70 being the only American rifle made for it.

When the Browning line of centerfire rifles was introduced, the .375 Magnum caliber was included. The Remington Model 700, the Steyr-Mannlicher Model S Rifle (imported by Stoeger Arms), and let's not forget the Winchester Model 70, are available in this caliber. And I might add, the .338 Winchester Magnum will do just about anything the .375 will do.

In case you are not familiar with the .375 H & H Magnum cartridge, let's compare it to the .30-06, which is well known to most every shooter. The heaviest loading in the .30-06 is with 220-grain bullet—in .375 with 300-grain bullet. Velocity and trajectory figures of these bullets are quite similar. The 220-grain bullet leaves the muzzle at 2,410 feet per second, the 300-grain bullet at 2,550 feet per second. At 300 yards, the .30-06 bullet is perking at 1,790 feet per second, while that of the .375 is at 1,830 fps. The mid-range trajectory for both is under an inch for 100 yards, slightly over three and a half inches for 200 yards and a bit over nine inches for 300 yards.

But in the developed-energy department, there is a vast difference in favor of the .375. And sheer energy delivered and expended within the body of a game animal is the big factor in killing power. The 220-grain, .30-06 bullet is given 2,830 foot pounds of energy at the muzzle, while the 300-grain bullet of the .375 delivers 4,330 foot pounds of energy at the same place. At 200 yards, the .375 slug has retained 2,770 foot pounds of energy (more than the .270-caliber cartridge with 150-grain bullet delivers at the muzzle), as compared to 1,910 for the heavy .30-06 bullet.

When sighted in to shoot about three inches high at 100 yards, the .375 bullet will print about on the nose at 225 yards and you won't have to hold high at 250 yards on big game. And in case you meet up with an old *panthera-leo* varmint, you'll be well prepared with the .375. In a pinch, you'll have enough power for an unexpected elephant or rhino. And if you want something more powerful for your varmint hunting, the .458 Winchester Magnum is the ticket!

Most always, an individual's first rifle is a .22 rimfire of one kind or another. This is as it should be because the .22 is the very best for teaching people to shoot. It is highly accurate, has practically no recoil, which eliminates the development of flinching—a deadly enemy of accurate shooting—and it permits a lot of low-cost practice—the big element in becoming a good shot.

Within its scope, the .22 Long Rifle, in a good rifle, is one of our most accurate cartridges. Although extensively fired in specialized rifles for serious target shooting, the great mass of .22 ammunition is expended in small-game and small-varmint or pest hunting and in plinking or everyday fun shooting. For best results and practical trajectory in hunting small game and varmint, the .22 probably should be sighted in at seventy-five yards with Long Rifle, high-speed ammo. This puts the bullet an inch high at fifty yards and about three inches low at 100 yards.

When the .22 rimfire shooter goes out after woodchuck, prairie dog and crow, he soon learns that it is very difficult to connect with a killing shot at much over 100 yards, even with a scope-sighted, high-grade rifle. Bullet drop is enough to make it imperative that distance be judged accurately. Also, due to its low velocity, as compared to centerfire varmint cartridges, the .22 rimfire bullet is wind sensitive and a puff over the 100-yard range can put it well off the aiming point. Among 100-yard, small-bore target shooters, accurate wind doping is the element that separates the champs from the runners-up.

The .22 Winchester Magnum Rim Fire is between the .22 Long Rifle and the .22 Hornet cartridges on the ballistics chart. I have found it to be accuate and performance in the field is excellent. The forty-grain, hollow-point bullet is given 2,000-feet-per-second muzzle velocity. Remaining velocity at 100 yards is 1,390 feet per second, or more than that of the .22 Long Rifle at the muzzle. The .22 Magnum Rim Fire has caught on among shooters in great style. Marlin, Model 980 and Mossberg, Model 640, both bolt action; Savage, Model 24 over and-under, .22 Magnum and .410 or 20 gauge shotgun; and the Winchester Model 255 lever-action and 275 slide-action repeaters are all inexpensive rifles designed especially for this cartridge.

This rimfire cartridge also is popular among those who like to hunt small- to medium-size varmint with the handgun. The reason? Its bullet develops a muzzle velocity of 1,550 feet per second in a six-and-a-half-inch revolver barrel. This puts the .22 Magnum Rim Fire way out in front among rimfire cartridges and quite a bit ahead of most centerfire handgun cartridges in the muzzle-speed department. Revolvers chambered for this hot little number include the Colt's Single Action Frontier Scout; the Smith & Wesson Model 48, K-22 and the Model 51, 22/32 Kit Gun, and the Ruger Single Six for .22 Winchester Magnum Rim Fire. The Single Six also is furnished with interchangeable cylinder for the .22 Short, Long and Long Rifle cartridges at a slight extra cost.

So, the logical step forward, after thorough grounding with the .22 rimfire, is for the shooter to secure one of the long-range, centerfire varmint rifles. There are plenty to choose from and some will double as a deer taker.

Ingenious chuck hunters of the 1930s, who did a lot of experimenting with wildcat cartridges, were the pioneers in development of flat-trajectory varmint cartridges, and can be said to be responsible for our ultramodern varmint calibers.

The little .22 Hornet, originally a wildcat, was introduced in 1932 and it was the first of our specialized varmint cartridges. The Hornet was, and still is, a good accurate proposition, with low muzzle report and fairly flat trajectory. However, it, as well as the .218 Bee, the .219 Zipper and early wildcats such as the .22-3000, the Lovell cartridges, the Wasp, the .22 Gebby, and many others, are little heard of today. The Hornet does not have the range of more recently introduced varmint cartridges, but it is effective at 150 yards—maybe 175.

Woodchuck or "groundhog" is our most sought-after rifleman's pest or varmint target, requiring patience and high-level rifle accuracy, as well as stalking ability.

Even the deservedly famous .220 Swift has been on a steady decline. The Swift, with a muzzle velocity of 4,110 feet per second for the forty-eight-grain bullet, still is the fastest and has the flattest trajectory of our factory cartridges. When sighted in, with a scope-sighted rifle, to group about an inch and a quarter to an inch and a half high at 100 yards, it is just about on the nose at 250 yards and only about three inches low at 300 yards. That really is flat trajectory, and for my money, the Swift is still a great varmint rifle!

Today, our most popular of the .22 centerfire cartridges is the .222 Remington. It has a lot in its favor—low muzzle report, little recoil and superb accuracy. The cartridge caught on rapidly among varmint and bench-rest shooters. The fifty-grain, soft-point bullet of the factory load is given a most respectable muzzle velocity of 3,200 feet per second. Mid-range trajectory for 200 yards is only about two and a-half inches with an iron-sighted rifle. The very favorable point-blank range of 200 yards, or slightly more on woodchuck-size animals, can be obtained with a scope-sighted rifle. Sighted in at 180 yards, the bullet will print less than two inches high at 100 yards, a hair low at 200, and will require a holdover of slightly less than five inches at 250 yards. That makes the .222 a good 225-yard chuck rifle—maybe even 250 for the rifleman who can judge distance accurately.

The .222 is a natural for reloading with a number of precisely made bullets produced by Speer, Sierra, Harnady, Remington and Winchester available for the shooter who likes to roll his own.

The Remington bolt-action Model 722 was the first rifle to be introduced in .222 caliber. Since then, Models 725 and 40X bolt-action, as well as the 700 rifles have been chambered for this cartridge by Remington. Other rifles in .222 caliber that I have fired include the Marlin Varmint King (an excellent rifle, now discontinued), Sako, Savage Model 340 and the little Krico Carbine, imported by Stoeger Arms Corporation.

The new Remington .222 Magnum is a lengthened version of the regular .222. Slightly flatter trajectory and a gain in developed energy is achieved with a fifty-five-grain bullet at 3,300-feet-per-second muzzle velocity. This is an excellent cartridge and it may take some of the popularity away from the regular .222. Most existing rifles now chambered for the .222 can be converted to the .222 Magnum.

Next in the scale of varmint cartridges are those of 6-mm or .24 caliber. The .243 Winchester, introduced in the Model 70 Winchester rifle, is based on the .308 cartridge necked down for .24-caliber bullets. It is factory loaded with eighty-grain bullets at 3,500-feet-per-second muzzle velocity, and with 100-grain bullet at 3,070-feet-per-second muzzle velocity. The .244 Remington was first brought out in the Remington Model 722 rifle.

It is based on the .257 cartridge case; the ninety grain bullet leaves the muzzle at 3,200 feet per second.

The 6-mm Remington cartridge is similar to the .244, with chambering in the Remington Model 700 rifle. The 6-mm is loaded with 80-grain bullet, 3,540 f.p.s. and 100 grain at 3,190 f.p.s.

The combination of light recoil, flat trajectory and effective killing power makes either the .243 or 6-mm an excellent choice for the hunter who wants a good long-range varmint job that also will double for deer and antelope.

The latest cartridge in the varmint-deer class is the .25-06 Remington, which is loaded with an 87-grain bullet at 3,500 f.p.s. and a 120-grain bullet for big game.

Popular cartridges with commercial loadings for both big game and varmint include the .264 Winchester Magnum, .270 Winchester, .308 Winchester and the .30-06. Others, such as the 6.5-mm Remington Magnum and 7-mm Remington Magnum, can be used for this purpose.

There are a variety of rifles available for most of these calibers and almost without exception, they are the handloader's delight.

9

The .22—Any Man's Rifle

ALMOST ALL OF US DID our first shooting with a .22 rimfire rifle of one kind or another, and I doubt if there is anyone of shooting age who has not heard of or used that caliber rifle for fun plinking or small-game hunting. Today a great many more .22s are popped off than all other sporting ammunition. Also, more money has been spent on development, perfection and quality control of the .22 than on any other non-military cartridge.

Regardless of the fact that the .22 rimfire is our most popular cartridge, there seems to be a good deal of confusion in the minds of many shooters regarding it. And the issue is made more perplexing by the so-called .22 centerfire cartridges, such as the .22 Hornet, .218 Bee, .222 Remington, .22-250 Remington, .224 Weatherby Magnum, and .225 Winchester Magnum.

I have received letters from many sportsmen that indicate lack of understanding on such subjects as trajectory, cartridge construction and pressures developed by them, interchangeability of cartridges, and so on.

A common question is one from a person who wants flatter trajectory from bullets fired in a .22 rimfire rifle, so that he can reach out farther to knock over woodchucks. Seventy-five yards is about the range limit for the .22 Long Rifle cartridge on woodchucks. Please don't write in to tell me that you have killed them at longer range. I know that has been done many times, but nevertheless, it is not very sporting to shoot at a woodchuck beyond that range with a .22 rimfire rifle.

The question from such an aspiring rifleman usually reads something like this: "I want to have my .22 pump gun changed so that it will shoot the .220 Swift cartridge. I hear that it will kill chucks at over 250 yards. Will the factory do this job for me, or where can I get it done?"

The answer to that one is easy. No gunsmith or anyone else can convert a modern .22 rimfire caliber rifle to handle the .220 Swift, or any other of the .22 centerfire cartridges. The working breech pressure of the .220 Swift is in the neighborhood of 53,000 pounds per square inch—in the general class of the .30-06, .270, and .300 Magnum. The .22 Long Rifle develops a pressure of only about 24,000 pounds per square inch. Pressures developed by the .22 Hornet, .218 Bee and .219 Zipper are about 40,000 pounds per square inch. Rimfire rifles simply are not designed and made to stand such stress and strain.

The .22 Short and Long Rifle rimfire cartridges are most used today. Others, such as the .22 BB Cap, .22 CB Cap, .22 W.R.F. or Special, .22 Winchester Automatic, .22 Remington Autoloading and the .22 Extra Long, now obsolete, have seen quite some popularity in the past.

The .22 Short, patented by Smith and Wesson in 1854, was the pioneer .22 cartridge. The original little BB Cap or Bullet Breech Cap contained no powder, but was loaded with a .22-caliber round ball propelled by the fulminate priming compound in its case rim. Later this tiny cartridge was loaded with a light charge of powder and what amounted to a conical ball weighing eighteen or twenty grains. The BB Cap and the CB Cap (which had a similar case loaded with a twenty-nine-grain conical bullet and a charge of powder) just recently have been discontinued. The .22 Short was the first really successful self-contained metallic cartridge.

At twenty-five and fifty yards, the .22 Short, with its twenty-nine-grain bullet, gives good accuracy, especially so in some of the fine old single-shot target rifles that were made for it. Although the .22 Short cartridge is made and used in great quantities in rifles designed for firing the Short, Long and Long Rifle cartridges interchangeably, there are no rifles now being chambered and rifled especially for it.

The .22 rimfire rifle is the most used of all our sporting firearms. Here are three Winchester Model 121s: Deluxe, Standard, Youth.

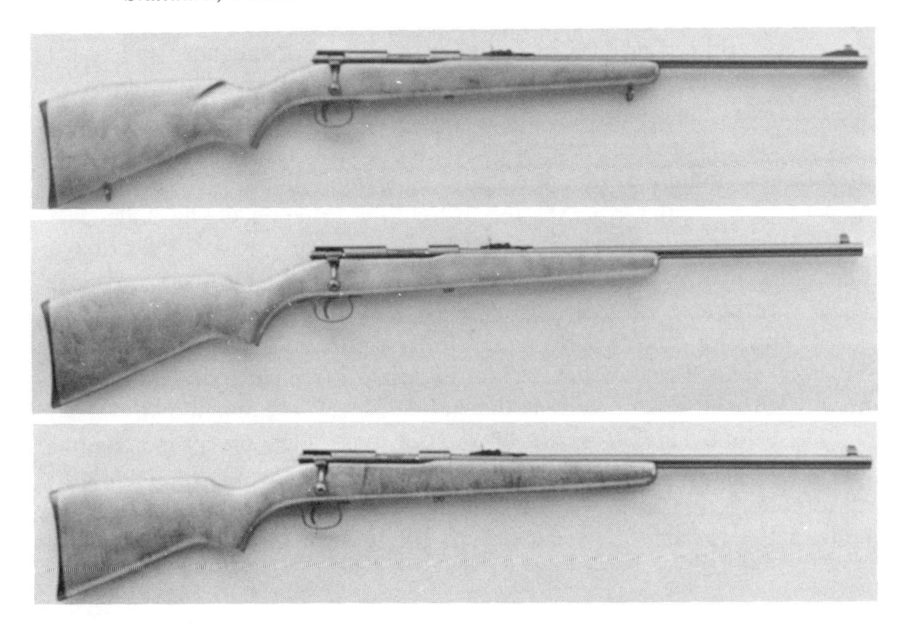

The .22 Long was designed to meet the demand for a cartridge with more punch than the Short, for killing small game. It has a longer case, similar to that of the .22 Long Rifle cartridge, loaded with more powder than the .22 Short bullet. It develops more velocity than the Short, but usually gives poorer accuracy.

The .22 Long Rifle cartridge is by far the most useful of all .22 rimfire cartridges now being produced. It gives superb accuracy in a good rifle, and the ammunition makers are super-careful to maintain a very high level of quality control in its production. Special target cartridges receive even more attention in their precise manufacture to insure almost unbelievable uniformity from cartridge to cartridge. They give tack-driving accuracy in match rifles, such as the Winchester Model 52 and Remington Model 40XB, and usually are decidedly more accurate than other types of Long Rifle cartridges in sporting rifles chambered and rifled especially for Long Rifle ammo.

The Long Rifle bullet weighs forty grains and is given a muzzle velocity of 1,145 feet per second with regular loading, and 1,335 feet per second with high-speed loading. The Long Rifle hollow-point bullet, especially for small-game hunting, weighs thirty-six or thirty-seven grains and develops a muzzle velocity of 1,365 feet per second. For comparison, the .22 Short has a twenty-nine-grain bullet with 1,045-fps muzzle velocity in regular loading, and 1,125-fps muzzle velocity in high-speed loading. The twenty-nine-grain bullet of the .22 Long has a muzzle velocity of 1,240 fps.

Rifle and pistol barrels are rifled by cutting or forming spiral grooves in the bores. After drilling, the hole through the barrel is reamed to finished size—termed the bore diameter. Then the rifling is formed, either by cutting or displacing metal, in spiral grooves of from one-thousandth to five-thousandths of an inch in depth, depending on the caliber and type of rifling used. The distance or diameter from the bottom of one groove to the bottom of the opposite groove is called the groove diameter.

The ribs between the grooves, technically called lands, bite into the bullet as it enters the bore to give it a spiral or turning motion, which continues as a rapid spin after it leaves the barrel. The rotation of the bullet is so fast that it becomes, in effect, a small gyroscope or gyrostat, the principle being that a body rotating steadily about an axis will tend to resist changes in the direction of the axis.

The spinning top often is pointed to as a good example of the gyrostat. You well know that if a top is spun just right it will spin straight upon its point, and spin in one spot if the floor is level. If spun too fast it will wobble a little until its speed of rotation has fallen the proper amount and it has gyrostatic stability, when it will "go to sleep," until the speed of rotation is too low, when it will wobble and fall over. The spinning bullet acts in exactly the same way. If the twist of the rifling is right, and other conditions correct, a rotating cylindrical bullet flies straight, with its point to the front, in continuation with the axis of the rifle bore, but less the drop or fall due to gravity pull and any deflection caused by wind or drift.

The business of the bullet beginning to fall, due to gravity, as soon as it leaves the gun muzzle, seems to create a little confusion in the minds of some shooters. I have received letters from a number of readers who maintain that this is not true with their rifles. The latest is from a fellow who recently bought a Winchester Model 70 rifle in .243 caliber. He said that at near range the rifle shoots exactly where he aims, but that at longer distances, such as 100 yards and over, the bullet hits higher on the target. So how could the bullet be falling?

At first glance that statement may seem logical. The only trouble is that his conception of what actually happens is a bit haywire. All of us should understand that as soon as the bullet leaves the gun muzzle, gravity begins its pull downward toward the center of the earth, and it follows a curved path called a trajectory. So, to hit a distant object, the axis of the barrel bore actually is pointed above the target. The sights of a rifle are arranged so that when they are aligned on a target at a predetermined sight-in distance, the bullet will hit the target. In other words, the line of sight is straight to the target, while the path of the bullet begins in an upward direction as compared to the line of sight. It intersects the line of sight at some near distance and continues upward until it reaches the vertex or highest point in the trajectory. Then the bullet begins to move slightly downward in its path toward the target until it hits it at the line of sight. Remember, all movement of the bullet after it leaves the gun muzzle is below an extension of the line of axis of the barrel bore. So, from the standpoint of the direction in which the gun is pointing, the bullet is falling all the time until it reaches the earth.

When sighting in a rifle, it pays in ammunition saving to do the initial shooting at the near distances where the bullet first crosses the line of sight in the upward portion of the trajectory. It is not unheard of for a rifleman, who wants to sight in his rifle at 200 or 250 yards with a scope sight, to shoot a box or more of ammunition without hitting the target, and with no idea of how to adjust his sights, as he does not know where the bullets are landing. Take our friend's new .243-caliber rifle, for example. Say he is using the cartridge loaded with the eighty-grain bullet and wants to sight in for 250 yards with scope sight. If he first shoots at forty yards and adjusts his sights so that the bullet impact is at the point of aim, the bullets will strike about one and three quarters inches high, or above the point of aim, at 100 yards; about two inches high at 150 yards; approximately one and a half inches high at 200 yards, and just about at the point of aim at 250 yards. At 300 yards the bullet will strike about two and a half inches below point of aim, and in the neighborhood of six and a half inches low at 350 yards. Brother, that's mighty flat trajectory, and when holding on fair-size game, the point-blank range can be considered at about 300 yards, without aiming high or low.

We were talking about .22s, remember? Seventy-five yards is a practical distance to sight in with the high-speed .22 Long Rifle cartridge when using a scope sight. If initial targeting is done at sixteen and a-half yards, the bullet will strike approximately an inch high at fifty yards, just about at point of aim at the zero range of seventy-five yards and about three inches low at 100 yards. When sighting in at the nearer distance, it is important that the rifle be check-fired at the zero range because peculiarities of the individual rifle may cause the trajectory to vary slightly.

Degree of pitch or twist of rifling in a rifle bore has varied from around one turn in six and a half inches to one turn in seventy-two inches. The longer the bullet in comparison to its diameter, the quicker the twist must be to maintain gyrostatic stability during its flight. That is, to keep it flying accurately, point on, and not tumbling. Also, to a certain extent, the higher the velocity of a bullet, the slower the twist necessary to stabilize it.

Now let's see what rifling twist is necessary to stabilize the lead-alloy bullets of .22-caliber rimfire cartridges. Barrels for the bullet of the .22 Short cartridge have been rifled with a pitch of one turn in twenty, twenty-four and twenty-five inches. Today the standard is one turn in twenty-four inches, with six groves. However, at the present time there is no American rifle made for exclusive use of the Short cartridge.

The bullet of the .22 Long Rifle cartridge weighs forty grains, over a third more than the Short; so, being of the same diameter, the Long Rifle bullet is much longer and requires faster spin for stabilization. One turn in sixteen inches gives best results and is standard.

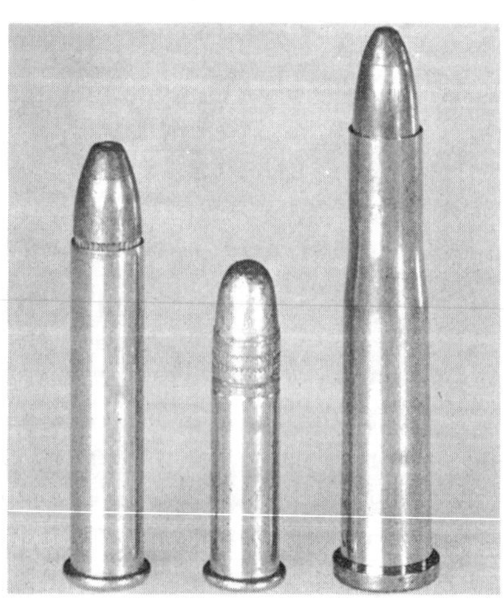

At left is the popular .22 Winchester Magnum Rim Fire cartridge, next is the .22 Long Rifle, and the .22 Hornet, our first modern .22 centerfire varmint cartridge.

Rifling pitch varies slightly for the so-called .22 centerfire cartridges, which, like all high-intensity cartridges, are loaded with jacketed bullets. The .22 Hornet, .218 Bee barrels are rifled with one turn in sixteen inches. While the .220 Swift and .222 Remington barrels have a twist of one turn in fourteen inches.

The minimum figure for bore diameter of the .22 Long Rifle and .22 Hornet barrels is .217 inch, with groove diameter at .222 inch. There are certain allowable variations in the dimensions of practically all machined parts made for our assembly-line type of production, and there may be slight variations in barrel dimensions. Actual measurement of the groove diameter of a number of Hornet barrels show this dimension to vary from .222 to .224 inch. Standard for bullet diameter is .2235, but some of them run close to .224 inch and weigh forty-five or forty-six grains. Hornet muzzle velocity is 2,690 feet per second.

Bore and groove dimensions for the .218 Bee, .220 Swift, and .222 Remington are standardized at .219 and .224 respectively. Bullet weight for the Bee is forty-six grains, and muzzle velocity is 2,860 feet per second; the Swift, forty-eight grains, with muzzle velocity at 4,110 feet per second, and the .222 Remington, fifty grains, with muzzle velocity at 3,200 feet per second. Bullet diameter is standard at .2245 maximum, but all that I have miked measure .224 inch.

Marlin-Micro-Groove barrels have sixteen grooves and very shallow rifling, which necessitates slightly different dimensions from those of the normal six-groove barrels. Standard for Micro-Groove barrels for .22 rimfire cartridges is a bore diameter of .220 inch and a groove diameter of .222 inch. And barrels for the .222 Remington have a standard bore diameter of .2215 inch and groove diameter of .2237 inch.

Well, sir, I certainly have given you a lot of figures, and I hope that you have been with me all the time. Why all these variations in dimensions of .22-caliber rifle barrels, bullets and velocities? I once asked that question of a ballistics engineer. I don't know what answer I expected, but I already knew the one he gave me. In effect, he said that these cartridges were developed to meet the demand of shooters at the time, and were the result of experiments and calculations which indicated best results under conditions for which they were intended.

As I said before, the .22 Short was our first successful self-contained metallic cartridge. Other rimfire cartridges were developed in an effort to improve on it. The .22 centerfire cartridges were brought into being by efforts to produce more effective varmint cartridges and rifles. Some of them are almost unbelievably efficient!

Today there are more than a hundred rifle models and model variations for the .22 rimfire cartridge alone.

10

Sharpshooting: From Bunker Hill to the Bulge

LATE IN THE AUTUMN OF 1873, the Irish Rifle Team, which had just won the championship of the British Isles and had made a clean sweep of Canada and Australia, challenged "any American team" to shoot a match the following year for the sum of 100 pounds. The match was to consist of three rounds, fired on targets at 800, 900 and 1,000 yards, by each member of a six-man team.

The veteran Irish team was armed with the finest of English muzzle-loading match rifles made by John Rigby, the famous Dublin gunsmith, who was a member of the team. The Americans, with little experience behind them—they had never shot at ranges more than 600 yards—had no special rifles, or money to buy expensive equipment. E. Remington and Sons and the Sharps Rifle Manufacturing Company came to their aid. They agreed to make the rifles for the match at no cost to the shooters, and even put up the $500 to make up the American side of the bet.

The Remington rifles were built around the Remington rolling-block action and the Sharps rifles around the conventional side-hammer, falling-block Sharps action. They were delivered early in March, 1874, and were the first of the world-famous Creedmoor target rifles.

American amateur riflemen practiced throughout the spring and summer, contesting for the honor of being selected for the team. The match was finally held on a hot and muggy September day.

The turnout was great. Few people believed that a breechloader could be made that would equal a muzzle-loader for accuracy. But the vast crowd made the trip to the range by every conceivable means of transportation, just to cheer the Americans on. Interest was about on a par with what it would be for the World Series today, and crowds stood in front of bulletin boards across the country, watching the score as it was relayed by telegraph.

The Americans, thanks to some fine shooting by the six-man squad—and to the mishap of a member of the Irish team who fired on the wrong target—won the match by three points: 934 to 931. It was much too close to be decisive, but the Irish, who would have won by one point had it not been for the errant shot on the wrong target, had to admit that the American riflemen could shoot with the best in the world. Yet the argument—breechloader versus muzzle-loader—continued until the Americans beat the Irish again in 1875 and 1876.

Sharpshooting, as such, has an interesting and colorful past. It has shaped our country's history from Bunker Hill to the Bulge. According to my dictionary, a sharpshooter is one skilled in shooting, especially with the rifle. That covers a lot of ground. Ordinarily, we think of sharpshooters in terms of the military, skilled riflemen trained to play important parts in the strategy of modern warfare. Actually, there are a great number of highly skilled shooters among sportsmen.

Guns were first employed for military purposes, probably early in the fourteenth century, and adapted to sporting purposes a century or so later. Early firearms were crude and unreliable, and strange as it may seem, there were sharpshooters long before the gun came into general use. For instance, during the Hundred Years' War of the fourteenth and fifteenth centuries, sharpshooting English archers, with their "longbows" and "cloth-yard shafts," demonstrated the superiority of accurate aim, combined with rapidity of shooting, over the slower crossbow and paved the way for the overthrow of armored knight. Outnumbered by the French knights, by as much as five to one, in the land battles of Crécy, Poitiers and Agincourt, the English archers won overwhelming victories. And it's a fact that the longbow was so much a part of the English scene that it was believed to be superior to other small weapons until well after the reign of Queen Elizabeth. It was not accepted as obsolete in England until about 1638.

To go back an even longer step—say, to the tail-end of the earliest period of savagery or to the beginning of the second period of savagery, when man discovered the use of fire—many a toothsome meal was clobbered and brought to hand by an accurately thrown stone. And some of our early ancestors were real sharpshooters. Rock throwing passed out of the picture with the development of the sharp-pointed spear, which could be thrown more accurately and with greater damaging effect. However, the bow and arrow was the invention that gave man control of his world. With it, he could kill the larger game animals and drive off his fiercest enemies, the saber-toothed tigers, cave bears, mammoths and wild bulls. He could strike the swiftest creature at a distance. The point I'm getting at is that there have been sharpshooters since the first steps in civilization, and efforts have been constant, not only to increase the range at which man could strike, but to increase the power of the blow.

As history proves, the trained rifleman has contributed greatly to the development of our country. Our earliest sharpshooters used a type of arm first made in Pennsylvania and now usually called the Kentucky rifle. This eighteenth-century American flintlock rifle was the result of evolution made necessary by conditions of the American frontier, which at the time was but slightly inland from the North Atlantic seaboard. The Kentucky rifle was a long, lightweight, easy-to-load and streamlined descendant of the heavy, short-barreled, large-caliber rifles popular in Europe late in the sixteen-hundreds and well into the next century. Early Kentucky rifles averaged about .45 caliber and fired round balls that weighed about forty-eight to the pound, or near 146 grains each. The spiral-groove rifling of the barrel spun the round, patched ball for good accuracy, and muzzle velocity was probably around 1,500 feet per second.

During the Civil War—a transition period in arms development as well as in military tactics—there were some almost unbelievable feats of marksmanship. Up to that time, target rifles were almost in the category of scientific instruments (as are many today) and were used a great deal in experimental work pertaining to accuracy.

On both sides, it was usual to detach any soldier with a reputation as an expert shot for special sniper duty. Rifles furnished these sharpshooters were either extra-accurate service arms, especially made heavy target rifles, or similar weapons collected from civilian experimenters. These latter rifles, in off-hand form, weighed from about ten to twenty pounds, and the bench rifles went to well over thirty pounds. They fired long lead bullets in front of heavy charges of fine-grain black powder and were equipped with either peep or high-power telescope sights.

One story about fabulous shooting concerns a heavy-percussion bench rifle and one shot that won a battle. The rifle was mechanically set up and adjusted for shooting with scientific precision for the range it was to be fired. Secret shots were taken in the opposite direction on a practice target before the shot for the record was to be tried. The plan was to incapacitate the enemy commander, who was the only opposing officer having battle experience. After the careful preparation, the shot was fired at a range of over a mile; all variables involved co-operated in perfect order for the marksman. The living target was hit, his troops dispersed and the battle won. Maybe so.

Colonel Hiram Berdan's sharpshooters were about the most famous marksmen of the Civil War. He organized two regiments in 1861. Only men of proven superior marksmanship were signed up. The original idea was to give each man a bonus of sixty dollars, if he furnished his own accurate rifle. However, the calibers of these guns varied so much that the supply of proper ammunition was next to impossible, and standard arms were issued. Some Colt revolving rifles saw service in Berdan's command, but in 1862, at his insistence, Sharps breech-loading percussion rifles were furnished for his men. This was a major victory for Colonel Berdan, because his requisition for Sharps rifles was stubbornly opposed by the

Assistant Secretary of War, the Chief of Ordnance and several other high-ranking officers who wanted to issue muzzle-loading Springfields for his men. Berdan's Sharpshooters, with the Army of the Potomac, were used as advanced skirmishers as well as for special sniping duties, and gained world fame for their shooting.

As the war developed, repeating arms, such as the Spencer and Henry rifle, became available—they were opposed by the "generals" almost as much as had been the breechloaders—and the percussion Sharps declined in popularity.

Up until well after the Civil War, the arms of Americans in many parts of the country were tools of everyday living, tools for defense and for securing food. With the days of buffalo hunting and general expansion in the West came a great demand for small arms, and business ordinarily would have been good for the gunmakers. But, as an aftermath of the war, the United States market was swamped with secondhand guns—many of them not so good, but still shootable. The arms companies had a tough time of it and some turned to foreign markets.

Popularity of Spencer and Henry repeating rifles during the latter part of the war whetted appetites for repeating arms throughout the country, and the first arm bearing the Winchester name—the lever-action Model 1866 rifle—was introduced. This rifle, an improved version of the Henry and chambered for the old .44 Henry rimfire cartridge, did not have the power for general use, so Winchester brought out the famous Model 1873 rifle for a newly developed and more powerful cartridge, the .44 Winchester Center Fire, usually called the .44-40. Shortly afterwards, the Colt Patent Fire Arms Manufacturing Company announced the Single Action Army Revolver in .44-40 caliber. This meant that the men who were winning the West needed only one type of ammunition for their rifles and revolvers. The Winchester '73 was discontinued in 1924.

Though the '73 gained immediate and brilliant success, it could not compete with the large-caliber Remington and Sharps single-shot rifles in big-game hunting and target shooting, where long-range accuracy and more power were more important than rapid fire. The most successful of the professional buffalo hunters used these heavy rifles and it was not unusual for one of them to sneak up to within two or three hundred yards of a small herd and kill every animal with heart and neck shots.

After the Sharps and Remington single-shots defeated the Irish in our first international target shooting match, a group of shooters (mostly of the military) got together in 1871 and formed the National Rifle Association of America. The purpose was to improve the shooting of the Regular Army and to encourage target shooting for sport among civilians. (For almost 100 years, the N.R.A. has successfully followed these aims.)

In 1907 Ad Topperwein shot at 72,500 two-and-a-quarter-inch-square wooden targets, thrown in the air by three assistants, with three Winchester .22 rifles. He missed only 9—a record that stood for 52 years.

With the popularity of repeating arms came a new kind of marksman, the exhibition shooter. This breed of sharpshooter was a development from the sport of live-bird shooting with the shotgun.

Captain A. H. Bogardus, a New Yorker who moved to Illinois and became a market hunter in the early 1860s, was one of the first exhibition shooters of note. Skilled with the shotgun by constant shooting of game for the market and at live-pigeon matches, he got the idea of holding shooting marathons in which 200 to 500 birds were the targets. At first, these contests were between several shooters. Before long, Bogardus, a powerful man not particularly bothered by the strain and severe physical punishment of shooting so large a number of shots in one day, was unable to find contestants who would go through the ordeal. So he began shooting to see what kind of score he could make. Naturally, for a while he made many records, because there were none to break but his own.

Bogardus' first long score was made in 1869 shooting at 500 live pigeons

In 1959 Tom Frye of Remington shot at 100,000 thrown two-and-a-quarter-inch-square wood targets. He missed only 6.

(some accounts mention 605 birds) in eight hours and forty-eight minutes from a trap at twenty-one yards' rise and fifty yards' boundary. He used one 12-gauge, muzzle-loading shotgun and missed only 105 birds.

In England and on the Continent, shooting thirteen birds straight was quite a feat and winners of the *Grand Prix du Casino* at Monte Carlo were considered for really top shooters. Killing of twelve birds without a miss won the shoot in 1887 and 1888. Yet in 1880, Captain Bogardus won a match with an Englishman, scoring ninety-nine birds out of a hundred.

Captain Bogardus claimed to be World Champion shooter, basing his assumption on his outstanding feat of breaking 5,500 thrown glass balls with a shotgun in a few seconds less than seven hours and twenty minutes. (The quickest time recorded at the time for breaking 100 glass balls with a double-barrel shotgun was under five minutes.) He used an English double-gun with two sets of barrels, one 10-gauge and the other 12-gauge, and changed barrels fifty-five times. The captain loaded for himself and missed only 356 targets. This was in 1879, and it is particularly interesting to find that there were only three misfires in the whole series of 5,856 shots. Later, with two 12-gauge guns, he shot at 5,000 targets in six hours and twelve minutes and missed only 156.

In the meantime, a young girl, Annie Oakley, strolled into the picture and began attracting attention as a sharpshooter. Perhaps her greatest bit of shooting was when she tried to break Bogardus' record in 1884 when she was twenty-four years old. She shot at 5,000 glass balls, using three 16-gauge shotguns, and missed only 228, not good enough to break the Bogardus record, but great shooting.

I well remember examining some of the arms, both plain and fancy, that belonged to Buffalo Bill and his partner, Pawnee Bill (Major Gordon W. Lillie) at the latter's trading post in Pawnee, Oklahoma, when I was a youngster. One was a smooth-bore .44-40-caliber Winchester Model '73 that had seen quite some use. Another one that fascinated me was a high-grade Remington rolling-block rifle of .50-70 caliber that Major Lillie told me had belonged to General Custer.

A big Westerner, Dr. W. F. Carver, a dentist who, like Wyatt Earp's deadly friend, Doc Holiday, did more shooting than teeth pulling, maintained that anyone could bust 5,500 glass balls with a shotgun and that he, Dr. Carver, would shoot 60,000 glass balls in six days—not with a shotgun, but with a rifle. He did just that at New Haven, Connecticut, in 1885. In order to make the record, he fired 64,865 shots, missing 4,865. He repeated the show (remember, these shooting events were before large audiences) in Minneapolis, and broke 60,000 balls while firing 60,650 shots.

However, Dr. Carver's record didn't last too long. In 1889, a little-known shooter, B. A. Bartlett, in six days shot at 64,017 composition balls two-and-a-quarter-inches in diameter and missed only 280.

The business of shooting a large number of targets against time died out for a while. Next, two young six-footers, Captain A. H. Hardy, of Nebraska and Ad Topperwein, of Texas got into the act. Both were expert with shotgun, rifle and handgun. They began their marathon shoots with a comparatively small number of targets. In 1904, Topperwein broke 3,507 two-and-a-quarter-inch clay discs without a miss. The time was two hours and ten minutes. He used one .22-caliber autoloader rifle. In 1906, Hardy clobbered 5,152 two-and-a-quarter-inch wooden balls without a miss. He used two .22-caliber repeating rifles. The next year, he shot 13,066 wooden balls without a miss.

Finally, on December 13, 1907, Topperwein did the big job. Equipped with three .22-caliber Winchester Model 1903 autoloading rifles, seven wagonloads of two-and-a-quarter-inch square wooden blocks and three assistants to throw them, he shot for ten consecutive days. It was cold, and on the last two days he shot in a drizzly rain. He missed only four out of the first 50,000 targets, which was all the seven wagons carried. His assistants picked out blocks that were not broken too badly and the marathon continued. At the end of the tenth day (sixty-eight and a half hours of actual shooting time) this iron man had shot at 72,500 targets and missed only nine. This record stood unbeaten for fifty-two years.

What guns did these old-time exhibition sharpshooters use? The early marathon shotgun shooters mostly favored fine English double-guns. Annie Oakley, who married Frank Butler (a Remington salesman and exhibition shooter), naturally was partial to Remington arms, but did have a Marlin lever-action rifle of .32-20-caliber. Dr. Carver shot a variety of guns. Ad Topperwein worked for Winchester from 1901 until his retirement and used Winchester long guns and Colt revolvers.

On October 3, 1959, Tom Frye, while on vacation (he is a Remington field representative), began shooting at the traditional two-and-a-quarter-inch square blocks in an effort to break the old Topperwein record. In ten days, he shot at 75,250 of these targets with but four misses. In fourteen days, he shot at 100,000 targets and missed only six. The longest run was 32,860 consecutive hits.

Frye's trigger finger was taped each morning and the worn-out tape replaced at noon. He started with two Remington Nylon 66 .22-caliber autoloading rifles, which are made of structural nylon and ordnance steel, and used a third when the original guns became so hot from shooting 1,000 or more shots per hour that they burned his hands. Debris from burned powder was cleaned from the guns five times during the shoot, the first cleaning after 40,000 rounds had been fired. There was no malfunctioning during the 100,000 shots. My guess is that this great record never will be broken.

The late Herb Parsons, known as the "Wizard of Winchester," not only was world-famous as an exhibition shooter and super-fast gun handler, but was a great entertainer. His shooting exhibition with rifle and shotgun ran for about an hour, mostly a display of aerial shooting, with a variety of targets ranging from quart cans filled with water, through cabbages, grapefruit, oranges, pieces of coal, eggs, grapes and small nuts—anything that gave a spectacular display when hit in the air with a bullet. One amazing bit of fancy sharpshooting consisted of shooting a .22 autoloader and then shooting and hitting the ejected cartridge cases.

Herb Parsons was with Winchester-Western for thirty years and used twelve or more Winchester rifles and shotguns while firing up to 600 or 700 shots during his feature display of fast, but safe, gun handling. He performed before more people than any other shooter in history. His film, "Showman Shooter," has appeared on television and theater screens and before sportsmen groups throughout the world.

Which reminds me, that "Showman Shooter," as well as four other films on hunting and shooting, is available free for showing before sportsmen groups. For details, write to Motion Picture Department, Winchester-Western, Olin Corp., New Haven, Conn. 06504.

Remington also has several excellent films of interest to shooters: "Gunning the Flyways" and three others. Write Remington Arms Company, Advertising Department, Bridgeport, Conn. 06602.

Lyman Gun Sight Corporation, Middlefield, Connecticut, has five films available, two made in Africa, one on wing shooting and two for the cartridge reloader.

Why not plan to show these at meetings of your local sportsmen group? They are color, 16-mm sound films and run from twenty to forty minutes. They should be booked at least two months ahead.

11

The Single-shot Target Rifle

SOME OF THE FINEST American rifles ever produced were made during the period beginning shortly after the Civil War, when the primed cartridge was in its early developmental stage, and ending just before the beginning of World War I. They were single-shot, mostly the progeny of certain arms made famous during the War of Secession, and reached a state of perfection before the turn of the century. The real heyday of the single-shot rifle was from the early 1870s until the early 1900s.

A great many makes and models were produced. There were rifles for every purpose—military rifles, large- and small-game hunting rifles, sporting rifles, and highly specialized target rifles. The single shots that I want to talk about are in the latter category. They were the cream of the crop—wonderfully well designed and made, some engraved, all of exquisite craftsmanship. Actually, there were comparatively few of these top-grade arms manufactured, so that today they are hard to find. A single-shot enthusiast will put on a nationwide hunt in order to locate a specimen to help fill out his collection.

These thoroughbreds of the single-shot clan fall roughly into three types—the Short or Mid-Range, the Long-Range or Creedmoor, and the Offhand or Schuetzen rifle. The very choice ones are of Creedmoor and Schuetzen variety.

The Long-Range rifles were of .40-, .44-, and .45-caliber, with the case portion of some of these cartridges being as long as 3¼ inches and holding 100 or more grains of black powder behind long, heavy bullets weighing as much as 550 grains. The other types of target rifles usually were of smaller caliber, running from .22 to .40 for the Short and Mid-Range rifles, with the Schuetzen rifles being of .32- or .38-caliber in many instances.

In the 1870s, if you saw a dyed-in-the-wool rifleman stretched out on his back, he was not taking an afternoon snooze. Actually, he was getting into the Creedmoor position for some long-range shooting.

The Creedmoor back position, which seems mighty strange today, was common during the latter part of the nineteenth century and gets its name

Fine Frank Wesson, Creedmoor-grade long-range rifle, made about 1876, Malcolm telescope sight.

from the famous old Creedmoor range, near New York City, where many international matches were held. This uncomfortable-looking position (actually it is not) was developed for very steady holding or support of the rifle, and for longer sighting radius to minimize any variation in sight picture while aiming and shooting.

The rear sight was attached to a special mounting base along the top edge of the buttstock near the butt plate. It could be moved and secured into position on another base located just behind the rifle's hammer for other position shooting.

The Schuetzen rifle, from the German word *Schützen* meaning "to defend," was of different design and made especially for shooting from the standing position. Its buttstock had extreme drop with perchbelly and horned butt plate that immediately identifies the Schuetzen. Many were equipped with palm rests, which extend below the forearm. The Schuetzen technique of shooting, developed in Germany and Switzerland during the muzzle-loading days, required this specially designed rifle that looks odd to those not familiar with it.

Today there are very few Schuetzen fans who delight in firing those old time rifles, even though the method is quite interesting. When shooting, the rifleman assumes a firm stance, with his legs spread apart. The butt of the rifle is held against the upper portion of the right arm with the horns, or prongs, of the butt plate around the arm, which acts as a pivot. The palm rest, in its down position, is grasped by the left hand, the muzzle of the rifle meanwhile pointing upward. The rifle is then lowered until the sights are aligned with the target, with the left elbow of the shooter coming to firm rest against his body. The palm rest is adjustable so that this is possible. The cheek comes to rest against the cheek piece of the buttstock, the hair triggers are set, and aim is carefully taken while the marksman holds his breath. Shooting from this position is slow and deliberate, but some amazing scores were made when it was in vogue. I understand that some records still stand from those almost forgotten days.

Single-shot cartridge rifles were manufactured in great quantities in the United States, mostly by Sharps, Remington, Ballard (Marlin), Stevens, and Winchester. Single shots made in smaller quantities were the Wesson, Farrow, Whitney and Phoenix, Maynard, Peabody and Peabody-Martini, Hopkins and Allen, Wurfflein, and the Bullard. When these arms were on the market, prices ran from about three dollars for some of the inexpensive little .22 rimfires, to $300 or more of some of the fine Creedmoors. Brother, even today, that ain't hay!

Some really great single-shot rifles are as follows. If you see one floating around, grab it but quick.

F. Wesson No. 1 Long-Range Rifle. The Creedmoor-grade is elaborately engraved and it is beautifully made throughout. Originally it was equipped with a spirit-level, wind-gauge muzzle sight and full vernier peep rear sight with sight bases at the upper receiver tang and at the upper rear end of the buttstock. I have one of these rifles with a William Malcolm telescope sight of about twenty-five power—probably the finest Wesson falling-block rifle in existence. It was made probably around 1876. Frank Wesson, a brother of Daniel Wesson, founder of Smith & Wesson, made a number of different model rifles and pistols, all of excellent workmanship.

Sharps Creedmoor Long-Range Rifle, Model 1874, made in .44 and .45-caliber. This is the very best in side-hammer Sharps, and is the best-known of all single-shot cartridge rifles. Christian Sharps was in business long before the Civil War. His first patent was issued in 1848, and the company bearing his name went out of business in 1881. During that period a huge quantity (probably well over 100,000) of Sharps rifles and pistols were manufactured, including thousands of rifles and carbines made for the government during the Civil War.

Sharps Borchardt Long-Range Rifle, Model 1878. From a design standpoint, the Sharps Borchardt is just about the perfect single-shot rifle. Hugo Borchardt, a Connecticut Yankee, also designed the pistol bearing his name which is the basic action of the famous Luger pistol. The sides of the action of the better grade Sharps Borchardt rifles often were paneled with hard rubber, fancy walnut, horn or other hard material. The delicate sights of the target-grade, single-shot rifles usually were removed and carried in leather-bound boxes.

Ballard (Marlin) Creedmoor A-1 Long-Range Rifle No. 7. This is a real prize when chambered for the 2$^{13}/_{16}$ inch, .44-caliber Ballard Everlasting cartridge case which takes 100 grains of black powder and a 500-grain bullet. The Ballard, one of the most famous rifles in American history of shooting, began life as a sporting arm in 1861. The Ballard Military Carbine was produced in 1862 for use in the Civil War. By 1864 it was back in sporting form and continued with improvements, and in

Creedmoor long-range type target rifle made on the ultra-modern Ruger No. 1 single-shot action, stock and engraving by John Warren. (Photo: John T. Amber, *Gun Digest.*)

many models, until about 1890 or shortly thereafter when production was discontinued.

Remington Rolling-Block Creedmoor Rifle. Introduced in 1873 and discontinued in 1890. (Other Remington-Rolling Block models were made from 1865 until 1933.) Caliber, .44, 90 grains of black powder and a 520-grain bullet. This rare model was one of the most accurate and popular long-range target rifles of its day, sharing honors with the Sharps at the Creedmoor range where the famous first International Match with the champion Irish Rifle Team was held.

Before the shooting began, it looked hopeless for the Americans. The Irishmen, who issued the challenge to the American team, had swamped all competition in the British Isles, Canada and Australia, running up the highest score ever made at the old Wimbledon range up to that time. Veterans of many years, shooting their beautiful, long-range and especially equipped muzzle-loading match rifles made by the world-famous Dublin gunsmith, John Rigby, the Irish team had visions of becoming world champions.

The Americans were in a sad predicament. They had constructed the Creedmoor range only two years before and their rifles were a motley collection. E. Remington and Sons and the Sharps Rifle Manufacturing Company came to the rescue and produced special breech-loading rifles (the first of the Creedmoors) for the matches.

This shooting event was of national interest, similar to World Series baseball today, and excitement ran high throughout the country. After shooting the 800-yard stage, the Americans led the Irish by nine points. They dropped two points at 900 yards and three points at the 1,000-yard range, ending with a final score only three points ahead of the Irish—not a very conclusive victory. However, the following year, in 1875, when the teams met again, this time in Dollymount, Ireland, and again in 1876, the Americans handily won, thereby settling the question of breech-loading versus muzzle-loading accuracy.

All true Creedmoor rifles, regardless of make, weighed ten pounds or less and had single triggers with a pull of not less than three pounds to conform with rules of the era.

Remington-Hepburn Match Grade B Rifle—a falling-block action rifle operated by a lever located on the right side of the receiver frame. This is a Schuetzen type. Favorite calibers were .32-30, .32-40, .38-50 and .38-55. Remington-Hepburn rifles were manufactured from 1880 until 1907—in Schuetzen-style from 1883 until 1907.

The above target rifles were furnished with spirit-level front sights and vernier-peep rear sights. The spirit level at the rear of the front sight was positioned so that the shooter could detect the slightest cant of the rifle while aiming.

The vernier scale of the micrometer adjustable rear peep sight on the top-grade, single-shot target rifles was calibrated either in hundredths or thousandths of an inch to afford super-accurate adjustments. A rifleman could shoot and adjust his sights for the various loads and ranges, and record the exact settings for future use. A rare rifle is the Browning single shot. A beautiful one was obtained by Winchester's T. G. Bennett from the Browning Brothers of Ogden, Utah, at the time the patents for that gun were purchased for Winchester. Without doubt, this is the finest Browning single-shot rifle in existence. It is of .45 caliber and has seen little or no use. This action gun was changed very slightly in design to become the famous Winchester Single-Shot Rifle.

The Winchester Single-Shot Rifle, in one style or another, was listed in Winchester catalogues from 1885 until 1920; the Schuetzen rifle from 1910 until 1916. As a sidelight on the popularity of the Winchester Single-Shot, it is interesting to note that during its period of production it was made in approximately sixty different calibers, including the 20-gauge shotgun.

The advent of the long-range, single-shot target rifle, brought about by the Irish Rifle Team challenge in 1873, and the winning of the match in 1874 by the American shooters, caused a rebirth of target shooting in this country. It has been kept alive and flourishing with a gradual change in form, mostly through the efforts of the National Rifle Association (established in 1871) until today, with most of our target shooting characterized by four position matches.

12

Gun Safety First

I LEARNED THE HARD WAY to be super-suspicious of gun-barrel muzzles. When I was eleven, with several years of hunting behind me, a squirrel-hunting companion accidentally shot me through the left foot with his rusty .22 rifle. The little bullet angled through from the left side and lodged in the sole of my boot. I was lucky. That little pellet of lead could have crippled me for life.

Since then I have been ultracritical in the selection of hunting pals, and I will not go afield with a careless gun handler. It gives me a slow burn to read a newspaper account of how some silly muddlehead shot a hunting companion out of a tree because he mistook him for a porcupine. Such happenings are reported every year.

Please do not misunderstand me and get the idea that shooting is a fearsome and highly dangerous sport. Actually it is one of our safest participant sports; the problem is to completely eliminate firearms accidents. It can be done.

All shooting mishaps are in the "could-have-been-avoided" category; safe gun handling is nothing more than plain common sense, including a little ordinary courtesy.

Self-inflicted wounds, of the accidental type, are without exception due to ignorance or to a moment of thoughtlessness on the part of the individual. Pulling a gun toward oneself by the muzzle obviously is a wacky and stupid act, yet each year a number of gunners are maimed or killed in this manner. Standing or leaning a loaded gun against some object is another dull-witted trick that may result in the same kind of disaster.

Reliance on, or absolute faith in the mechanical safety of a gun often breeds carelessness. With the safety on, the gun still should be handled as though it were ready to fire. In some instances the safety only blocks the trigger of a cocked firearm, putting the burden of safety on the sear mechanism. A sudden jar or bump, with a gun of this type that has seen a lot of use or misuse, might cause it to fire unexpectedly.

Knowledge of gun construction and operation is of utmost importance in knowing when a firearm is slightly out of order. A gun with any of its parts broken or badly worn may be unsafe to use. For this reason all guns should periodically be returned to their makers for a check.

When hunting in groups, the problem of the unseen Nimrod or other individual is an element that must be controlled by having certain knowledge of the area to be hunted and accurately knowing where each person in that area is located at all times. This is particularly important when after big game because of the power of the rifles used. Plans should be made and areas allotted to each hunter from day to day. Definite rules of behavior should be agreed on and carried out to the letter.

I believe that there would be no gun accidents if all hunters were thoroughly grounded in proper gun handling—which should be established as habit—and were so familiar with the habits of the game hunted that they need not consciously think of them. Considering today's hunting problem, maybe this is asking too much, but I doubt it. Anyway, this kind of training should be given to all of our youngsters. It would stay with them for life.

Careless gun pointing is the sure sign of an inexperienced, untrained and stupid shooter. Alertness, and a conscientious and continuous effort in keeping the gun muzzle pointed in a safe direction will result in safety in the game fields.

Today, the large majority of American hunters are factory workers, brick-layers, professional men and white-collar workers whose hunting is confined to a few days each year. Despite their urban existence they still have the old inherent instinct of the chase. Unfortunately, in some cases, the instinct is all that is there, unguided by any knowledge of, or aptitude for firearms.

No one is a natural-born good shot, nor is anyone born with a clear perception of gun safety. Every shooter should be trained in the proper way to handle a gun.

The task of target identification is of ultimate importance. Most of us certainly know that a deer does not wear a red shirt and cap, and walk on two legs. Yet, during past hunting seasons a number of hunters and bystanders have been shot—with the trigger-happy shooter maintaining, "I thought it was a deer."

Here the answer also is quite simple, but more difficult to put in operation. It is a matter of education and training with firearms until every hunter has the know-how for positively identifying the target, the ability to shoot accurately, and the self-restraint to withhold fire until certain of properly placing the shot.

The National Rifle Association of America deserves a great deal of credit for promoting the Hunter Safety Training Course throughout the country. Public demand for such instruction has become so great that the course is required by law in an ever-increasing number of states. Classes in hunter safety also are being offered as part of the curriculum in numerous high

Youngsters who learn safe gun handling retain the habit for life.

schools, where this early training will do the most good. In localities where the program is in effect there has been a substantial reduction of accidents. In fact, accidents have been almost nonexistent among those taking the course.

Gun accidents will become nothing more than a nightmare of the past if each of us religiously observes the following few rules:

Always know where the gun muzzle is pointing and be sure that there is no person in front of it, whether the gun is empty or loaded.

Be absolutely sure of the target before aiming and pulling the trigger.

Never take any gun into camp, a vehicle, or home, unless that gun is empty with the action open, or it is taken down.

Always be positive that the action and barrel are clear of any kind of obstruction, no matter how small.

Never leave a gun anywhere unless it is unloaded.

Never attempt to climb a tree, fence, cliff, or steep bank with a loaded gun.

Never shoot at any flat, hard surface, water, ice, or over a hill into unknown and possibly inhabited territory.

Never point an empty gun at anything at which you would not point a loaded one.

And above all—treat every gun as if it were loaded, whether it is or not.

The very least the novice hunter can do is to study and obey the "Ten Commandments of Safety," a copy of which may be picked up at any sporting-goods store or found packed with practically any gun of American manufacture. Let's keep shooting a safe sport!

13

Your Gun Has Hot Spots

IT'S A SHAME TO SPOIL a fine spring day with talk of work, but the fact must be faced that this is the time when the gun fancier has lots of work to be done. As much as I would like to be moseying through the woods at this very minute, I do not intend to set foot off the property until I have given every gun around the place its spring cleaning and whatever repairs it needs.

Rebarreling and other major operations will require more time and skill than I can give them. They can be done better by the maker of the gun, whose service department is going through its slack season right now and will appreciate the work I send to them.

As to the work I can do myself, I don't anticipate any back-breaking amount of it. There shouldn't be for anyone who takes proper day-to-day care of a gun, cleaning not later than the evening of the day it's used, and keeping the bore and outside surfaces well greased against rust.

I find that a lot of people, though, through ignorance of gun construction or a lack of equipment, neglect the really vital points in gun maintenance.

In a turn-bolt-action rifle, for instance, a lot of people neglect cleaning the bolt locking-lug recesses. Gunk and dirt accumulate, resulting in wear on the lug-locking surfaces, resulting in excessive head space, resulting in a gun that is as dangerous at one end as it is at the other.

The recesses usually are located within the upper and lower section of the receiver ring. They can be cleaned and slightly oiled with canton flannel patches and a pair of long-handled tweezers, but it's better to make a special tool for the purpose.

The tool is simple to make: Get a ½-inch-by-10-inch brass rod, and bore a 5⁄16-inch hole across the circumference ⅛ inch from the end. To use it, tightly roll a cylinder of cotton to measure about ⅜ by 1½ inches. (If there are females around the house, they sometimes have on their dressing tables little cotton squares called Coets, which are perfect for the job.) Push the cotton cylinder through the hole with ½ inch protruding from each side of the rod. Remove the bolt from the rifle, and place the tool inside the receiver so that when you turn it the cotton cylinder moves into the bolt-lug recesses for the cleaning and oiling.

In cleaning the chambers of rifles taking bottleneck cartridges, you can do an atrociously poor job without even knowing it. The bore-size cleaning-rod button, with a flannel patch in place, simply doesn't have the bulk to scrub the larger chamber as it should. What you need for this is a bristle brush of proper size.

I find that with lever-action rifles that have to be bore-cleaned from the muzzle, you have to be very careful not to damage the delicate lands of the rifling at the muzzle. To avoid this wear, which can ruin the rifle's accuracy, I use a collar on the cleaning rod. You can make this yourself out of brass. Mine is outside-tapered to fit any bore from .22- to .45-caliber.

There's a special problem with shotgun barrels. You can scrub the bore with patches and powder solvent and swear it is immaculate when it really isn't. The shot passing through the bore usually leaves lead streaks that can cause after-rusting. To get these thin washes of lead out of the bore, apply a layer of blue ointment (the mercury in it will amalgamate with the lead) and leave it there for several days before removing it. Or, most gun stores carry a cleaning-rod accessory with brass gauze that contacts the entire surface of the bore as it passes through. (Tomlinson makes them for various gauges; the Tri-pak is adjustable from 20- to 10-gauge.) You can

The sporting firearm should be thoroughly cleaned not later than the evening of the day it is used or handled.

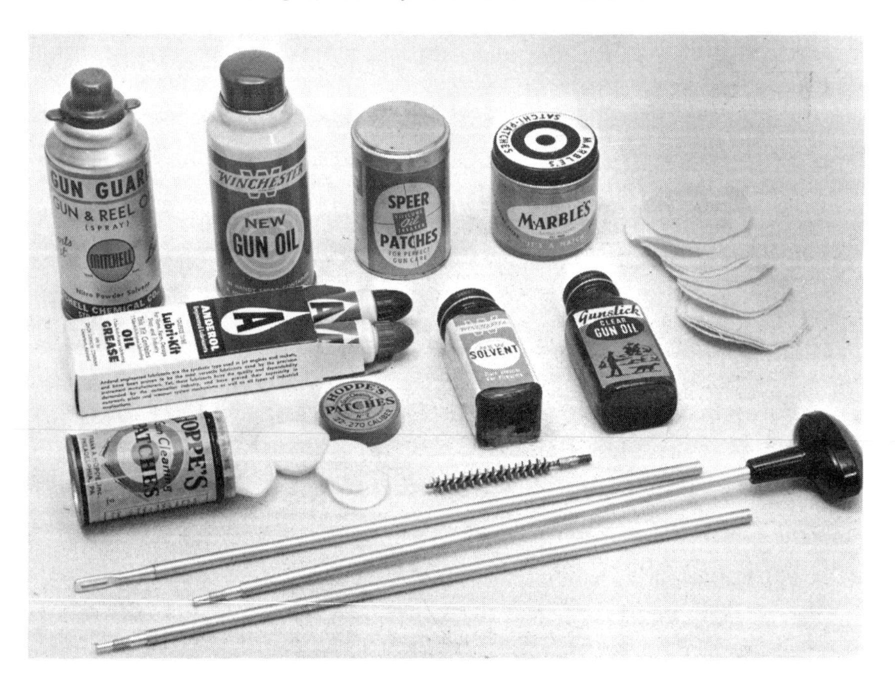

also do the job with a leather bore polisher and a mild polishing compound, but I find personally that I am too lazy to do that much scrubbing. The steel-bristle brushes that come with some shotgun-cleaning outfits should never be used on a fine shotgun; they will scratch the bore.

In cleaning revolvers and pistols, certain parts are awfully easy to overlook. In autoloader pistols, they are the sliding-bolt face and the breech surface of the barrel proper, including the extractor cut. In revolvers, they're the recoil plate, the breech portion of the barrel, and the rear and front faces of the cylinder. These should be scrubbed with an old toothbrush saturated with powder solvent or light gun oil. Gunk and dirt, inside and around the chamber portion of a handgun, can cushion the cartridge, cause uneven ignition and a disastrous loss of accuracy.

I always keep at least two or three screwdrivers (the shooter's screwdriver kit is excellent and inexpensive) at hand to fit the various screws on sporting arms. Any gun that gets normal use is taken completely apart once a year and cleaned with white gasoline or benzine. Then I wipe all the metal surfaces with a lightly oiled rag and lubricate all the working parts with gun oil. This latter must be done lightly; a gun must never be saturated with oil. Also, powder solvent is not a lubricating oil.

In case you're hazy about the proper way to clean a gun bore, here is old Dr. Kuhlhoff's recipe:

Put a snug-fitting flannel patch, saturated with powder solvent, on the cleaning rod and push it slowly through the bore—from the breech, if possible. When it emerges from the other end, dirty and gritty—as it will—throw it away. If you're going to use the gun again in a few days, that's all the bore cleaning it needs. If you don't intend to use the gun again in the next week or more, coat the bore and chamber with gun grease. (Anything lighter is apt to run and leave the steel unprotected.) If the gun is to be stored for a considerable length of time, all its metal parts should be well covered with a heavy gun grease. Before the gun is fired again, all this oil or grease should be removed from the bore and chamber. A grease-clogged bore or chamber can cause the piece to blow up.

There's one other cleaning point to bear in mind. All recent commercial and government priming is non-corrosive, which means that the priming compound does not produce salt when fired. But some government ammunition contains potassium-chlorate priming; when the cartridge is fired, the potassium chlorate is changed into something pretty much like ordinary table salt. Even when covered with grease, this attracts moisture and causes rust. To cleanse the bore of such fouling, give it a good scrubbing with hot, soapy water.

Going over a gun, I always check to see if certain minor adjustments are needed:

In the interests of accuracy and reliability, all screws should be kept turned up tight, especially those that secure the receiver sight and the scope-sight mount.

In a bolt-action rifle, a slight swelling in the wood stock may bind the trigger so that the firing pin will fall as the bolt is closed. I have had this happen several times, and I find it's an easy job to cut away a little wood where the trigger is rubbing.

If the trigger pull of a gun is not to your liking, take it to a good gunsmith and let *him* adjust it. The majority of us kitchen-table gunsmiths can ruin a trigger mechanism quicker than you can say "Jack Robinson."

Gun stocks should be carefully examined to see if they need refinishing. Most factory stocks are finished with varnish or lacquer, which looks good when the gun is new and is relatively waterproof—until the surface skin is broken and those little bumps and scratches start showing up. During the hunting season last fall, I had trouble with three guns: two rifles and a scatter-gun. We had some very wet weather; the guns got soaked several times, and the finish flaked off in gobs. Any of these finishes will scratch or flake off in time if the gun has hard use, and there's nothing that can be done about it. Sooner or later, you will have to refinish it.

Remove the old finish completely with varnish remover, being careful not to gum up the checkered areas. Then smooth the wood by sanding it lightly with very fine garnet paper. (Ordinary sandpaper is not sharp enough, and it wears out quickly.) Rub the stock with a wet rag and dry it quickly over a gas flame, taking care not to scorch the wood. When little whiskers rise on the surface, lightly sand them off with the garnet paper. Repeat the process—wetting, drying and sanding—until no more whiskers come up.

When the stock is absolutely smooth, apply a half-and-half mixture of white shellac and boiled linseed oil. Work this into the wood a few drops at a time, rubbing briskly with a woolen cloth. Don't just caress it; give it the elbow grease. When the stock is completely covered, allow it to dry thoroughly; this may take a week or longer. Repeat the process four or five times, and you'll have yourself a handsome and durable finish.

Once a year, clean the stock surface with benzine and give it an application of the mixture.

When all of this is done, you and your gun will really deserve each other; then you can go moseying through the woods.

Myself, I intend to sleep the rest of the afternoon.

14

The Gentle Art of Indoor Shooting

THE CHANCES ARE that you have played ping-pong or tossed darts on a target-board, friendly and most always good-spirited and competitive fun. But have you tried target shooting indoors at home? I'm a ping-pong and dart enthusiast, but indoor shooting is even more fun.

There is little or no noise involved in this kind of shooting because no gunpowder is employed. With proper equipment correctly managed, the danger element is nil. The sport of indoor shooting is inexpensive and it has grown so rapidly that there is a wealth of gear available, including guns and projectiles which have been developed especially for safe indoor, at-home shooting contests and target practice. Shooting distances usually are from fifteen to twenty-five feet. Projectiles range from the ordinary B-B, about .17-caliber, through five-mm or .20-caliber, and .22-caliber skirted pellets, to be fired from air guns, pneumatic and CO_2 gas guns.

Also, we have special cartridge cases and bullets made of plastic and designed for us in .38- and .44-caliber revolvers, with the bullet propelled by an ordinary pistol cartridge primer.

The majority of youngsters experience their first shooting with the perennial B-B gun. After going through several cork popguns, my first shootin' gun was a Daisy air rifle, taking the conventional B-B. Youngsters in our rural neighborhood gave it an almost continuous workout. The majority of our targets were tin cans, but now and then, we shot on homemade paper targets having fair-sized bull's-eyes. That B-B gun certainly gave good service and was still in use when we graduated to .22 rifles.

That first Daisy of mine was built according to the time-tried principle, propelling air force developed by a compression spring, which is used in many current Daisy B-B guns.

A variety of Daisy air guns is available at prices from about $10 to near $170 for the super-accurate match air rifle that is used in International Shooting Matches. The less expensive of these are especially valuable for training youngsters in gun handling and the art of shooting—of course, under strict supervision. The inexpensive Daisy Model 99 Target Special, a fifty-shot repeater with rear peep sight and hooded front sight having four interchangeable discs, is a National Rifle Association Approved Training Rifle.

Of particular interest to young shooters, as well as to adults who enjoy plinking and informal target practice with a low-velocity gun, is the Daisy "Spittin' Image" series of B-B rifles. These are realistic reproductions of popular cartridge rifles. For instance, the Model 1894 Daisy "Spittin' Image" B-B gun, while in one of my gun racks, has often been mistaken for the Winchester Model 94 Carbine. The giveaway, of course, is when the B-B gun is picked up, it weighs a little over three pounds, as compared to six and a-half pounds for the Winchester .30-30.

The Daisy 1894 has a number of meaningful "firsts" to its credit: It was the first B-B gun made to the exact scale of a famous rifle; the first with port loading, through a side port of the receiver, as with the Winchester 94, with a capacity of fifty B-Bs; the first with two-way-lever cocking action, cocking load is divided to minimize the effort needed to prepare for each shot, half on the forward stroke and half on the return stroke; first B-B gun with a ten-shot selective feed, reservoir or main magazine is tapped by pulling back a tab which automatically meters out 10 B-Bs and holds them in the force-feed magazine ready for firing; first B-B gun with compression spring action designed for both adult and youth usage.

Muzzle velocity of the Daisy 1894 is over 315 feet per second. That is enough to make a healthy dent in a pine board at fifteen feet distance.

The second in the Daisy "Spittin' Image" series is the Model 572 Slide Action Repeater. It looks similar to the well known Remington "Fieldmaster" .22 pump action. This Daisy has a capacity of forty-five shots and the tubular magazine under the barrel is loaded through a port in the conventional manner. The cocking load is divided, half on the forward motion of the sliding forearm and half with the return stroke.

Both "Spittin' Image" B-B guns are available with 4-power scope sight.

During recent years, the Daisy Manufacturing Company has produced a couple of CO_2 (carbon dioxide) gas-operated semi-automatic pistols. The latest is the $CO_2$300. It has a capacity of approximately 200 B-Bs. A five-shot primary feed (magazine) makes it easy to keep track of the number of shots fired when target shooting. The $CO_2$300 takes either the 12-grain CO_2 cylinder or the 8.5-grain Jett by use of an adapter which comes with the pistol. The 12-grain cylinder supplies enough carbon dioxide gas for about 160 shots.

We have used several of the Daisy guns, including the three mentioned above, for fun target shooting in our playroom, and for instructing beginners, both young and adult, in gun handling, the proper method of aiming and so on. These B-B guns are smoothbore and the accuracy distance for target shooting is fifteen feet.

To back up our targets for B-B shooting, we have employed a corrugated cardboard box, stuffed with tightly wadded newspaper, backed by discarded magazines. Behind this, we almost always place a large piece of half-inch-thick synthetic building board, just in case someone misses the box.

Included in the National Rifle Association shooting program are qualification courses for air, gas and pneumatic-type guns. The air guns with smoothbore barrels are fired on targets at fifteen feet, while air guns with rifled barrels, gas and pneumatic guns are shot at a distance of twenty-five feet. Though less formalized than other types of NRA competition, many NRA matches are open to these guns and pistols. Details of this element of the shooting program may be obtained by writing The National Rifle Association, 1600 Rhode Island Avenue, Washington, D.C. 20036. The NRA also has the Home Firearms Safety Program, which is important to all gun owners. After all, there is much more handling of firearms around homes than in the field, and at home, many persons who have no direct contact with their recreational or other uses come in frequent contact with firearms. When you write to the NRA about the qualification courses, ask about this program.

In our game-room shooting, we have also shot a number of other no-noise guns, including pneumatic and CO_2 types.

A pneumatic-type rifle that we have used is the Sheridan Blue Streak Model CBS. The Silver Streak is similar except, instead of being blued, it is nickelplated and buffed to a soft, satiny finish. By use of the Sheridan mount base, scope sights with tip-off type mounts may be added to this rifle. I prefer a scope, so I installed one of the new Weaver V22 scopes, which is continuously variable from 3 to 6 power of magnification. This Weaver creation has a ⅞-inch diameter scope tube to take larger lenses for better illumination, a help with indoor shooting. This scope is intended for .22s and other light-recoil rifles. Although designed for longer-range shooting, it worked out very well for the short range of our indoor shooting. The 1⅙-inch bull of the NRA Official Fifteen-foot Target is but slightly blurred when the scope is adjusted at 3-power, and the target at twenty-five feet is but slightly blurred when the scope is adjusted at 6-power. This slight blurring has not bothered us in our target shooting and we regularly make better scores with the scope than we do with iron sights.

The Blue Streak, without scope, weighs about five pounds and is very pleasant to aim and shoot. It has a rifled barrel and gives excellent accuracy. The open sights are adjustable for windage and elevation and the rifle is available with Sheridan-Williams receiver sight.

Of pneumatic type, the Blue Streak's power is controlled by the number of strokes given with the forearm. Maximum is eight strokes and this gives enough velocity for the 5-mm diameter bullet to go through an inch of

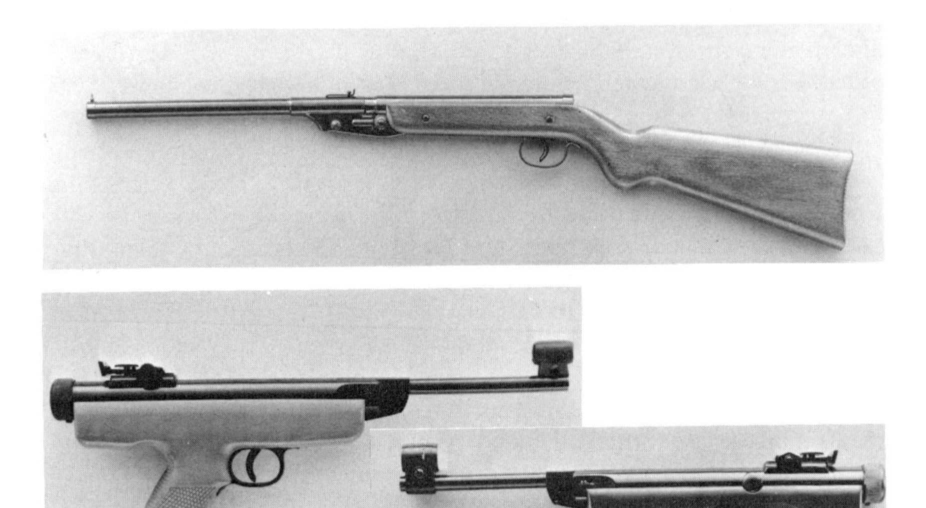

Inexpensive air rifles and pistols are available from many manufacturers. Here are the Winchester Model 416 (top) and Models 353 and 363 (bottom).

pine or more. For fifteen- and twenty-five-foot target shooting, we give the gun three pumps. This gives quite some power and for any pump-up or CO_2-powered gun we regularly shoot into the Sheridan Model 22 Target-trap which is a backstop and target holder intended for pneumatic rifles and those of .22 rimfire caliber. We do not allow beginners or youngsters to shoot the pneumatic and CO_2 guns until they have proven their ability in safe gun handling and fairly accurate shooting with the B-B guns. It is important to remember that the pump-up and CO_2 guns should not be used with the cardboard box stuffed with wadded newspaper, but a more substantial backstop should be set up. Bullet traps are made by several companies, including Sheridan, and your dealer can furnish information.

In international match type air rifle shooting the standard distance is 10 meters or 33 feet. Highly refined, super-accurate rifles are used on official targets having 10 rings. Rings 4 to 9 inclusive are black for an aiming bull (approximately 1$\frac{3}{16}$ inches in diameter) with the 10 scoring ring a small white dot. Rifles for this sport, capable of scoring on the 10 ring with each shot, are available from Daisy, Savage Arms, Winchester and others.

Speaking of Winchester, that company has a complete line of single-shot pellet guns from low cost types for plinking, informal target shooting indoors or out, pest and small game shooting, on to the more expensive competition models. Calibers include .177 and .22, with precision-manufactured, highly accurate Winchester pellets available.

Speer, Incorporated, well-known bullet makers for reloaders, produces the Target—38 and 44 components for indoor subvelocity handgun shooting. Originally developed by Speer for an Air Force training program, this ammo consists of reusable cartridge cases and bullets made of high shock-resistant plastic. The large pistol primer is the propellant. Loading these cartridges is accomplished by hand without the use of tools, excepting a pencil or nail for depriming fired cases. Muzzle velocities developed are approximately 500 feet per second and the bullets can cause bodily harm at distances of at least seventy-five feet. Accuracy at twenty-five feet is sufficient for serious target practice and best accuracy is obtained in revolvers having barrels of from four to ten inches long.

To keep the plastic bullets in good shape for re-use, the best bullet trap is a paper board carton with toweling or rug draped in the middle suspended by a dowel.

These various kinds of indoor fun shooting are convenient, relaxing and healthful and they develop precise co-ordination. If you contemplate getting into the act, be sure to check all laws and ordinances pertaining to shooting in your locality.

The paramount element of indoor shooting, whether for fun or serious practice, is safe gun handling—just as it is for every other kind of shooting.

As I mentioned earlier, more guns are handled around the home than in any other specific location. So it seems only logical that the home is the place to begin the all-important training for gun safety. Once the habit of safe gun handling is acquired by a youngster, it remains with him or her throughout life. As a matter of fact, when a youngster gets the idea, he is more conscious of gun safety than an adult who has not had the proper kind of training early in life.

I have seen concrete evidence of this in a shooting club that I am connected with. A great many teen-agers have been trained by the members. These kids pick up the least infraction of safety rules and let the fact be known in no uncertain terms.

While speaking of youngsters, it may be pertinent to mention that outdoor sports, such as recreational shooting, can be an effective preventive for juvenile delinquency. Judge William G. Long, of Seattle's Juvenile Court, who heard 45,000 cases over a twenty-year period, says that not one of the boys or girls that came before him had a wholesome outdoor hobby.

Safe gun handling is a matter of common sense, but it comes only with knowledge and experience. This talent is not acquired in minutes. Here are three fundamentals that every person should know and practice with full understanding and appreciation for the necessity of each rule:

1. *Treat every gun as if it were loaded.* Never take anyone's word that a gun is empty. Check for yourself and keep your finger off the trigger. If you don't know how to open a gun to check its chamber, don't guess. Leave it alone!
2. *Always point the gun muzzle in a safe direction.* Never allow a gun muzzle to point at anyone, or yourself, or at or near anything that could be injured. Remember that bullets will penetrate walls, floors and windows, and will ricochet from flat surfaces, including water.
3. *Be sure of your target.* Identify your target with certainty before you touch the trigger. Determine where your bullet will go if it passes over, under or through the target. You are responsible for starting the bullet. Make certain you know where it will come to rest.

In conjunction with these rules, the gun owner must never lend a gun, or allow others to handle or shoot it without properly instructing them in the fundamentals of its operation and safe use. Never leave a gun unattended, and never lean a rifle or shotgun against a fence or car—in fact, never against anything, excepting a properly constructed gun rack.

While speaking of safe gun handling, mention of a more or less kindred subject may be in order—that of ill-advised or thoughtless gun legislation. It has been proved time and again that crime cannot be legislated out of existence. So the inanimate gun itself has been and is taking the brunt of righteous indignation against the misuse of firearms. Many foolish anti-firearms laws have been proposed, and some have been made into laws, in practically all instances penalizing and putting hardship on law-abiding gun owners.

Congressman Robert Casey of Houston, Texas, proposed some common-sense legislation that, when passed, would strike at the crux of the problem.

"Mr. Speaker, I ask this Congress to stop the harassment of the legitimate gun owner—and instead to open war on the illegal use of firearms by the criminal preying on society."

With these dramatic words, Congressman Casey introduced two bills in the House which are welcome news to more than 20,000,000 hunters and shooters in America.

He told Congress, "I introduced legislation to set a twenty-five-year mandatory Federal sentence for anyone guilty of using or carrying a firearm during the commission of a robbery, assault, murder, rape, burglary or kidnaping. We in Congress can swiftly enact a model program of crime control for our own crime-ridden home base of the District of Columbia, and one bill pertains solely to it. The second invokes the authority of the interstate commerce clause and pertains to the Nation as a whole."

Bills similar to those of Representative Casey—aimed at criminal misuse of firearms with no harassment of law-abiding, recreational shooters—have been entered in the California and Illinois Legislatures.

I believe that Representative Casey's strong and thoughtful words on the subject should be known to all citizens.

"The criminal, Mr. Speaker," he told Congress, "is the cause of the problem facing our Nation today—not the sportsman, the gun collector, the decent, law-abiding citizen who happens to own one or more guns. And it is this problem that we should attack.

"There are pending before Congress proposals calling for registration of all guns, and I tell my colleagues now that this is a completely ineffectual way to strike at the problem of illegal gun use. I see little need to further harass the legitimate gun owner when the problem is caused by the criminal, most of them repeat offenders, often using stolen weapons to commit a crime.

"Mr. Speaker, no man in his right mind can expect a criminal planning a robbery with a stolen gun to register the weapon with Federal authorities, or to be alarmed because he has not done so."

Representative Casey further stated, "We, in Congress, are being asked to justify the need for such a sweeping proposal. We should know, before we pile unworkable and unnecessary restrictions on the decent citizen, the nature of the criminal causing the problem."

Representative Casey said he realized the reluctance of Congress to invade the field generally left to the States to prosecute and punish for crimes of violence.

"But the problem of outlaw gun use is nationwide, and the States have failed to deal with it effectively," Representative Casey stated. "The Federal Government sets mandatory sentences for trafficking in narcotics, and the illegal use of guns by criminals touches far more citizens than dope."

Representative Casey told Congress, "Here in the District of Columbia, as over the Nation, the serious problem of illegal gun use has been severely aggravated by extreme laxity on the part of the courts in meting out punishment to violators. The time has come to meet this problem head on, and to take from the courts the power to turn loose on society the second and third offenders to continue preying on our citizens. My bills leave the courts no discretion in sentencing the guilty, and I think this legislation will go a long way in solving a growing problem.

"How many times, Mr. Speaker, have we read of the ex-convict with a long string of arrests and convictions for armed robbery finally killing an innocent businessman in the course of another crime? How many times have we read of a criminal free on bond while awaiting trial being caught in the act of committing a similar offense."

Elaborating on the laxity of the courts, Representative Casey said, "How many times, Mr. Speaker, have we sat idly by and watched the courts repeatedly turn loose these vultures to continue preying on society, while the hue and cry mounts against those of us who happen to like to hunt . . . to like to own guns, and who abide by all of the laws of our society?"

Representative Casey said that the passage of his legislation will stop the hysterical cries to unduly penalize the law-abiding citizens through imposition of rigid and unworkable restrictions on sale, registration or taxation of firearms, when the heart of the problem is to find a way to protect these same good citizens from the criminal in our midst.

"I have no quarrel," Representative Casey stated, "with those who wish to place needed and workable restrictions on the easy availability of firearms to the mentally incompetent, the criminal or the unsupervised teenager. . . .

"But I shall vigorously oppose any effort to impose sweeping restrictions upon the law-abiding citizen, while this Congress and the respective States blandly ignore the cause of our Nation's most serious problem. I urge my colleagues to join with me in this effort."

Unfortunately, for everyone except the criminal, Congressman Casey's proposed legislation has received the thumbs down treatment. I don't know why!

15

Sharpen Your Eyes with Live Targets

AN EXPERIENCED WOODSMAN was hunting deer in New Brunswick, Canada. A native of the country, he knew the game trails, the habits of the game, and could move noiselessly through the woods. This chap usually hired out as a guide with an established camp operator in the vicinity where he worked at lumbering most of the year. At the moment, he was on his own, wanting to tag a deer for family use.

Traveling was not exactly quiet. The weather had been dry. Twigs and hardwood leaves snapped and rustled with a careless step. The hunter moved around a slight curve on the trail. About sixty yards away, at a fork in the run, a whitetail buck stood looking at him, ready for instant flight. The stalker slowly raised his rifle, aimed carefully at the motionless target with the open sights and squeezed the trigger. There was no resounding thump of bullet striking flesh. With a whistling snort and a bound, the deer was out of sight. The woodsman carefully searched the area around where the buck had been standing and in the direction he had taken off. There was no evidence of a hit!

Somewhere along the coastal range in northern California, an old pal of mine, a resident of suburban Los Angeles, was deer hunting with several celebrated members of the movie industry. As luck would have it, my friend jumped a blacktail at what seemed to be about thirty yards. The deer, evidently taken by surprise, leaped about fifteen feet and stopped for a look back. The hunter shouldered his scope-sighted rifle, placed the cross hairs for a lung shot and fired—a complete miss! The blacktail sprang away with a characteristic stiff-legged, high hop and was gone before a second shot could be made.

In some very heavy cover, in New Hampshire, a hunter was moseying along, up the side of a mountain. Near the crest, he found an open spot and proceeded to glass several thinly vegetated spaces below him which probably had once been mountainside pastures. The mid-afternoon, late-fall scene was magnificent and the weary huntsman, fascinated, watched the motley colors for perhaps half an hour. Again he glassed the scope and picked up a whitetail buck, standing and looking around, no doubt in the act of leaving his siesta bed. The hunter figured the distance to be about 200 yards. He picked a rest for his rifle against a dead and needleless evergreen tree, found the target in his scope, held for what he hoped would be a chest shot just back of the shoulder, and touched off the shot. The deer left the scene in high gear. Tying a red bandanna to a branch of his rifle rest, just in case he might have to return to do a relocating job, the hunter took a bearing to mark the spot where he saw the deer and headed for it. Without too much difficulty, he found where the deer had bedded down and where he was standing at the shot. There was no sign of a hit!

These are pretty sad tales. Being nearby during each incident, I had to listen to them. The three Nimrods had one thing in common. They all missed shots that should have been fairly easy for them. And even sadder, those were the only chances that they had on those particular hunts!

"Are you sure they were misses?" you query.

Yes, as sure as I can be under the circumstances. I certainly know that with deer hunting, all reported misses are not really misses, usually due to ignorance or lack of experience on the hunter's part, and that it is of utmost importance for a hunter to follow up his shot with careful and intelligent observation. Also, a running deer, scared and with the adrenal glands sending adrenalin in to the bloodstream, is much less likely to show signs of being hit than a standing, unfrightened deer. Not a one of these animals were really scared up to the time of the shots, and knowing that those hunters ordinarily show quite some woods savvy—each had searched the scene of action for evidence, including the tiny tuft of deer hair that usually can be found with a hit, and according to their stories, they had been able to trail the deer for a hundred yards or more without seeing any evidence of a wounded animal—I would say that the chance of hits were very remote indeed.

Why did these shooters miss their shots? In each instance, and for different reasons, the hunter did not know where the bullet would print at the particular range.

In the first instance, the shooter needed a new rifle and some experience in shooting it so that he would know its ballistic characteristics. He was using an old rifle that had belonged to his father, maybe his grandfather, too, only useful as a wall decoration, and a poor one at that. The venerable piece, well beyond the age of retirement, hadn't been used for many years and was in the hands of the hunter simply because it was the only rifle available to him at the time. It was of .44-40 caliber, worn and rusted, with only a trace of rifling in the barrel. Afterwards, its owner told me that, by check firing, he found that it wouldn't group into a wash tub at fifty feet.

The second hunter was carrying a .257 Roberts-caliber, Remington bolt-action rifle with 4X hunting-type scope sight. He had bought the outfit with the idea of hunting the big hares we call jack rabbits, in this case, the blacktail and antelope variety of the Southwest and West. A year earlier, he had sighted in the rifle for 100 yards and had managed to shoot a few jacks. His intentions were good, he wanted to get in a lot of practice on running jack rabbits, but never got around to doing it. At the time of the deer hunt, he assumed that the rifle was sighted in, but he actually did not know where it was shooting.

The third hunter had just bought a new Winchester Model 88 lever-action rifle in .358 Winchester caliber. With scope sight in place, he had sighted in to put the 200-grain bullet about two inches above the point of aim at 100 yards. Now this is a flat shooting cartridge, with mid-range trajectory for 100 yards being less than an inch. Thinking the deer to be about 200 yards away (it very well could have been closer), he, on a wild guess, held the cross hairs about a foot above the animal's back. That probably is where the bullet went. Actually, the bullet would print only a little low at 200 yards with his sight setting. Had he realized that the mid-range trajectory for that 200-grain bullet of the .358 is only a hair over three and a-half inches and had held just about where he wanted to hit, he no doubt would have had meat in the bag.

There is another element, which hunters are prone to forget, that could have been a contributing factor to that miss. A bullet fired uphill or downhill at a steep angle will overshoot the target even though the sight setting of the gun is correct for the distance between the rifle muzzle and the target. This is especially important at very long range and can cause a miss with perfect sighting and hold. Roughly, the reason for this overshooting is that the distance uphill or downhill is greater than the horizontal distance, with the bullet drop being that of the horizontal range, instead of the greater distance of the slant range.

I was always under the impression that bullets strike low with uphill shooting and high with downhill shooting. About ten or fifteen years ago, Dr. Charles S. "Chuck" Cummings, II, who at that particular time was Chief Ballistic Engineer for Remington Arms Company, tried to explain this business to me, but I was lost in mathematical formulae. (By the way, if you are interested in gun and ammunition behavior, pick up a copy of Cummings' inexpensive book, "Everyday Ballistics," published by Stackpole and Heck.)

In case of our mountainside shooter, if he was shooting downhill at an angle of thirty-five degrees and at a range of 200 yards, as he thought, according to a set of figures worked out by Cummings, his sight should have been adjusted for a distance of about 164 yards to be dead on the point of aim. You can understand what a great difference this would make with high-trajectory, rifle-cartridge combinations, and at extreme range with even the flattest-shooting cartridges.

Each of our three hunters needed more shooting experience with the rifles they were using—shooting at various taped distances as well as at unknown ranges, and probably more practice in judging distance.

Every year, a large number of big-game hunters find themselves in the same boat with the fellows mentioned. They spend a tidy sum and a lot of time getting together equipment, making necessary arrangements and traveling to a favorite hunting spot—remote or nearby—and come home without even a snack for the table.

Excellent practice in the various phases of shooting can be accomplished with varmint hunting.

As you no doubt know, there are a great many shooters who, as a hobby, go in for varmint hunting with highly specialized equipment—heavy rifles and various cartridges designed particularly for long-range work on very small targets and with high-power varmint or target scope sights, some with as much as twenty-five- or thirty-power magnification. Early devotees of this sport are the ones who developed organized bench-rest shooting. Outfits that are common to these fellows would be practically useless to the average big-game hunter, so I'm talking about varmint hunting with rifle and equipment ordinarily used by the individual in big-game hunting. This brings up some interesting problems.

First, let's take a brief look at the most easily located of the pest species of wild life called varmint.

Exactly what is a varmint? He is any one of a number of creatures of a size, with characteristics that make him a sporting target and whose good traits are outweighed by those which are at odds with the activities of man. These include the woodchuck, the crow, the prairie dog and a few others.

The woodchuck, called ground hog, marmot, whistler and pasture pig, and the prairie dog are members of the squirrel family and date back twenty-six million years. The woodchuck's range is over most of Canada and about a third of the United States—eastern, except the deep South, while the yellow-bellied marmot sticks mostly to rocky areas in western mountains.

The prairie dog hangs out in the West Central states. I have read that near San Angelo, Texas, there was once a prairie-dog town measuring 250 by 100 miles, with a population estimated to be around 400,000,000 of the sharp little barkers. The prairie dog and his vast, complicated and well-engineered system of burrows is not at all helpful in farming and stock-raising localities and he has been poisoned and shot in vast numbers. But he is plentiful in many places, especially in arid areas of little commercial value.

Jack-rabbit shooting is the finest possible training for the big-game hunter. These big-eared, powerful-legged members of the hare family are found in great abundance in many areas from the plains to the Pacific and from Mexico to the plains of western Canada. He can thrive in barren and arid lands where any other animal would starve to death. The antelope jack rabbit probably is the largest of the tribe, weighing up to around ten pounds, and the blacktail variety is the most numerous and widely distributed of the jacks. Second only to the pronghorn antelope in the speed department among North American animals, he makes an elusive and very difficult target for riflemen. Any marksman who can, with a fair degree of regularity, make hits on running jacks will have no trouble at all with any species of big game. Almost any rifle can be effective on these hares. Over the years, I have shot them with a number of different caliber rifles, including the .22 Long Rifle with hollow-point bullet, the .22 Hornet, the .22 K Hornet, the .218 Bee and Mashburn Bee, the .219 Zipper and several wildcat variations, the .22-250 (.25-3000 necked down to .22 caliber, now commercially made as the .22-250 Remington), the .220 Swift, the .250-3000, the .270, the .30-40 Krag, the .30-06 and several other wildcats. I haven't had a chance to try the .222 or .243 on these runners, but they should be great.

Just about any big-game rifle that will group into two inches or less at 100 yards will do a job on jack rabbit. And one of these jumpers mobiling along at a distance of forty yards makes a tough target for most shooters. And as the range increases, so do the misses.

The wily, old, black-marauder crow is the most exciting target for many varmint hunters. Although a migratory type, the crow is found the year round in most of the United States and in the great southern area of Canada during the summer. He is shot at with both rifle and shotgun, the great majority being taken with the latter. As many as 5,000 have been taken by an individual during one year.

I started shooting crows at an early age, first by hiding in bushes alongside a sprouting corn or wheat field and catching them on the ground with my .22, later in the air with a shotgun. The crows' damage to crops was so great that the idea was to eliminate as many as possible. We would stand behind a field barn and shoot until our supply of shells was gone. That summer, I shot approximately 500.

Our shot size was small, Number 8, as I remember. Later, I shifted to size 6, believing that the close-feathered cawers could be knocked down at farther range with the larger shot. However, the crow's body is as small or smaller than that of the familiar pigeon and the smaller 8s and 9s, with a larger number to the load, make a more concentrated pattern to work better at longer ranges. Those are the sizes used by most crow hunters in our part of the country today.

Sometimes crows seem to be a bit demented. One time several years ago, we located a roosting area on a hillside above an apple orchard. Having depended mostly on the crow call, I never had used artificial crow

This youngster is on his way to becoming a successful big-game hunter.

or owl decoys. So, with neither at hand, we looked around for a substitute and found a child's toy in the form of a fair-sized furry kitten. We secured this thing in one of the small trees at the roost and returned that afternoon with our shotguns and a good supply of shells. I had little faith in the program and we didn't even build a makeshift blind, but hid under some bushes. The crows began to come in. When they spotted that phony cat, they went mad. They frantically squawked, dove, zoomed and darted about, paying absolutely no attention to the two of us. We shot up all our ammo, and still they came in.

Successful crow shooting most always is done with the shooters well concealed in a blind, usually on the edge of a flyway. If the wind is directly in the face of incoming birds, so much the better. Calling is of utmost importance and the tyro crow hunter should practice cawing as often as possible, first under the guidance of an experienced caller or following the directions that come with the call and developing a technique by watching the birds' reaction. A poor caller will chase away more birds than he brings in. I have used many calls, including the various models made by Olt, Pekin, Illinois, and lately, several made by Lohman Manufacturing Company, Neosho, Missouri.

Crow shooting with the shotgun is a great way for the upland bird and waterfowl hunter to get in almost year-round practice and keep in the groove. It sharpens gun pointing and improves rhythmic co-ordination in swinging with and leading the target. With short open seasons and small bag limits on most upland birds and waterfowl, it is almost impossible for the beginning hunter to get in enough practice on eating game to become a competent gun handler. Skeet and trap shooting help, but there is nothing like the real thing, and crow seem to me a good substitute.

Shots at woodchuck, prairie dog and crow with the rifle are most always taken when they are feeding and moving slowly if at all. For long-range shooting on these animals, a rifle of gilt-edged accuracy is needed. However, fairly close-range shots (from offhand is better practice) often can be obtained with a little careful stalking. Cracking big woodchuck at fifty yards is about like doing the same with a big whitetail buck at in the neighborhood of 180 yards.

Good practice in judging distance can be gained while stalking small game, or while walking most anywhere. You just pick out a rock, bush, tree or other object at some distance, guess how far away it is and count the steps to it, trying to make each stride a yard long. With a little practice, you will be surprised how accurately you will be able to judge the range. A change of locality may foul up your judgment a little at first. For instance, an Easterner going out West can easily be led to underestimate distances due to seeing better in clear mountain air or flat or slightly rolling terrain.

Hunting, to most American sportsmen, is recreation, fulfilling a deep yearning to get away from humdrum of everyday life, to enjoy the exercise of life in thc open, to follow the instinct of matching wits, senses and skill with game. I ask practically everyone I know why they like to go hunting; that, in effect, is just about the answer that all of them have given.

16

Teddy Roosevelt's $42 Rifle

WHEN PRESIDENT THEODORE ROOSEVELT wrote to the Chief of Ordnance in November, 1903, asking that one of the new Model 1903, Springfield service rifles be adapted for sporting purposes, he set a precedent for high-velocity hunting rifles in America. T.R.'s Springfield no doubt was the first modern American military rifle remodeled into a sporting arm in the United States. Teddy directed the ordnance boys to fit Lyman sporting sights and to make the butt stock exactly like that of his Winchester lever-action rifle, only one inch shorter. The cost of the remodeling job was $42.13, which the President paid with his personal check. Roosevelt took his Springfield, a Winchester Model 95 in .405 caliber, and a powerful .450 double rifle (a gift from fifty-six of his English friends) on his African hunting trip in 1909.

As near as I can determine, the second Springfield to be slicked into a sporter belonged to Stewart Edward White, the famous writer of Western stories. The actual work was done by an old-time Los Angeles master gunsmith named Wundhammer, with lots of advice and suggestions given by the novelist and a number of his hunter friends. White took the rifle to Africa and, using 165- and 172-grain pointed bullets, killed 185 game animals, 112 with one shot each. The Springfield sporter was his favorite rifle and he maintained that it would take any African game, but actually was not heavy enough for the big five. Of course, in his shooting, he was backed up by a rifleman with one of the cannon-like English double-barrel rifles. White had a heavy .465 double-barrel Holland & Holland rifle for the big, thick-skinned animals, and a .405 Winchester as a spare.

Roosevelt fired the .30-06 service cartridge with its 150-grain pointed, full-jacket bullet, in his Springfield on game of African-antelope size with good results. He evidently was lucky in almost every instance. He reported that the bullets keyholed and windmilled through the game to cause a slashing wound and kill quickly. Later, experiences of a large number of hunters definitely proved that the full-jacket, 150-grain service is not reliable for taking big game of any kind. T.R.'s favorite was the .405-caliber Winchester rifle.

Inasmuch as the Springfield can be called the grandpappy of our modern high-velocity, bolt-action sporting rifles, let's take a look at it. Over 2,000,000 in various forms were made from 1903 until 1944, and many thousands of them, in service or sporting style, are in the hands of sportsmen throughout the world. Around a dozen types or styles were produced at Springfield Armory, including several for service, special rifles for National Matches, sporters, International Match, and heavy-barrel target rifles. Springfields also were made in .22 Long Rifle caliber.

The original 1903 cartridge was loaded with a 220-grain round-nose bullet given a muzzle velocity of 2,300 feet per second. Soon after it was in production, the French and Germans came up with sharp-pointed bullets having superior ballistic characteristics. To compete, our boys developed a lighter bullet weighing 150 grains and having a sharp "spitzer" point. It was adopted in 1906. The .30-caliber, 1903 (.30-03) cartridge case had a long neck to hold the lengthy 220-grain bullet. The shorter spitzer bullet required only about half the seating depth in the cartridge case, and it was found desirable to shorten the neck of the case by approximately one-tenth of an inch. All Springfields in service were called in and the barrels cut off at the breech and rechambered to take the new cartridge, designated .30-06, 30 for caliber and 06 for the year of adoption.

The Springfield rifle quickly began gaining a reputation for accuracy. Soon it was known as the world's most accurate arm. Although this modified Mauser military weapon was carefully made by expert workmen, a great deal of the credit for its fine accuracy should have gone to the very excellent ammunition made for it.

At the beginning of World War I there were not enough Springfields on hand (only about 600,000) to arm our troops, and we needed rifles but fast! When we entered the war, five American concerns were making rifles on large foreign orders. Three of them were the Winchester Repeating Arms Company, of New Haven, Connecticut; the Remington Arms-Union Metallic Cartridge Company, of Ilion, New York, and the Remington Arms Company of Delaware at its enormous war-contract factory at Eddystone, Pennsylvania. These concerns were producing the Enfield, pattern of 1914, for the British Government, with an estimated combined capacity of 11,000 rifles per day. The 1914 rifle was a highly advanced design, originally planned for a .276-caliber cartridge. Before it was in production, Britain was at war, and there was no time for changing to a new caliber, so it was made in .303 British caliber.

By the spring of 1917 England was doing well at home manufacturing small arms and her American contracts were nearing completion. Rapid mobilization of our forces really put the pressure on for rifles (it's a fact that many of our men in training actually were drilling with broomsticks).

Springfield Armory had a capacity of only 1,000 rifles per day and Rock

Island only 400 per day. Tooling other plants for producing the Springfield would have taken too much time. It was fairly easy to change the Enfield to take the .30-06 cartridge, and we were in business with the above three great plants making the U.S. Rifle Caliber 30, Model 1917, popularly called the 1917 Enfield. During the nineteen months the United States was in World War I, more than 2,500,000 Springfield and 1917 Enfield rifles were produced, with 2,193,429 of them 1917 Enfields. Twenty-two years later, after the Dunkirk evacuation of World War II, the United States Government gave Britain a million of the Enfields in anticipation of an invasion of the British Isles.

Almost 4,750,000 Americans in World War I became more or less familiar with the bolt-action military rifles, and after the war there was a strong demand for a sporting arm of that type. At that time our most

Teddy Roosevelt in Colorado with his custom Springfield rifle.

powerful hunting rifles were of autoloading, pump or lever-action, and none of them, excepting the Winchester Model 95 and the Savage Model 99, were chambered for cartridges as powerful as the .30-06.

The major arms companies recognized the demand for bolt-action, high-velocity sporting rifles and they got busy. Savage was first on the market with the very graceful Model 20 which represented the latest and highest development of American bolt-action hunting rifles at the time. It was the first of a long line of improvements to keep the Savage line completely modernized. Model 20 was made in .250 Savage, .300 Savage and .30-06 calibers.

When the war ended in 1918, Remington had quantities of partly finished 1917 Enfield military rifles, actions and barrels on hand. Utilizing the very strong breech mechanism of the arm, Remington engineers designed, developed and introduced the Model 30 rifle in 1921. This highly successful sporter was announced in .25, .30 and .35 Remington Rimless, and .30-06 calibers. Later it was made in 7-mm Mauser and 257 Roberts calibers, and a few in 8-mm and 7.65-mm Mauser.

Winchester started from scratch to develop not only that company's first bolt-action rifle for heavy high-velocity ammunition, but a new cartridge for it. In 1925 the Model 54 was put on the market in two calibers, the .30-06 and the brand-new .270 Winchester. The 54 was greeted with enthusiasm by the shooting fraternity and it soon achieved great popularity. Eventually it was made in ten calibers and was the first repeating rifle chambered for the .22 Hornet varmint cartridge.

Those first three bolt-action models for heavy, high-velocity cartridges are long gone, but in each instance they have been replaced by rifles of greatly improved design. Shooters have demanded more and more specialized ammunition, and those demands have been met.

Around the turn of the century, thinking riflemen were becoming concerned with higher bullet velocity for flatter trajectory and longer point-blank range. The .30-40 Krag was best-known and most popular with those interested in high velocity. The 220-grain bullet of the .30-40 was given about the same velocity as the 170-grain .30-30 bullet, for greater killing power. Quite early, hunters discovered that the 220-grain full-patch service bullets of this Spanish-American War veteran were not ideal for taking big game. While they killed well if the brain or spinal cord was struck, hits in other parts of the body often made small wound channels, and the game escaped and died a lingering death. However, once in a while an animal would be killed instantly when hit in a more or less soft part of the body. This phenomenon was a mystery until someone advanced the theory that hydrostatic pressure, sometimes called hydraulic action, was responsible for those quick kills—the idea being that when a high-velocity bullet strikes an organ distended by fluid it may produce a deadly bursting or sort of explosive effect. This action of natural mechanics is one of the reasons for developing the modern ultra-high-velocity cartridges. Now a number of types of bullet points are used to control expansion.

By the time the .270 Winchester cartridge was put on the market, in 1925, the .30-06 was well established as a reliable big-game taker, and jacketed sporting bullets in various calibers were being engineered especially for the speed that they were to be driven and for the particular job for which they were intended. At first, the .270 did not catch on among sportsmen. But in time its very excellent performance in the game fields, especially with the 130-grain bullet at over 3,000-feet-per-second muzzle velocity, became better known and more popular.

The .280 Remington is another high-velocity job that is proving very successful among hunters. It is one of the group that may be termed all-around cartridges.

For years, rifle buffs dreamed of cartridges giving velocities of 4,000 feet per second. In 1936 such a cartridge became a reality. Winchester introduced the .220 Swift with a forty-eight-grain bullet at over 4,000-feet-per-second muzzle velocity. Almost immediately after the Swift was announced, hunters gave it a workout in the field and all kinds of game on the American continent were killed with it. Varmint-sized animals were really clobbered, but with larger animals, from whitetail deer to moose and big bear, the tiny super-velocity bullet proved to be unreliable. The Swift definitely is not for big game, and some states outlawed it—and other light-bullet cartridges like it—for use on deer and larger animals. But it certainly is great for varmints.

Our very latest in medicine strictly for varmints are the Hi-Speed Remington .222 and .222 Magnum cartridges. The standard .222 has seen extensive use by woodchuck hunters and bench-rest shooters. It holds an arresting number of world's records for accuracy. The .222 Magnum has not enjoyed the field use of its slightly less robust, but older companion. Quite some shooting indicates that the magnum is very accurate and is slightly less sensitive to wind than the standard .222.

One of the first really high-speed numbers to be put on the market was the .250 Savage cartridge. It was introduced in 1913 with an eighty-seven-grain bullet that left the rifle muzzle at the then amazing speed of 3,000 feet per second. Later, in 1932, Peters brought out the cartridge with a 100-grain bullet, at 2,850 feet per second. The .250 Savage was—and still is—a good cartridge for the hunter who wants a rifle for every sort of game.

The 6-mm cartridges (.243 Winchester and 6-mm Remington) are ammunition for the one-rifle sportsman who hunts nothing larger than whitetail deer.

With the .220 Swift indicating that high velocity evidently cannot be entirely substituted for bullet weight, favorable efforts have been made to up the velocity of heavier bullets. In recent years, Roy Weatherby probably has done more in the interest of high velocity than any other one man. He developed his line of powerful magnum cartridges in calibers from .257 to .460. All of them have proved their worth in game fields throughout the world. The .300 Weatherby Magnum, a medium-power cartridge of the line, is probably the most popular of Weatherby cartridges. It has taken practically every species of game from elephant on through the list. The .378 and .460 WM cartridges are strictly for heavy African animals.

More recently, Winchester has introduced a new family of magnum cartridges. First was the .458, for the world's largest game animals. Next came the .338 for medium to large game—Alaskan brown bear, grizzly bear and moose, and general African and Indian game, including lion and tiger. The .264 Winchester Magnum is a flat-shooting, high-velocity cartridge built on the belted magnum case of the .338 and .458. It is designed for long-range shooting on medium game, such as goat and antelope.

The 7-mm Remington Magnum has become very popular because of its effectiveness on game from coyote to moose and bear.

There is no doubt about it, we have a great variety of American high-velocity cartridges, medicine for every kind of game found in the world. Look them over at your favorite gun shop, decide what you need and make a choice. And, by the way, all of our highly refined bolt-action sporting rifles have been directly influenced by the Springfield which Teddy Roosevelt ordered in 1903.

17

Choke: Your Shotgun's Secret Weapon

IF YOU'VE BEEN DOING a lot of missing with your shotgun lately, perhaps you are having what the boys call tight-collar trouble—too much choke.

The choke of a shotgun is nothing more or less than a constriction, or narrowing of the bore of its muzzle. By increasing or decreasing the amount of choke in the barrel, the range at which the shot pattern is most effective is increased or decreased.

Every shotgun barrel is factory-bored to one of a number of degrees of choke. The degree of choke determines the percentage of the shot charge that strikes within a 30-inch circle at 40 yards. Full choke puts 65 to 75 per cent within the circle; improved modified (¾-choke) 55 to 65 per cent; modified (½-choke) 45 to 55 per cent; improved cylinder (¼-choke) 35 to 45 per cent; and cylinder bore 25 to 35 per cent.

In the past a lot of shooters have put their money on the line and lugged home a full choke-barreled shotgun for all-round field shooting. For long shots on ducks, geese and turkeys (say up to 50 or 55 yards) with heavy shot such as size 2 or 4, a full choke barrel gun in the hands of an experienced hunter can really do business. But taking shots normally within 40 yards, say, at ducks over decoys, doves and pheasant, an improved modified or modified choke is better for many shooters. As a matter of fact, modified is pretty good for all-around use. A more open pattern such as improved cylinder is good for up to 30-yard shooting on quail, ruffed grouse, woodcock and maybe rabbits.

Since World War II there has been improvement in shotgun ammunition. The new shells, with wadless crimps and gas-seal powder wads, pattern closer than pre-war ammo. A gun that once patterned 65 to 70 per cent may now pattern 75 to 80 per cent or more, which is great for pass shooting at the quackers and doves, but these dense patterns when well centered on the target will do a mangling job at the usual 20 to 35 yards upland range. You can well imagine the concentration of about 400 Number 7½ shot within a 15-inch circle at 20 yards. Such a small pattern also means very close holding to get the shot on the target.

When you pull the trigger and the shot charge leaves the muzzle, it is on its own. If you have properly pointed the target and it is within the effective range of your gun, the score should be a "dead bird." With the shot in the air there are two elements over which you have no control. One is the above-mentioned shot pattern and the other is what ballistics engineers call shot column or string.

Shot pattern is the arrangement of the pellets as they travel through the air and strike a flat target perpendicular to the line of flight. The 10, 12, 16, and 20-gauge shotguns ordinarily are patterned at 40 yards. A large piece of paper is put up and fired on at that distance. The shot should show a fairly uniform distribution at the most densely peppered section and a 30-inch circle is drawn around that area. Then the pellet holes within the circle are counted and the percentage figured.

After looking at a shot pattern, whether it was made on paper or on the side of an abandoned barn, some shooters get the mistaken idea that the load of shot flies toward the target in the form of a sort of wheel or disc of pellets.

All pellets of a shot charge fired through a shotgun barrel do not travel to the target at the same speed. The choke, near or at the barrel muzzle, works something like the nozzle on your garden hose and squirts out the shot charge at somewhere between about 850 and almost 1,100 feet per second, depending on the load. Some pellets speed up as they go through the choke, others manage to become slightly deformed and air resistance slows them down more rapidly. The lack of absolutely uniform speed causes the pellets to string out and form a shot column as they fly through the air.

A short shot string is desirable, for no matter how evenly the pellets may be distributed on a flat piece of paper, if they are strung out too far it might be possible for a target to fly through, between the shot, and never be touched. With a fairly short, concentrated column, many pellets get to the target at the same time.

It always has been quite a chore to measure the shot string as it flies through the air and not too many years ago no one knew if the majority of the shot was in a 10-foot or a 30-foot string out where the game was moving.

Now the technicians at Remington and Winchester-Western take high-speed motion pictures to get exact measurements of the length of shot strings. They set up the camera, which takes 6,000 pictures per second, so that it is focused on a lead foil screen backed by powerful lights. The shotgun is fired at a distance of forty yards and as each pellet perforates the foil it is photographed as a pin point of light. Knowing the speed factor of the photographs and the speed of the pellets it is a cinch to figure the length of the shot string.

It has been determined that about 90 percent of the pellets of a high-velocity load of Number 4 shot form a shot string measuring approxi-

We spent a week shooting on fields of blown-up balloons to check shotgun patterns. This particular full-choke, 12-gauge gun delivered an excellent round pattern at 40 yards, with but few stray pellets at the upper edge, and averaged 73–80% on the board–great for pass shooting on waterfowl.

mately 9 feet in length at 40 yards. (In case of No. 7½ or 9 shot at shorter ranges, and with less choke, the string measurement would be even less.)

With the shot traveling the 9 feet in less than $\frac{1}{100}$ of a second, a canvas-back or Mallard duck flying at top speed of 90 miles per hour could move only about halfway through a 30-inch shot pattern and certainly would be lambasted every time if well-centered in the pattern.

Degree of choke has a definite effect on shot pattern and string. With certain degrees of choke more nearly perfect for certain kinds of shooting, the all-around scatter-gunner needs several shotguns with degrees of choke suitable for his hunting conditions. One single-barrel gun with a device that will give the degree of choke needed will do the trick also.

The first contrivance of this kind was the Cutts Compensator, originally designed to reduce recoil by dispersing the powder gas through fins or slots at the end of the barrel. The marines found it of great value on their submachine guns and today it is used on many rapid-fire guns to soften recoil and hold muzzle climb to a minimum.

The Cutts was adapted to shotguns with the addition of interchangeable tubes to control the shot pattern.

The Cutts Compensator has no effect on the breech pressure nor on the velocity of the shot charge. About forty years ago ballistic engineers of the Hercules Powder Company did exhaustive tests with the Cutts and found that it reduced recoil up to about 40 per cent or slightly more. By use of the six interchangeable Comp tubes, shot patterns for all shooting from 20 to 60 yards may be obtained.

The Lyman Gun Sight Corporation introduced an adjustable Comp tube for their Cutts Compensator that gives the degree of choke desired by a quick twist of a knurled collar.

The new "Winchoke" interchangeable steel choke tubes (improved cylinder, modified, and full choke) are available in barrels of Winchester Model 1200 Field Guns (not magnums) and Model 1400 Field Guns. The tubes screw on or off in seconds with spanner wrench.

The first of the "twist of the wrist" type of adjustable choking devices, the Poly-Choke, was invented by the late E. Field White. Taking the familiar garden hose nozzle as his inspiration, he split the end of a cylinder-bore shotgun barrel lengthwise in a number of segments and applied a screw collar to compress the segments and form a choke.

The original (now the Standard) Poly-Choke has nine degrees of instantly adjustable choke. In 1948, the Ventilated Poly-Choke was introduced. It features reduced recoil by diverting the powder gas through slots which are forward of the constriction section of the device.

Now there are several choking contrivances on the market.

The POWER-PAC employs separate pattern tubes. They are designed so that they lie inside the compensator body, rather than extend forward as with the Cutts.

Some of the gun companies have their own adjustable chokes. Savage-Stevens have the Savage Adjustable Choke for instant choke selection. With gas dispersing sleeve, which reduces recoil and prevents blow patterns, it is known as the Savage-Super-Choke. O. F. Mossberg and Sons have the C-Lect-Choke. It can be adjusted by rotating a sleeve.

An adjustable choke is a boon to the "one gun" shooter and this device may be attached to any single-barrel (autoloader, pump, bolt-action, or single-shot) scattergun.

18

See Why You Miss

A TRACER SHOT SHELL has been developed by Winchester-Western Division, Olin Corporation. I have fired several hundred rounds of this very desirable shooter's helper.

Such a shell is fascinating to contemplate, not only because it can be used as a shotgun-pointing aid during regular day shooting or during night shooting under lights, but because of the very great help it could be for training beginner shooters in the art of effective shotgun handling. And it would be a god-send for the experienced gunner when old demon slump has stomped him into a mass of quivering indecision and he has no idea of what he is doing wrong.

I certainly could have used a couple of those tracer shells during an afternoon last week. A neighbor—who seems to do fairly well on pheasant in the field, but never has been able to connect when after ruffed grouse—came over "to sharpen his eye" by blasting a few clay targets from the practice trap. He was shooting from a position that simulated Station Three, High House, in skeet. He nicked the first target, little more than a duster, but he seemed well pleased. The second target sailed away without a pellet touching it. I was standing near his gun side and remarked that he shot behind the target.

He gave me a glassy stare and said, "Yep, maybe so."

The third shot was a duplicate of the second.

He mumbled, "I was right on it. Must have been a hole in the pattern."

This business continued for some half-dozen shots.

Finally I said, "You really have been shooting away behind the targets. Try to get the shot off when you are swinging about five or six feet in front of the bird."

I figured that with a good long lead in mind, he might actually point out ahead of the target and clobber it.

He did get ahead of the clay with his next try and powdered it. But, sad to say, with his next shot, he tracked the target, swung well ahead of it, evidently decided he was too far ahead, stopped the swing and put the shot charge into the air behind the target.

Now the point is, if I could have supplied a couple of the tracer shot shells for him to shoot, the track or trajectory of the shot charge would have been obvious to him and he would have known, without a doubt, that he would have to lead the target in order to hit it.

In the past, quite some years ago, there were a number of tracer-type shot shells on the market. I monkeyed around with some of them. Those I tried were useless for the purpose they hopefully were intended—that is, showing the trajectory of the shot charge in flight.

It may seem that the production of a reliable tracer shot shell would be fairly simple. Not so! For instance, those early tracer shells, which had a pellet of pyrotechnic mixture that burned in flight, did not give a true indication of the trajectory or shot flight. The tracer element did not stay centered in the shot cloud, but turned out of line one way or another. Those shells had other serious faults. Sometimes, the burning tracer would get ahead of the shot cloud, at other times, it lagged behind, and once in a while it burned out very quickly. But more serious, it often continued to burn well beyond the target area and, as a result, created a very definite fire hazard where there were dry grass or brush areas near the shooting layout.

The Winchester-Western shell is of true tracer type and it does what it is intended to do: the shooter or observer can tell where the shot cloud is flying in relation to the target.

How did this development come about?

The first step in any research project is to determine the specific design and performance specifications of the product which is desired. Winchester-Western engineers therefore established the following, and I quote:

"A. The tracer vehicle must have the same ballistic characteristics as that of the shot and therefore must travel with, and accurately indicate, the true trajectory of the shot cloud.

"B. The tracer vehicle must be so designed and located that it prevents the propellant gases from entering the shot column and producing blown patterns.

"C. The tracer vehicle must maintain proper orientation during handling and during its flight to the target.

"D. The burning time of the tracer must be designed to constitute a minimum or no fire hazard, i.e., the tracer must burn out before hitting the ground under normal shooting conditions.

"E. The design must be such that it can be manufactured at a cost which will permit the finished product to be marketed at an acceptable price."

The first of these conditions is of paramount importance. Without it, the others are meaningless.

It was easy enough to make the tracer vehicle large enough to hold the tracer compound. The problem was, what to make it so that it would have

Tracer shot shells in action on the range.

flight characteristics of the individual pellets of the shot charge, and how to shape it so that it would fly base rearward to show the burning mix plainly to the shooter.

A number of materials and shapes were tried. Finally, aluminum was used in making the vehicle. The proper shape turned out to be a sphere with a protrusion or hollow tail to hold the tracer mixture and to act as a rudder —in flight. An aerodynamic study was made to determine just what dimensions the vehicle should have in order to meet the basic in-flight requirements. The aluminum vehicle which I took from one of the experimental shells has a diameter of about .40-caliber—.409-inch, to be exact. The tail is .192-inch in diameter and .147-inch in length. The unit, with tracer compound, weighs 27.3 grains.

In shooting the tracer shell at trap and skeet, the trajectory (curve in flight) of the vehicle can be seen clearly and brilliantly during day time or night shooting under lights. Occasionally, the tracer vehicle of the shells struck the clay targets. With a missed target, there was no doubt whatever about where the shot cloud traveled in relation to the target.

We wanted some photographs showing the tracer in flight and with the target in fragmentation. However, our ammo supply was limited and, while we got pictures of the trace, we obtained none showing the busted target and the tracer streak. With night shooting under lights, the powdered targets flicked away like glowing diamond dust, almost with the appearance of a Roman candle.

Winchester-Western ballistic engineers did extensive research testing to determine exactly where the tracer vehicle is located in the shot cloud at all times during normal range flight. High-speed photographs plainly pictured the tracer vehicle in the forward area and well centered in the shot cloud at various distances. Rifle accuracy cannot be expected with the tracer vehicle, but extensive shooting on the pattern board at forty yards by Winchester-Western technicians indicates that the tracer vehicle may wander around a little in the shot pattern, but not too much. A typical pattern sheet with ten shots, each aimed on a centered, small bull's-eye, shows an extreme spread of 23½ inches for the tracer vehicles, all within the shot pattern, with seven within fourteen inches and well centered.

This means that, if a miss occurred, even the widest placement of the tracer vehicle in the shot pattern, it would be possible to tell where the gun was pointed in relation to the target.

I was a little apprehensive about the tracer shell from the standpoint of fire hazard. But I evidently had not given the Winchester-Western engineers enough credit in the foresight department. I tried to start a fire by firing into a pile of very dry hay which had been in barn storage since last summer. The hay was fluffed and the shooting was done at twenty and forty yards. At the near distance, the tracer vehicle glanced away and evidently landed in a dry grass field. Next, I poured some gasoline over and through the hay, let it stand for a couple of minutes, so the fumes were throughout the hay, and fired again at distances of twenty and forty yards. Nothing happened! I'm not flat-footedly saying that it would be impossible to start a fire, under conditions that I cannot imagine, but that gasoline-hay bit seemed a sure-fire way (no pun intended) to start things burning. And we must remember, the tracer mixture is metered in an amount that will completely burn out before hitting the ground under normal skeet and trap shooting conditions.

The experimental tracer shot shell is constructed somewhat similar to the Mark 5 shell, excepting the filler wad has a central hole with the tracer vehicle seated at its upper side in the bottom portion of the shot charge. In firing, flame from the burning propellant powder ignites the tracer mixture in the tail of the vehicle. With the ballistic characteristics of the vehicle being similar to those of the individual shot pellets, the vehicle becomes a part of the shot cloud and stays well centered in it.

That is the story of the Winchester-Western experimental tracer shot shell. It would be very useful indeed for any shotgun shooter, beginner or not, who is having trouble connecting on moving targets.

19

Gun Games

"BANG!" SHOUTED THE SHOTGUN, "but the flashing bird didn't get the word." That is the way my friend described his first shot at a ruffed grouse. Now this fellow—we'll call him Joe, because that's his name—had little experience behind him when he made that shot, but in less than a year he has become an avid and fairly accomplished shotgun shooter. How? Simply by indulging in a few shotgun games.

As a sort of prologue, before telling you about Joe's first hunting experience, let me mention a few facts.

First, I'd like to say that fun shooting—which includes plinking and all kinds of shooting at lifeless objects, as with skeet and trap, the running deer and rising bear, on to busting clay targets from a hand trap—is probably the most fascinating and enjoyable of all participation sports; definitely so for those who have the shooting yen.

Sometimes a person will not realize that he has the inclination and natural co-ordination for becoming a fine shot. But it usually takes little more than an introduction to shooting to awaken the basic instinct (which all of us have) and to develop him into a true enthusiast.

There has been a steady growth in hunting and shooting among Americans. For instance, a national survey made by the United States Department of Interior indicates that from 1955 to 1960 the total increase in hunters was twenty-four per cent. More than 14,637,000 Nimrods went afield in 1960. An estimated 20 million hunters went afield in 1970. The sad thing, however, to my mind, is that a high percentage of these shooters did not get the full enjoyment out of their guns that is possible with a little effort and small expense. Now let's see what happened to my friend, Joe.

One morning early last fall, Joe and I were out looking for ruffed grouse. We had a couple of pointer dogs with us. One of them, a pup, was fast, careless, rather wild and difficult (in his enthusiasm) to control—just about everything not needed for grouse hunting. The other, an old dog, worked close, slow and careful, but he was frustrated by the actions of the youngster he had sired. Among other things, the pup would flush birds almost out of hearing distance. Finally and rather harshly I'm afraid, I ordered the pup home. His dejection was sad to behold, but he headed for the house a mile or so away. In about an hour, the little rascal returned, all full of biz. Fortunately, while he was away we got in some fair shooting.

Now as you probably know, the ruffed grouse really is cunning and wild-acting—a wily customer in much-hunted areas. He will take amazing advantage of all natural elements of the woods for outwitting the hunter. Although his flying speed is about half that of a speedy duck in high gear, he will buzz behind a bush or tree and disappear in an instant. Or he will dive away low, veering and dodging in dazzling flight, to shock the gunner into momentary paralysis.

In our part of the country, the woods partridge (as the oldtimers call them) evidently have taken post-graduate work in the ways of the hunter. Bluntly, they are very difficult to take but experienced hunters will tell you that they are the sportiest of all shotgun game. Reflexes have to be fast and gun pointing instantly accurate if the sportsman is to have the pleasure of the tastiest of all bird eating. This is certainly not a species of upland-game birds for the beginner to try his mettle on.

While the pup was absent, old man luck was with me and I scratched down two birds. My hunting companion—who, as I said, was not too familiar with the shotgun and certainly never before had launched a charge of shot at a ruffle—didn't see a feather. But he was enthusiastic and wanted to get in some shooting practice, so we spent the remainder of the day busting clay targets from a practice trap and thrown with a hand trap.

As it happened, while hunting we were using a Winchester Model 59 and a Remington Sportsman-58, both autoloaders with improved cylinder choke barrels, and very fast-handling shotguns. Joe insisted on trying both guns on the clays, and in just one afternoon, his sharpness in gun pointing improved amazingly. He really was bitten by the gun bug.

Our practice trap, a Remington Blue Rock, hurls one target at almost any angle, or two birds with a departure angle of about fifty-five degrees between them. A shooter has to be fairly fast to clobber both targets, especially if the right-hand long bird is taken first. With the trap in its present setting, the right-hand bird, if untouched, is in the air for around forty-five to fifty yards, while the left-hand target travels only about twenty-five yards before hitting the ground.

Two or more sportsmen can very easily work out a number of games using such a trap, or one person can handle it by kicking the release bar and then shooting the flying target or targets. When the trap is so operated, the shooter is off balance as the targets take off—as quite often happens with grouse, quail and other upland hunting; this makes for even more fun and better simulated-hunting practice.

Over the years, shooters have invented a number of games for shotgun, rifle and pistol—from do-it-yourself types to the more complicated sort.

Excellent practice for field shooting—throw target, recover from swing, mount gun and . . . clobber same!

The two best-known shotgun games which require a special layout and equipment, usually afforded only by organized clubs, are skeet and trap. A wealth of information is available from the major arms companies on measurements and construction of layouts, as well as shooting tips.

Do-it-yourself shotgun games require nothing more than the desire to shoot, a hand trap or a practice trap, a supply of clay targets and shells, a safe place to shoot and a shotgun of any gauge.

Two well-known and popular hand traps for launching regulation clay targets are made by Remington and Winchester-Western. Both are lightweight and easy to handle for a variety of shots, from straightaway to very tricky ones. Skimmers, fast and close to the ground, are difficult targets for many shooters to hit. They simulate a speeding rabbit or perhaps the transitory outburst in flight of such game as quail or grouse, and they furnish wonderful practice. Or towering targets, as often encountered in the field, are easy to learn to throw.

Also, hand trap shooting is a game that can be managed by one person. The shotgun is held at the forearm by the left hand (for a right-hand shooter), the loaded trap in the other. When the target is thrown, the shooter is off balance. He has to recover, bring the gun to shooting position, point on the target and bust it quickly. This not only is an enjoyable pastime, but is good exercise for quick recovery and fast gun mounting.

The Remington hand-trap target thrower is of cocking type with spring tension, while the Western hand trap gets its snap from a sturdy, coiled, flexible spring ferrule. They are inexpensive, and with a little care they will last almost indefinitely. Both companies also produce more elaborate and very excellent practice traps, which throw a single target.

Miniature clay target shooting works out particularly well as a game for a group. Several advantages are immediately apparent. The .22-caliber smoothbore, using shot cartridges, gives no recoil to bother the beginner or youngster; noise level is very low, and comparatively little space is required, due to the limited range of the .22-shot cartridge. The tiny No. 12 shot pellets will penetrate cardboard at fifty yards. Miniature skeet and trap fields can easily be laid out.

It certainly is true that most of us do not get enough practice with the shotgun to develop and maintain the skill necessary for consistently hitting moving targets.

Other fun games, for two or more sportsmen, can be worked out with the aid of the inexpensive Targeteer, a power-actuated launcher, which throws empty beer or soft-drink cans as targets. It uses only .22 Short blank ammunition for launching power and will send a can from thirty to forty yards out and thirty to forty feet high. If a little flour or white powder is put in the can, a white puff will appear when it is hit by a charge of shot.

Shotgun games requiring more elaborate installation of equipment include

Quail and Quail Walk, which simulate upland bird hunting, and "High Tower" and "Oh, Shucks" which make fine practice for waterfowl shooting. Many shooters prefer these games to actual hunting because of the constant action.

The game, Quail, requires two traps, preferably of automatic type, as made by Winchester-Western and Remington. The course consists of shooting twelve pairs of targets. The contestant starts walking forward. When he is at a point sixteen yards or so from the traps, which are located side by side in a pit or trap house, one target is thrown from each trap, two seconds apart, and it is up to the shooter to clobber them with the two shells loaded in his shotgun. He reloads for the second pair. Perhaps halfway in his first stride, or maybe after a couple of steps, the targets are released. As the angle of target departure is constantly changing, Quail requires alertness and fast, accurate shooting. Naturally, the ornery character operating the target-release buttons does his best to catch the shooter off stride or in an awkward position when he sends the birds on their way.

The Quail Walk throws targets to duplicate shots often encountered when upland bird hunting. One of the best I have seen is operated by the Williams Gun Sight Company on their home grounds near Davidson, Michigan. A round consists of firing on twenty-five targets. The traps are well hidden, but the shooter knows approximately when to anticipate the flight of a clay bird because a silhouette of a bird dog is placed facing the direction of the trap. Here again, the chap who releases the target tries to take the shooter by surprise.

The Quail Walk is a natural for club operation. In laying out a course, the terrain should be studied for best arrangement of target flight pattern, and the element of safety should be borne in mind at all times. By using each trap at least twice on a round—that is, with each approach from a different direction—cost of equipment can be kept at a minimum. But regardless, each round of twenty-five shots should consist of as many different shooting problems as is practical.

The High Tower event is almost always managed with one trap. A tower is constructed, the higher the better within reason. Small bluffs or cliffs are a help in keeping down building expense. The layout should be such that shots at targets from various stations are taken at distances of from fifteen to thirty or forty yards in the air. Stations should be located for a variety of shots, some so that targets are visible to the shooter for only a very short distance, if practical. A committee of ingenious club members can work out the details. The course consists of five single targets and ten pairs of doubles.

The pioneer installation of "Oh, Shucks" was at Remington Experimental Farm in Maryland. The name came about naturally because practically every shooter utters the expression, or words to that effect, when "lost bird" is called at any one of the five shooting positions or stations. The traps are arranged so that the thrown targets simulate the flight pattern of waterfowl. The original idea was to offer a sharpening-up exercise for hunting guests. Competition and scoring quickly developed, however, and ground rules were established to enlarge on the difficulties that characterize live-game hunting.

Five shooting positions of five shots each are located to provide a full range of target angles—right and left crossing shots, incoming and going away. Any number of shooters may compete. Each one shoots his five shots at one station and is followed by others in turn.

In all possible respects, the setup and ground rules are designed to approximate conditions of hunting. A minimum of cover is removed, just enough to permit free flight of the targets. Intervals of release are randomized and at least one set of doubles (two targets in rapid sequence) are thrown from each position. Targets not seen or shot at score a miss. While waiting for the target, the shooter must hold his shotgun at waist level in normal hunting position.

The random path of targets provide for endless variation and no one round is a duplication of the one before. This element of surprise, together with the close approximation to actual flight of birds, provides realistic hunting practice.

For the rifle and pistol shooter, there are also a variety of games, all the way from simple do-it-yourself plinking type with .22s, and combat scoring games with the handgun, on to longer-range contests for centerfire rifles which furnish big-game-hunting practice.

Almost every .22 rifle owner has indulged in the simple plinking games, such as shooting at swinging tin cans, Bustible Targets (obtained from the National Target Company, 7050 Spring Pl., N.W., Washington, D.C. 20012) or other setups invented on the spur of the moment—all with a safe backstop, of course.

An easy-to-manage .22-caliber scoring game for two or more shooters is played with a life-size woodchuck, squirrel, pheasant or other animal game target. Five shots are fired in ten seconds or less by each contestant at a distance of twenty yards. In case of ties, the distance is increased by increments of five yards until a champ emerges.

Besides the well-known running deer, where a full-size target is arranged on a track or trolley to simulate a running animal for shooting practice, a couple of other games can be great fun and training for the centerfire rifle enthusiast.

The Rising Bear utilizes a full-size target for offhand shooting at 100 yards. It is exposed to the shooter for three seconds. A heart shot counts ten; a body hit, eight, and a leg shot one point.

Sheep or Goat simulates long-range hunting from the prone position. A one-third-size sheep or goat target is placed at 100 yards from the shooting point—in effect, 300 yards marksmanship. Five scoring rings, which cannot be seen from the firing point, are located in the forward chest area of the target. The center ring, measuring ½-inch in diameter, scores five points when hit. The remainder of the rings are ¼-inch apart and score from four to one point for the outside ring. Shots not within the rings are counted as misses. Scopes of up to four-power are permitted. This game requires accurate shooting, and a score of fifteen or sixteen will usually take the event.

Rifle and handgun games give variety to gun-club shooting where normally the regular courses of competitive firing are most common. The shotgun games are naturals for shooting preserves, and all of them add zest to shooting programs of gun and hunting clubs. Or several congenial fellows can get together for such fun. With a little imagination, terrain of almost any sort can be adapted—always with the safety element uppermost in mind—in ways to provide challenging shooting of an offbeat character.

20

Slugging with Your Shotgun

I HAVE NEVER been one to shout huzzas about the virtues of hunting big-size game with a shotgun. To me the shotgun, in its rightful place, is meant for upland game and wildfowl shooting; the high-power rifle is for big game. In some states and places, however, the law states that deer, for instance, may be shot only with a shotgun. There isn't much you can do about that. Either you stay home and sulk or you get out the shotgun.

It is highly fortunate that manufacturers have done a good job developing the rifled slug. This slug has been designed especially for the problem of hunters who, either by choice or by law, will be gunning for big game with a shotgun. The rifled slug is definitely more accurate than the lead sphere or the round ball. For those of you who go out in brushy, timbered country after deer or bear in the fall the rifled slug is a boon.

In those places where the law requires use of the round ball, the rifled slug or buckshot to shoot deer, the idea is that such slugs will not travel as far over flat land as high-speed bullets and as a consequence will not be nearly as likely to pot some unsuspecting hunter a mile or more away from the nearest deer. The idea is true—and it works.

For example, the popular 150-grain, .30-'60 bullet will fly about two miles with an angle of departure of 31 degrees. With a shotgun barrel raised at an angle of between 25 and 31 degrees, the rifled slug is computed to have an extreme range of 1,800 yards, or slightly over a mile. However, if the slug tumbles in flight, which is likely at long distance, the extreme range may be cut down to 1,200 yards.

From the standpoint of accuracy, I had always considered the rifled slug to be a very short-range proposition—and not an able one at that. Only once before had I used the rifled slug when deer hunting, and that was for one day, about eight or ten years ago. I carried a 12-gauge gun that I had fired for point-of-impact at 50 yards before taking to the woods. As I remember, five shots grouped high and to the right in a vertical string measuring about nine inches. Not too reassuring, but maybe good enough for close shots.

As luck would have it, my one and only chance came at what I judged to be slightly over a hundred yards. A delicious-looking buck was moseying through a little evergreen-cluttered valley. It would have been a fairly easy rifle shot, but I had no idea of where to sight and hold the shotgun for a killing hit. When the buck came to a small opening, I held high on his shoulder and squeezed off the shot. As I slammed back the slide to chamber another shell I saw snow fly beyond and over the deer. Up went his flag and he disappeared into the cedar as I smacked another slug on its way. Net results, two clean misses!

Remember well the moral of this little episode. Every hunter should know exactly where his gun hits at all ranges likely to be encountered. And here is the question to be considered: Is the rifled slug accurate enough for big-game hunting at ranges up to 100 yards? Judging from that one sad incident, which really represents no experience at all, I would have given out with a definite no. Now the answer is a qualified yes.

Several years ago, while visiting Shelly Smith at the Ithaca shotgun plant, the subject of rifled slugs came up, and we did some plinking at slightly over a hundred yards. We used a 16-gauge, modified choke, Model 37 Ithaca pump gun, equipped with adjustable rifle sights. The accuracy of that gun was amazing. With two shots, I twice hit and moved a Dixie cup at about 115 yards. Because of the terrain we couldn't actually measure the distance, so it was figured by triangulation. Lady Luck was at my shoulder for those two shots but Shelly showed me a number of hundred-yard targets made with similar Ithaca Model 37 shotguns which indicated accuracy as good as that of quite a number of rifles used for deer hunting. Then and there I decided to dig into the rifled-slug business and find out what they would do in various scatterguns.

The rifled slug is a round-nose, short, conical bullet with hollow base and slanting fins along the side. The fins or rifling on the outside are supposed to make it rotate on its axis in flight, supposedly with much the same result as when a bullet is fired from a rifle. Slugs can be used in shotguns with any degree of choke because the hollow bases contract when they hit the constriction toward the muzzle. Also, the hollow base and heavy nose tends to stabilize the slug and keep it from tipping or pinwheeling in flight. Rifled slugs are made in 12, 16, 20 and .410 gauges.

The 12-gauge slug weighs 437.5 grains. It is given a muzzle velocity of 1,600 foot seconds with a muzzle energy of 2,485 foot pounds (the .30-30, 170-grain sporting rifle bullet has a muzzle energy of 1,860 foot pounds). The 16-gauge slug weighs 340 grains and has a muzzle velocity of 1,600 foot seconds and muzzle energy of 2,175 foot pounds. The 20-gauge slug weighs 272 grains with a muzzle velocity of 1,600 foot seconds and muzzle energy of 1,555 foot pounds. The .410 rifled slug is the weak sister and, in my estimation should never be used on deer. Its 93-grain bullet has a muzzle velocity of 1,830 foot seconds, with but 650 foot pounds of energy at the

The rifled slug, in any shotgun, has tremendous short-range power.

muzzle—only a bit more than that of the .38 S&W Special high-speed revolver bullet.

All rifled slugs have poor ballistic shape and lose energy very fast. At 50 yards the 12-gauge slug is traveling at only 1,175 foot seconds, with about 1,300 foot pounds of energy. However, it is made of soft lead and mushroom or expand very well to do great damage. A hit in the chest cavity with either the 12- or 16-gauge slug will put a buck down for keeps, and a hit most anywhere will usually put him down long enough for the hunter to finish him off.

I tried rifled slugs in practically every type of shotgun. Practically all makes were used. They included Winchester, Remington, Marlin, Browning, Ithaca, Savage, Stevens, Mossberg, and Harrington & Richardson—also a Parker and an L. C. Smith, both double-barrel guns. In a couple of instances identical examples of the same model gun were tried to find if they differed in shooting characteristics.

When shooting at 50 yards with regular shotgun sights not one of the guns I tried printed exactly at the point of aim. The groups centered anywhere from about five inches to twelve or fourteen inches away from the aiming point on the target. In one instance, the group was almost seventeen inches high and to the right. This means that practically every one of the guns would have to have adjustable sights installed and then be sighted in by actual firing before being taken out for big game. With receiver-type rifle sights, the group can be centered where the shooter wants it, and he can be more certain of accurate sighting.

I mounted Lyman, Redding and Williams adjustable receiver sights (they are inexpensive) on several of the shotguns and discovered that in some instances higher front sights were necessary—usually on guns without adjustable choking devices. My shooting was from bench rest, in groups of five shots.

After squeezing shotgun triggers for almost two weeks, I studied the groups and put them in table form. Here are my conclusions after what must be considered a comparatively limited amount of shooting:

1. The individual shotgun, when fired with rifled slugs, is almost without exception a law unto itself. One gun will shoot surprisingly well, while another, perhaps of the same model, will group into about eighteen inches at a hundred yards. But I must admit that most all of them did better than I expected. My smallest group at a hundred yards was a hair under five inches—which I consider phenomenal slug accuracy. The largest measured almost two feet.

2. Any of the guns I tried would usually put three of five shots within about five or six inches at fifty yards, with the other two scattered, and as far as a foot from the aiming point.

3. Guns with more open choke, such as modified, improved cylinder, or skeet bore, seem to group better than those with more constriction.

4. For accurate aim with a shotgun when using rifled slugs, it is absolutely necessary to have rifle receiver-type rear sight and flat-face front sight in place of the regular shotgun sights.

5. A shot from an unfouled barrel almost always printed higher on the target than normal.

6. The 12- and 16-gauge guns (especially those of 16-gauge) shot tighter groups than those of 20-gauge.

7. The one .410-gauge gun I used is a Remington Model 48, of skeet grade. From the bench rest it made groups as small as 2¾ inches at fifty yards with its regular shotgun sights. This gauge should be used on small game, say under fifty pounds. I'd like to give it a try on jack rabbits.

8. A gun that patterns exceedingly well with shot shells may not necessarily shoot slugs accurately.

Here is a tip. If you want to use the shotgun and rifled slug combo on big game, such as deer and black bear, try a few groups with your own gun. If it puts them all over the lot, search around until you find one that will shoot accurately—then do a little horse trading!

21

Shooting Eyes and Ears

FRIENDS, RIFLEMEN AND COUNTRYMEN, lend me your ears!

Of course, that's a take-off of Marc Antony's speech in Shakespeare's "Julius Caesar," but I really *could* use some new ears.

It was quite a shock when I learned that my hearing has been impaired by the noise of shooting. I'm sure that many others unknowingly are in the same boat. Such damage is permanent, and it is vital that every shooter protect his hearing. It is easy to do and comparatively inexpensive.

Here's how I learned the sad news.

Recently, I was visiting and discussing telescopic rifle sights at the Rochester, New York, plant of Bausch & Lomb Optical Company. Jack Brandt, one of my friends there, asked me if my hearing was up to par. My answer, in a lot more words, was that my hearing was excellent to perfect.

Jack said that, due to the fact that I do quite a bit of shooting, he would bet dollars to doughnuts that my hearing was impaired. But, if I believed my hearing to be good, it was an encouraging sign and any loss would probably be in the higher frequencies.

At that point, it dawned on me that for years it has been a fact—and somewhat of a standing joke around the house—that I cannot hear the singing of a cricket, which is in a rather high-frequency range.

Jack indicated an electronic-looking piece of equipment called a Zenith Audio-Rater 11, actually a special audiometer, and said, "Let's do a check on your hearing."

After putting an earphone in place on my right ear, he picked up a Zenith Audiogram Form and a red pencil. The blue pencil is for the left ear. The form, laid out for charting a graph, is calibrated vertically in units of 10, from 0 at the top to a loud 110 at the bottom, for establishing the hearing threshold level in decibels. Horizontally, the form is graduated for vibration frequency in cycles per second, from 125 to 8,000.

Human ears differ in their capacity both to hear sound and to recognize pitch. The limits of audibility at the lower end of the scale are approximately from 12 to 33 vibrations per second, and at the upper end, from 20,000 to 40,000. The musical range of tones lies between 30 and 4,000. Above

4,000 vibrations per second, sounds are heard as squeals and squeaks, practically indistinguishable in pitch. The normal range of the human voice is from 60 per second for low base to about 1,300 vibrations per second for high soprano, which is over four octaves.

Jack started manipulating the instrument. My right ear first heard the low pitch, 125 frequency cycles per second, at 30 decibels, which is fairly loud. I understand that a person with normal hearing picks up this sound at well under 10 decibels. With first pickup at the 30-decibel level, as in my case, a person is supposed to begin having trouble hearing normal conversation on the telephone. My hearing stayed at that level through 500 cycles per second. Then it gradually got a little better. At about 1,500 cycles per second, the level was at about 15 decibels—not too bad, but not good. It dropped to 20 decibels at 2,000, then really plunged to a loud 80-decibel level (which is nearing what usually is considered total deafness) at a shrill 4,000 cycles per second. (That explains why I cannot hear the cricket.) Then the graph line dropped off the chart at 8,000 cycles, with the sound stronger than 110 decibels. In short, my hearing is not what can be considered great with my right or gun ear.

My left ear did slightly better up to around 750 cycles per second, about the same at 1,500 and then, as with the right ear, fell like a lead balloon.

The important frequencies in speech range are between 500 and 2,000 cycles per second. So, hearing loss usually is not noticed so much above 2,000 cycles per second. My loss is a fair amount, but evidently not critical in the voice range as I have not noticed any real problems in hearing on the telephone.

The facts are that frequent exposure to loud noise *will* cause permanent loss. A single exposure *may* cause a permanent loss. If you or I, or anyone else, has been doing an average amount of clay-target shooting with a shotgun, as at skeet or trap, or with centerfire rifles and handguns, and without adequate ear protection, hearing *has* been damaged to some extent.

The really tough part of any such condition is that the loss, as I mentioned earlier, is permanent. Nerve cells in the ear have been damaged and they cannot heal themselves, nor can they be repaired by any surgical technique or medicine.

Many shooters believe that stuffing a small amount of cotton in the ears, or perhaps inserting an empty .38-caliber cartridge case in each ear, will do a good job of protecting hearing ability. It was my habit to follow such procedure, and I mentioned this to Jack. In effect, he said that sticking things in the ears does some good, and that the little ear plugs, especially made for noise reduction, are better than inserting odds and ends in the ears.

"Okay," I said, walking right into it—and I'm glad I did. "What is the best and/or easiest way to protect the ears when shooting?"

To avoid inner ear damage and permanent hearing loss, every sportsman should protect his hearing when shooting. Bausch & Lomb Quiet-Ear Protector is earmuff-type hearing guard, while the Sound Sentry (Douglass) is plug-type.

"That's an easy one," Jack answered firmly. "The Bausch and Lomb Quiet-Ear Protector. It's an earmuff-type hearing guard."

All of us have seen people working around airfields, or at other occupations where the noise level may be high, wearing earmuff-type protectors, which is compulsory in many instances. There are a number of such hearing guards on the market. For quite some time, Bausch & Lomb has been supplying industry and the Government with this type of protector. The price has been around $25 each, which perhaps is on the high side for the average shooter.

An engineering program at Bausch & Lomb has resulted in a new design, the Quiet-Ear Protector, made in two versions, one with over-the-head or top band and the other with back band. Light in weight (7 ounces and 6¾ ounces respectively), they sell for only $7.95 each.

I have been using the back-band type. It is hardly noticeable after a few minutes, and it does not get in the way when shooting. Normal sounds can be heard—ordinary speech, such as range officer instruction and so on—but the Quiet-Ear is effective for loud noises and shrill sounds, giving protection throughout the noise range. A tight seal around the ears is the critical element with such muff-type protectors. Even a tiny leak will degrade performance. The cushions of the Quiet-Ear that go around the ears are vinyl-covered soft foam which readily adapt to the wearer's contours. They are removable and washable.

Another type of hearing protector that I obtained more recently is the Sound Sentry, available from H. E. Douglass Engineering Sales Company, 3400 West Burbank Boulevard, Burbank, California 91505, at $3.95 a pair. This is a plug type that seals the ear-canal opening to protect against permanent hearing damage by reducing sound intensity. Only extremely loud noise levels overcome the protection of the Sound Sentry. I was told that, when shooting, such a type is about 90 percent as effective as the muff type. The Sound Sentry is approved and is acceptable for industrial use by the California Division of Industrial Safety, Department of Industrial Relations. This unit weighs only 1¼ ounces, can be worn comfortably with eyeglasses and hat, and is adjustable for most comfortable fit. Component parts are resistant to all natural body oils, and they can be safely washed with any hand soap and water or they can be sterilized by standard wet-heat procedures.

Still another type of hearing protector is the SafEar. It is a custom made noise suppressant that is used in industry and in the transportation areas, such as air planes, airports, fire departments and even trucks and trains where jet engines, high speed motors, scream of sirens and the roar of diesels are a hearing hazard.

However, for most of us it is of utmost importance in the recreation area —the blast of sporting rifle, pistol and shotgun shooting; even the crash of bowling balls, the shriek and boom of rock and roll bands (that's my favorite for use of the SafEar noise suppressant), the howl of racing engines, the roar of crowds, the scream of model engines, etc.—all of which can cause immediate and severe damage to the ear or a slow but steady loss of hearing.

The SafEar is custom-fitted of soft pliable rubber, hand crafted for comfort and lifetime wear.

The people who make the SafEar tell me that it provides complete protection from damaging sounds by use of a scientifically designed, engineered and patented acoustical chamber, attenuating high decibel and high frequency sounds or continuous impact sounds down to a safe level below 85 decibels; it allows the ear to breathe, with no heat or pressure in the ear, and it allows normal conversation to be heard. There are no moving parts or electronic hookups, it does not cause dizziness, and it can be worn continuously, preventing exposure to damage at all times.

The way to obtain a SafEar set is to order one from Human Acoustics, Inc., 888 E. Williams St., Carson City, Nevada 89701 (they cost $27.50, and are guaranteed for 10 years). An ear impression kit is sent to you; your individual ear impressions are returned to the laboratory; impressions are trimmed, corrected and built up; impressions are placed in epoxy casting; casting is removed and trimmed; liquid rubber is placed in casting and rubber casting is cured with heat; ear mould is removed and trimmed; sound chamber is placed in ear mould and inspected; SafEar is sent to you.

At this writing, I have been using a SafEear set for several months while check shooting sporting rifles and handguns, as well as while shooting skeet and trap—no problems, very comfortable, in fact, I hardly know that I have them in my ears.

Now for your eyes!

Have you ever been sprinkled by bird shot from a distant and unseen shooter's shotgun while hunting? Many sportsmen have had such an experience. I know I have, quite a number of times. Nothing serious, not even a really sharp sting, but nevertheless, without shooting glasses, an eye injury could possibly have resulted.

Some ten or fifteen years ago, I started wearing the regular Ray-Ban shooting glasses made by Bausch & Lomb, designed to give maximum protection and maximum unobstructed field of view—that is, without the frame interfering with the vision. The lenses are toughened and made impact-resistant. Periodic checks are made to insure above-minimum performance. Each month, about fifty samples are selected at random from stock and given a ball-drop test. Quite some years ago, I watched the routine at the Bausch & Lomb plant. As I remember, steel balls measuring ⅝-inch in diameter were freely dropped on the horizontal upper or outside surface of the lens from a height of 50 inches. That's quite a whack. The balls bounced

Shooting glasses protected the eyes of Joe-Joe the dummy when he took a charge of No. 8 shot pellets at 50 yards. About thirty-five to forty pellets hit the head area, with at least six on the Bausch & Lomb glasses.

off without fracturing the glass in any way. And I might add, due to the fact that even the slightest lens irregularity can distress the eyes and cause excess body fatigue and nausea, every Ray-Ban shooting glass is ground and polished with the same exactness as if it were a prescription lens.

The latest Ray-Ban Decot shooting glasses have lenses that are shaped a little differently from the regular type. They ride slightly higher to avoid any check push-up by the gun butt and they give more ventilation area to eliminate fogging of the glass.

For cloudy and hazy days, the Kalichrome yellow lenses are excellent. They minimize haze and sharpen contrast to make it easier to see the target. I have worn glasses on not-so-hazy days with good success, too. However, in really bright sunshine during midsummer, or in the dazzlingly bright light of equatorial Africa, the Ray-Ban green or the gray (developed at the special request of the United States Air Force) reduces annoying and harmful glare and blocks infrared and ultraviolet light to give the shooter a visibility edge similar to the yellow lenses under dull conditions.

The regular Ray-Ban shooting glasses list at $25 and the Decot at $27. That may seem expensive but, with a little care, they will last almost indefinitely.

Just to see what would happen, I put a pair of Decot yellow-lens Bausch & Lomb shooting glasses on Joe-Joe the dummy and shot him in the head at approximately 50 yards. The load was low-base, 12-gauge, 1⅛ ounce of No. 8 shot. About 35 to 40 pellets hit the head area, not counting the cap, with at least six pellets on the glasses. Before shooting, I fully expected the lenses to be broken. However, where the pellets struck the glass squarely, there was a tiny white speck that in some cases could not be wiped off—actually a slight crater that hardly can be seen without a magnifying glass. Joe-Joe's face was sprinkled, and two pellets that squarely hit the edge of the cap's hard bill penetrated over a quarter of an inch. Two others traveled the full width of the bill and lodged at the body of the cap, but the eye area was well protected. Incidentally, Ray-Ban shooting glasses now can be obtained in your own prescription from your local optometrist.

Obviously, there are other excellent shooting glasses that I haven't had a chance to checkout.

There isn't a constant danger of an individual's eyes being badly sprinkled with bird shot, but ears definitely can be permanently damaged by continuous loud noise, or even by one loud blast. Remember the old saw: An ounce of prevention is worth a pound of cure. But what if there ain't no cure?

22

The Power in Your Gun

MODERN GUNPOWDER has come a long way from the days when black-powder manufacturers blasted the roof off the mill every now and then when they mixed a new batch, and its development has been helped along by all sorts of historical oddities—from a blacksmith who was interested in billiard balls to a cut on one of Alfred Nobel's fingers. Although practically every car owner can discourse intelligently about the types of fuels that power the engine of his automobile, surprisingly few shooters know as much about what has been done over the years to improve the fuels *they* use.

What gasoline is to your six- or eight-cylinder car engine, gunpowder is to your sporting arm. Gunpowder is the stuff that gives a gun its power. It is the fuel for the piston-type engines that we call firearms. The bullet of the cartridge is the piston and it is put into action and given power in the same way the pistons of your automobile are motivated.

The fuel or powder is probably the most important component of the cartridge. It is directly responsible for the bullet's power and for the proper functioning of the gun, just as gasoline is for the automobile. Too much powder, or too little powder, causes trouble and the type of powder has to be right for best results in the particular cartridge.

Actually, powder is a form of solid matter which, when confined in a cartridge case, will burn rapidly if ignited. It has been found by years of experimental effort that certain substances work better than others. Today we have two general kinds of gun powder—black powder (which is just about obsolete except for buffs who shoot the old ones) and smokeless powder. There are a number of variations of each type.

Black powder was used for several centuries as a propellent in firearms before smokeless powder was invented. Historians tell us that an explosive compound of saltpeter, sulphur and charcoal, in practically the same proportions used today for black powder, was being made in the Ninth Century. Strange as it may seem, guns came along much later, probably in the Thirteenth or early in the Fourteenth Century.

Black powder is a mechanical mixture of the three ingredients mentioned above—all highly inflammable substances. When mixed together, sulphur and charcoal burns readily if there is plenty of air present. Cut off the supply of oxygen and the mixture will not burn. Such a combination is useless for firearms, since there is very little oxygen in a sealed cartridge or shell case. The addition of saltpeter (potassium nitrate) which is rich in oxygen, turns the mixture into an explosive that burns instantly, whether in the presence of air or not.

Black-powder mills usually were constructed with a strong skeleton framework and roof. The side boards were barely tacked onto the structure —and for very good reason. The workmen assembled the ingredients, prepared them for mixing, and then left the building fast. The machinery was started by remote control from outside and allowed to run the proper length of time. Then the men returned to prepare for the next operation. When a "blow" occurred, the explosion naturally took the path of least resistance and cleaned the structure of the lightly attached boards. Operating in this way, it was seldom that anyone was injured and all that was necessary was to clean up the machinery, pick up the boards and tack them in place, and start operations again.

Originally, gunpowder actually was a powder—the ingredients simply being ground together. By the eighteenth century, however, it was being made in granular form, with the size of the grains determining the burning characteristics.

In production, charcoal, sulphur and saltpeter of proper purity and proportions are mechanically mixed together, water is added and the mass is milled or ground in special stone or iron mills and pressed into a solid cake. After drying, the cake is crushed and put through assorted sets of grooved rollers. It is sifted and glazed and polished by being tumbled with powdered graphite in a revolving barrel; then it is graduated on a basis of the size of the granulation.

Today black powder is available for shooters and reloaders in three different granulations, with Fg the coarsest and FFFg the finest. Fg grain size is used in large rifle cartridges—say .40-caliber up. FFg is the most used. It works well in almost all caliber revolvers and rifles. A rule usually followed is this: use this granulation when more than 20 grains is required. FFFg is used in very small-caliber guns.

Comparatively speaking, there is very little black powder used in small arms today. In fact no cartridges are now loaded commercially with black powder by the ammunition companies. Quite a quantity is burned each year, mostly by those who enjoy shooting the old muzzle-loading rifles and handguns, and the early black-powder cartridge guns.

Semi-smokeless and Lesmok powders were the result of attempts to take most of the dirt and smoke out of black powder. Semi-smokeless is a mixture of black and smokeless powders—the two being combined during manufacture. The semi-smokeless burns cleanly, and fouling does not build up as with black powder, but it is considered fairly dangerous to handle. I have used many a pound of it without trouble of any kind.

Lesmok powder is a horse of a different color and definitely should not be used in muzzle-loading guns or by the handloader. This powder was principally used in loading .22-caliber rim-fire ammunition and fortunately very little of it ever got into the hands of the shooting public. It is the only small-arms powder that I consider to be really dangerous to handle. Being a mixture of black powder and guncotton, it ignites easily and can be fired by friction or by a blow. Semi-smokeless and Lesmok powders were dangerous to make and handle. The ammunition loading companies have stopped using these hazardous powders.

Now we come to smokeless powder—which is a misnomer; it is not smokeless (although it develops much less smoke than black powder), nor is it a powder. It is made in granular form.

The development of smokeless gunpowder was closely allied with that of nitroglycerin, guncotton and plastics. In 1845 Professor Christian F. Schoenbein, at the University of Basle, Switzerland, produced a nitrated cotton which he called guncotton, and at the University of Turin, Italy, Professor Ascanio Sobrero invented nitroglycerin. In modified forms, these two discoveries, in time, were literally to alter the face of the earth and to give us the modern military and sporting small-arms powder that we use so successfully today.

Black powder, in several forms, was used for blasting. It was woefully lacking as an all-around explosive during the rush and development of the country in the middle of the Nineteenth Century. It had several shortcomings for use in mining. Instead of shattering rock and ore, it merely pushed out big hunks which had to be broken into pieces. This increased costs and retarded work when the need was for greater speed. Industry required a blasting agent that not only would push but also shatter whole mountains if need be.

Nitroglycerin and guncotton seemed to be the answer. Both exploded cleanly and had tremendous power. However, producing plants in England, France, Germany, Austria and Russia blew up with so heavy a loss of life and property that a great fear of these explosives developed and put a stop to practically all effort to manufacture them commercially.

Experiments continued. By midyear, 1866, Alfred Nobel had successfully mixed nitroglycerin with finely powdered earth (Kieselguhr), producing a material with great explosive power that was safe to handle. His invention —dynamite—was the nearest man had come to creating a manageable mountain wrecker.

Guncotton, which was too dangerous for blasting, either commercially or for military destruction, strangely enough was adapted by a Boston medical student, J. Parker Maynard, for the needs of medicine and surgery.

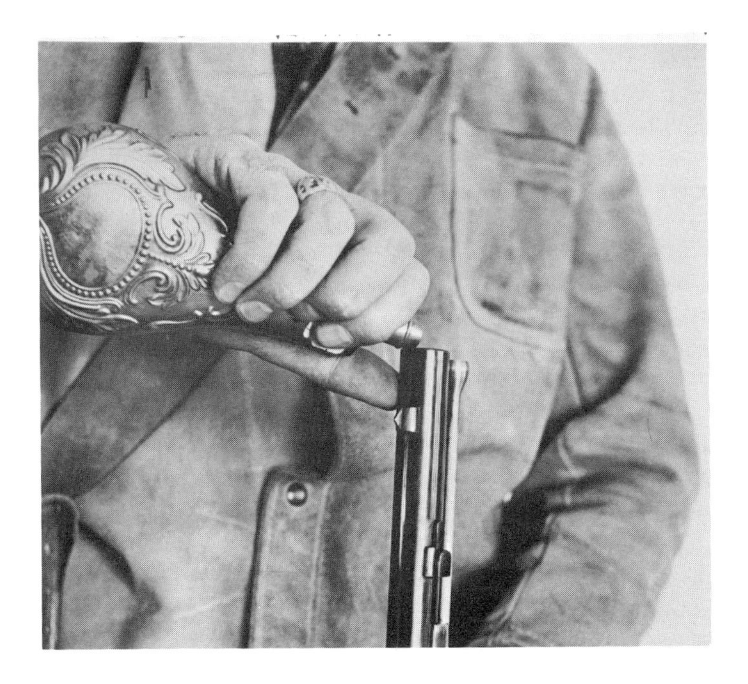

This shooter is putting the power in his rifle.

He put it in solution with ether and alcohol and produced a harmless chemical known as collodion. Coated over a wound, this concoction dried quickly into a thin, tough, protective film.

One night in 1873, Alfred Nobel, of dynamite fame, cut his finger. He applied collodion, watched it dry, and went to bed. But the paining finger kept him awake. He pondered over a new explosive he was seeking. Years before, he had combined guncotton and nitroglycerin, but the coalesce had not turned out well. The aching finger gave him the idea of using collodion. He hurried to his laboratory and by dawn had produced a jelly-like substance of yellowish tint that became known as blasting gelatin.

Blasting gelatin is almost waterproof and was found to be unsurpassed for use under water. Combined with materials such as are used in dynamites, graded gelatin dynamites were obtained that were suitable to most any sort of condition in wet mining operations.

Thus another step in the direction of smokeless powder was completed.

The correct chemical term for guncotton is cellulose nitrate. Chemically, cotton is almost entirely cellulose, as is the fibrous and cellular structure of most plants, including trees. This inexhaustible supply of cellulose made

Schoenbein's discovery of guncotton of interest in fields far removed from explosives.

In an effort to win a $10,000 prize for a new material to replace ivory in the manufacture of billiard balls, a young blacksmith, John Hyatt, invented celluloid while fooling around with collodion.

Next, cellulose nitrate, in the form of light, fluffy, lustrous filaments was used as the lighting element in incandescent light bulbs. By 1924, this material, now called rayon, was used to make cloth.

To cut a long story short, in 1886, a Frenchman, Vieille made the first military smokeless powder of the modern type. His Poudre B was a straight pyro-nitrocellulose variant of Hyatt's plastic, with certain chemicals added to promote combusion and stabilize the compound mixture. Poudre B was what we now call a single-base powder.

About two years later Nobel combined nitrocellulose and nitroglycerin and produced a double-base smokeless powder which was trademarked Ballistite. Some years later Du Pont brought out a double-base shotgun powder by the same name. Several countries hopped on the band wagon. Russia and Belgium each adopted a modification of the French Poudre B or single-base powder. England, Germany and Italy developed double-base powders on the principle of Nobel's Ballistite. The English powder, being in the form of long thin tubes, was called Cordite. The Italians called their similar powder Filite.

In the United States, the Navy experimented with single-base powders and the Army experimented with double-base powders, but neither got to first base.

In 1889, the Army's Chief of Staff asked the Du Pont Company, who had made black gunpowder for the government since shortly after the turn of the Nineteenth Century, to do something about the smokeless-powder situation. In 1890 a large tract of flat open land was purchased at Carney's Point, New Jersey, across the Delaware River from Wilmington, Delaware, the home of the Du Pont Company. A laboratory was built there and a plant was begun for the production of guncotton. In June 1892 the first guncotton was produced for the Navy. Soon, in 1893, a single-base smokeless powder was developed and put into production. It was on the market in time for the hunting season of 1894. This was the foundation of the Du Pont Improved Military and Sporting Rifle powders of today.

Other smokeless powder companies became busy in the United States. There have been a great number of them in operation at one time or another since 1893, but at present there are only three—Du Pont, Hercules Powder Company and Olin Corporation. Du Pont mostly makes a line of single-base powders, while Hercules produces double-base powders. Winchester-Western, a division of Olin, manufactures a comparatively new bullet propellant called Ball Powder.

Bulk smokeless powders were the early ones made to be loaded in the old black-powder cartridges in the same volume, or bulk, as black powders. The smokeless charges did not weigh the same as the black-powder equivalents, but could be loaded bulk for bulk with the black powder. Later, some so-called bulk powders were developed that produced greater pressures and could not be loaded bulk for bulk for obvious reasons. Bulk powders were not entirely satisfactory. They crumbled easily and in some instances properly hand-loaded cartridges, which had been carried around for some time until the powder was well crumbled or powdered, developed dangerous pressures when fired.

Dense powders have a much higher nitrogen content and are so powerful that they cannot be loaded in anywhere near the same volume as black powders. In the early days of dense powders many a gun was wrecked by home-rolled cartridges put together by handloaders who were familiar with black powder only and did not realize the power of the new powders.

Briefly, smokeless powder is manufactured in several basic steps. The process begins with the production of nitrocellulose (cellulose nitrate) from cellulose or vegetable fiber. The cellulose, called cotton, is nitrated by being stirred in a pot of a mixture of nitric and sulphuric acids in proper proportions. It is in this process that the cotton acquires the nitrogen that gives the powder its power.

The nitrated cotton is then pulped and put through several washings to remove impurities. The water is removed and the cotton compressed into solid blocks. The blocks are broken up and ether and a stabilizer are added to change the cotton to a colloid. The mass is then squeezed through a screen to mix it more thoroughly. The squeezing changes the mass from a coarse, porous substance into a hard, tough, hornlike substance of a yellowish or brown color which is pressed through macaroni machines into tube-like strings. Some powders come out as solid strings.

The hollow-tube formation of the grains promotes progressive burning. If the grains were solid, less gas would be thrown off as they burned smaller. This means that the pressure within the gun would decrease as the powder burns. With the powder grain burning within, as well as on the outside, the inside burning area increases while that on the outside decreases—thus maintaining a comparatively even formation of gas until the pellet is consumed. Coating of the powder grains with certain materials tends toward the same end. This retards the early stages of burning and as the coating is consumed the combustion rate increases to build up a continuous pressure in the gun as the projectile moves up the barrel bore.

The strings are cut into grains of the desired length. Next, the powder is coated, if desired (depending on the kind of powder being made) and dried. After drying, the powder usually is tumbled in graphite. This is an incomplete outline of how nitrocellulose powder is produced but I hope you get the idea.

There are a number of conditions encountered during the process that cannot be precisely controlled. This means that two lots of a similar powder may have slightly different burning characteristics. For this reason, the cartridge-loading companies carefully check and test each batch of powder received and determine the proper amount of powder necessary in a specific caliber cartridge to give its customary ballistic characteristics.

Double-base powders are made in a somewhat similar manner except that nitroglycerin is incorporated in the chemical compound.

Western Ball Powder, developed by Dr. Fred Olsen for the Western Cartridge Company, can be made in either single or double-base form. It comes from the production machines in small spherical grains. The spheres are coated with a material to delay or slow down the initial burning. In certain instances Ball Powder is run through rollers and flattened. This changes its burning rate. This new powder can be produced ten times as fast as regular, single and double-base powders.

Smokeless powders are produced with slightly different chemical compositions and in various shapes to meet the requirements of our standard cartridges.

A number of rifle, pistol and shotgun powders are regularly packaged by Du Pont, Hercules and others for those who want to load their own ammunition. Reloading is a fascinating and economical hobby, especially for sportsmen who do a lot of shooting. If you are interested in reloading, I suggest that you buy the Lyman Ideal Handbook, published by the Lyman Gun Sight Corporation, Middlefield, Connecticut, the Speer Handloaders Manual, published by Speer Products Company, Lewiston, Idaho, and the Hornady Handbook of Cartridge Reloading, as well as the Gun Digest publications and those of Stoeger Arms Corporation.

23

So You Think You Know Your Cartridges?

THE SYSTEM of names and terms used in identifying sporting cartridges can be downright confusing—actually in the realm of bewildering mystery for many sportsmen. Even the knowledgeable boys of the shooter's hotstove league often find themselves perplexed—and in fiery and sometimes bitter argument—over elements of cartridge nomenclature. Exactly what do such names as .22-250 Remington, .250-3000 Savage (now usually called .250 Savage), .30-30 Winchester, .30-06 Springfield and .44-40 Winchester mean? And how about the magnums? Why are they called magnums? A query put to me is responsible for this piece. The question was asked by a chap who, although not a confirmed gun bug, is a regular hunter and quite familiar with firearms. "Which is the more powerful, the seven-millimeter Remington Magnum or the .44 Magnum?"

If you can answer correctly, you know your cartridges. If not, read on.

To better understand our modern cartridges, let's examine the very earliest ones and take a look at a few high points in cartridge development over a period of around six centuries.

In order to invent guns and construct cartridges, it was first necessary to have gunpowder. This substance was used in celebrations as early as the ninth century A.D. and it has been established that the material we call black gunpowder saw use as a projectile propellant not later than the first part of the fourteenth century.

This first propellant was a mechanical mixture of saltpeter, sulphur and charcoal—rather than a chemical compound, as with our modern smokeless powder. "Smokeless powders" are produced by nitrating cellulose (cotton or wood fiber) in the case of a single base powder, and with the incorporation of nitroglycerine into the compound of what are known as "double-base powders."

The earliest cartridge was very simple. It probably was first used in the sixteenth century during the matchlock-ignition period. It consisted of a pre-measured charge of black powder wrapped in paper or other material, nothing more. However, it marked a great step forward, because it made loading the gun easier and faster when the shooter was under duress or while shooting from horseback. A little later, someone thought of including the ball or bullet in the package to make reloading even faster.

By about 1600, the paper cartridge, containing powder and ball, was more or less standard among well equipped troops. In use, the powder end of the cartridge was torn, ordinarily by biting, the powder charge poured into the barrel of the gun and the bullet seated on top. The pan of the ignition system (flint) was charged with a small amount of powder and the piece was ready to shoot. This cartridge system, but with caplock ignition, was still in use two and a half centuries later, and it was the mainstay of our American Armies during the Civil War.

Two important developments came during the early part of the nineteenth century—the conical bullet and the combustible envelope which was used in the production of cartridges. Materials for the envelopes, such as paper, linen cloth, collodion, skin, etc., were highly nitrated to make them readily combustible or inflammable. The unit—envelope, powder charge and bullet—was loaded into the gun to be ignited by the fire from a separate percussion cap or a pellet of a tape primer which was located in the gun mechanism.

A step nearer to our modern cartridge was the so-called "separate-primed" cartridge. In almost all instances, this cartridge was less fragile than earlier types. Some were made of brass with an extraction rim—our first metallic cartridge—and looked vaguely similar to modern cartridges. Others were cased in heavy paper, paper and brass, rubber or gutta-percha. All of them had a needle hole centered in the base to admit the igniting flame of the percussion cap, as with the combustible cartridges.

Up until this period, cartridges ordinarily were named for the bullet or barrel-bore diameter and for the name of the arm for which they were intended. Often the weight of the bullet and powder charge in grains was printed on the box label.

During the first half of the nineteenth century, a great deal of work went into the development of self-contained cartridges—one unit having powder, ball and priming for ignition. This effort resulted in a number of odd cartridges: lip fire, teat fire, cup primer and pin fire. The pin fire saw extensive world-wide use. A pin protruding from the side of the base of the cartridge was struck by the hammer of the gun to detonate an internal primer.

The Volcanic system, where the hollow base of a conical bullet contained the powder charge and primer of fulminate, was a high point in cartridge development. The Volcanic repeaters were the immediate forerunners of the Henry rifle and the famous Model 1866 rifle which was the first to bear the Winchester name. The Henry and the Winchester Model 1866 were lever-action repeaters, sixteen- and seventeen-shot, and fired the .44 Henry cartridge with a 200-grain, .44 caliber bullet propelled by twenty-six grains of black powder. If you are a .22 rim-fire shooter, you no doubt have noticed the H stamped on the head of Winchester rim-fire ammo. This is the Winchester factory tribute to B. Tyler Henry. His ideas completely revolutionized the firearms industry and made possible the immediate success of the Winchester rifle.

Most shooters do not know that rim-fire cartridges have been produced in calibers ranging from the tiny two-mm, with a bullet measuring about .08 of an inch, to the huge .58-caliber, with a bullet measuring over a half-inch in diameter.

A few of the rim-fire cartridges were identified by two numbers. Take the Spencer cartridges, for instance. They were for the Spencer rifle, which was one of the first repeating arms made for metallic cartridges containing their own priming. Probably more than 100,000 Spencers saw service during the Civil War, and more than 58,000,000 Spencer cartridges were bought by the War Department. There were several caliber Spencer cartridges produced—56-46, 56-50, 56-52 and 56-56. The first number (56) referred to the diameter of the cartridge case just above the rim, while the second number roughly indicates the caliber in hundredths of an inch.

The identifying numbers for the rare Sharps 52-70 rim-fire cartridge makes more sense. The 52 refers to the caliber in hundredths of an inch, and the 70 indicates the charge of black powder in grains. This system of identification was extensively used with center-fire cartridges, which came into being during the mid 1800s.

With the advent of center-fires, cartridges in various calibers were developed by the dozen, and with the increase came more confusion in identification of them.

As late as 1914, the Remington catalogue listed a total of 582 metallic cartridges. Exactly 100 were rim fires and three were pin fires. The 1913 Winchester catalogue listed 390 cartridge loadings, seventy-three of them being rim fire. (After World War I, a lot of deadwood was dropped from the cartridge lists. Late catalogues show that Remington lists 153 center-fire and rim-fire cartridge loadings, and Winchester-Western a total of 151.

At that time, such cartridges as the .41 Swiss rim fire and the four above-mentioned Spencer cartridges were regularly produced. In .40-caliber—now little known except among cartridge collectors—there were over twenty loads produced. This included the .40-60, .40-65, .40-70, .40-72 and .40-82. The .40 represented the caliber and the other numbers indicated the charge of black powder. When smokeless powder was loaded in such cartridges, the ballistic levels for black powder were maintained, obviously necessitating smaller charges of powder.

Sometimes a third figure was added to the name of a cartridge: the weight of the bullet in grains. Thus the .45 Winchester Express cartridge often was called the .45-125-300—.45-caliber, 125 grains of black powder and a 300-grain bullet. The famous .45-70 (now loaded only with a 405-grain bullet) was produced in six different bullet weights.

A number of center-fire-cartridge identifying terms included the name of the arm the cartridge was intended for, such as the .22 Extra Long Maynard and the .28-30-120 Stevens. Also, foreign-developed cartridges were produced by United States ammo makers to retain their metric designations—7-mm, 7.65-mm and 8-mm Mauser, 9-mm Mannlicher, etc. Cartridges of American development have been given metric designations—the old 6-mm U.S. Navy, as well as modern cartridges such as the 6-mm Remington and the 7-mm Remington Magnum.

The use of the term "Express" (as with the .45 Winchester Express mentioned above) added to the turmoil of cartridge nomenclature. It was used by the British to indicate that a cartridge was more powerful than usual for a particular caliber. This was okay, and many rifles were made for black-powder Express cartridges in .577, .500, .450, etc. calibers. But with the development of smokeless powders, double rifles and single shots were manufactured especially for much more powerful cartridges of these calibers and using similar cartridge cases. These cartridges were called "Nitro-Express Rifle" and they were unsafe for shooting in black-powder rifles. So the older loads were labeled "Black Powder Express," and smokeless loads at black-powder ballistic levels for the black-powder rifles were marked "Nitro for Black Powder Express Rifle." To compound the muddle, the word "Magnum" was also used by the British to indicate a powerful cartridge. Some cartridges were called "Magnum Nitro-Express Rifle," and were intended for strong rifles designed for them. Such cartridges for older black-powder rifles were named "Magnum Nitro for Black Powder Express Rifle."

Well before World War I, the British firm of Holland and Holland brought out the excellent line of "Belted Rimless Magnum Nitro-Express" cartridges in .240, .275 and .375 calibers. They were called H & H Magnums in America. At first, none of them gained popularity in the United States. A few hep guides in Alaska saw the light and carried the powerful .375 H & H Magnum for a backer-upper when hunting the big brown bear. It proved a real life-saver when a dude got into deep trouble with a poorly placed shot on a brownie.

Then, in 1935, Ben Comfort won the coveted Wimbledon 1,000-yard match at Camp Perry with standard Western .300 H & H Magnum factory loads. This put that cartridge on the map for long-range shooters, as the famous match customarily had been taken with the .30-06-caliber rifle.

American hunters gradually became magnum conscious. Roy Weatherby put the spurs to the lagging horse by developing his magnum cartridges and making custom rifles for them. Weatherby Magnums became world-famous, and Roy's line now consists of cartridges for everything from woodchuck to elephant—9 different calibers—all built with belted cases.

Winchester developed the now well-known family of magnum cartridges. The .264 Winchester Magnum, loaded in two bullet weights, is a long-range proposition—the 100-grain bullet for varmint from wolves down,

Nine once highly popular centerfire cartridges—.44 S&W American, .44-40 (.44 W.C.F.), .25-25 Stevens, .32-40 Bullard, .32-35 Stevens, .32-40 Remington, .32-40 Winchester, .38-55 Winchester, 45 Winchester Express (.45-125-300)—are all obsolete but two.

and the 140-grain bullet for big game, especially in open-plains hunting, maybe up to moose. With the 140-grain bullet, I took a number of large African antelope, several at quite long range, weighing as much as 750 pounds or more. It did the job perfectly. The .300 Winchester Magnum develops more bullet energy than the .300 H & H Magnum and has great knock-down power. The .338 Winchester Magnum is intended for almost any kind of game with the exception of African elephant, Cape buffalo and rhino. The daddy of the family, the .458 Winchester Magnum has the power for taking any animal found in the world. The .264 and .338 were named for the bullet diameters in inches. The .300 for the barrel bore diameter and the .458 for the approximate bullet diameter (actual diameter is .457"). The Winchester family, as well as the Holland and Holland and the Weatherby magnum cartridges, have belted cases and are headspaced in the rifle chamber against the forward edge of the belt at the base.

Practically all .30- or .300-caliber rifles have cartridges loaded with .308-

inch bullets, which is the groove diameter of the barrel. The .308 Winchester actually is .30-caliber, but is named for the bullet diameter.

The word "Winchester" or "Remington" on a cartridge indicates that the cartridge was introduced by that particular company. For instance, the .30-30 Winchester, .284 Winchester, .32 Special, etc., were introduced by Winchester, while the .222 Remington, 7 mm Remington Magnum, .35 Remington, etc., were introduced by Remington.

I must admit that nomenclature for modern cartridges is not as complicated as it was during the black powder and early smokeless powder days, but there still is confusion.

The question quoted at the beginning of this scrivening, "Which is the more powerful, the 7 mm Remington Magnum or the .44 Remington Magnum?" is a reasonable one that ordinarily would not occur to a ballistician or to a dyed-in-the-wool gun bug. My friend commented, "It seems logical that a .44 Magnum, with its larger and heavier bullet, would be more powerful than the 7 mm Magnum." Logical, yes—true, no!

The reason is elemental when we know the background of the two cartridges. The 7 mm Remington Magnum was named to distinguish it from the less powerful, but well known 7 mm Mauser hunting cartridge. Both of these cartridges have .284" diameter bullets, but the 175-grain one in the magnum cartridge is given the high muzzle velocity of 3070 feet per second, as compared to 2490 feet per second for the Mauser load.

On the other hand, the .44 Remington Magnum cartridge was developed as a super-powerful revolver cartridge. It was called magnum to distinguish it from the less powerful .44-40 and .44 Special cartridges. Ballistics of the .44 Magnum pointed the way to using it in the rifle for deer hunting in the usual brush cover and at ranges up to around 150 yards. The Ruger Carbine, with gas-operated mechanism was introduced, and a little later Marlin brought out the Model 336 Magnum—both in .44 Remington Magnum caliber. The cartridge has certainly proven itself highly successful as a deer buster!

Now, let's run through the other cartridges mentioned in the second paragraph. The .22-250 Remington is so named because it first was produced by necking down the .250 Savage cartridge case to take a .22-caliber jacketed bullet. The .250 Savage originally was called the .250-3000 Savage because its 87-grain jacketed bullet was given the then very high velocity of 3,000 feet per second at the muzzle. The .30-30 Winchester has a .30-caliber bullet and when introduced it was loaded with 30 grains of smokeless powder. The .30-06 Springfield cartridge has a .30-caliber bullet and was adopted as our service cartridge in 1906 for the U.S. Rifle, Caliber .30, Model 1903. The .44-40 Winchester (has been called .44 W.C.F., .44-40-200 and .44 Winchester) is near .44 caliber (actually .425" bullet) and was originally loaded with 40 grains of black powder.

24

What Type Bullet?

AMERICAN HUNTERS HAVE grown more and more bullet-conscious during the past thirty years. There was a time when even the fairly well-informed sportsman went into his favorite gun shop or hardware store and just asked for a box of such-and-such-caliber cartridges, regardless of whether he was going to hunt big game, shoot varmints or do a little paper-target shooting. Today the bullet-wise shooter not only names his cartridge by caliber, but he specifies the bullet type and its weight in grains. He knows that a particular bullet will do the job of shooting he wants; he also knows that there are other weights and types of bullets loaded in his particular cartridge that were designed for other kinds of shooting. This Nimrod expects that little consolidation of lead and gilding metal, called the bullet, to perform miracles—and it will—providing the right one is used for the chore at hand.

This interest in sporting arms projectiles possibly was stimulated by the wave of activity with wildcat cartridges which began sweeping the country back in the late 1920s. That wave still continues, but it has leveled off to the point where it is not much more than a gentle swell. I don't mean there is lack of interest in wildcat cartridges, but the overwhelming preoccupation with this breed of untamed kittens is not with us today as it was in the 1930s and 40s. At that time, practically every gunsmith worth his salt worked out from one to a dozen wildcat cartridges, and an advanced gun buff was not in the swim unless he had at least one to his credit.

Just what is a wildcat cartridge? It is one that has been cooked up by an individual, or group of experimenters, with the idea of filling a niche not quite covered by factory cartridges, or one that will do a certain job better than any existing cartridge.

Actually, the line of factory-produced cartridges now covers the field so thoroughly that there is little or no room for wildcats. But to give credit where credit is due, many very worthwhile wildcat cartridges have been developed, and some have been adopted by the manufacturing companies. Roy Weatherby's line of cartridges is the result of his interest in super-high velocities, and he started as a wildcatter.

The vast interest of gun enthusiasts in offbeat cartridges and in handloading ammunition, plus the fact that thousands of sportsmen with inquisitive minds have become interested in shooting and hunting has led to popular study of ballistics.

Ballistics is the science of moving projectiles, and is composed of three divisions. Internal ballistics covers what happens within the gun before the bullet leaves the muzzle. External ballistics concerns the movement of the bullet from the gun to the target. And terminal ballistics refers to what happens at the target. The real gun buff is interested in all three phases, while the hunter mostly is concerned with external and terminal ballistics.

The study of external ballistics probably began in the neighborhood of 300,000 years ago, maybe well before the Old Stone Age was in full swing. The first missile in flight no doubt was observed when one of our brighter-than-average forebears came down out of the trees to pick up a good-sized rock and heave it over the side of a cliff to clobber a hairy mammoth, or a cave bear, or perhaps a belligerent member of his own breed.

Much later, some unsung savage genius invented the bow and arrow, and a real advance was made in the science of the missile in flight. Toward the tail end of the Middle Ages, perhaps in 1313, gunpowder was invented. This simple mixture of saltpeter (nitrate of potassium), sulphur and charcoal, which we call black powder, helped change the entire face of European civilization, completely revolutionizing war and helping to form powerful nations. And it also put powder into the hands of the common guy.

At first, firearms development was slow, but by the time the twentieth century spun into view, black-powder sporting arms, in single-shot and repeating form, had reached a high stage of perfection, and the formal study of ballistics was well established. Some very fine target and game shooting has been done with black-powder cartridges. But black powder certainly had its drawbacks. The voluminous blast of smoke created was not much of a problem for outdoor target work, but indoors it was murder, and in the game field it sometimes made it impossible to see if a second shot was necessary. Due to the low power of black powder, the range of the bullet was limited. Its trajectory, or curve in flight was about like that of a rainbow and estimation of range had to be almost exact to make a hit at any great distance. And the rifle-cleaning problem was real misery.

Black-powder cartridges ordinarily were loaded with the simplest type of bullet. They were molded or swaged of lead, or lead alloyed with a small amount of tin to make a harder mixture, and they were greased to prevent them from leaving a lead deposit in the barrel.

Today, lead-alloy bullets are found in .22 rimfire and in many revolver cartridges. Handloaders, too, often use lead-alloy, home-cast bullets for reduced loads in rifles. When they are to be propelled at much over 1,400 feet per second, brass or copper cups, called gas checks, are fitted to their bases to prevent the lead from melting by the blowtorch-like action of hot, smokeless-powder gases and to prevent escape of gas around the bullet. Several firms supply molds for casting lead or lead-alloy bullets. For instance, the Lyman Gun Sight Corporation, Middlefield, Connecticut, besides making a complete line of reloading tools, produces more than 200 different molds. That certainly gives a wide choice of bullets for practically every kind of reduced-load rifle shooting and for handgun loads.

The invention of practical smokeless powders in the late 1880s brought about a lot of complications in the manufacture of sporting arms and ammunition, and intensified the study of metallurgy and internal ballistics by the producing companies. Dense, smokeless powder burns hotter when confined, as with a cartridge chambered in a firearm and, weight for weight, produces much higher pressures than black powder. To eliminate blow-up, cartridges for the great number of black-powder arms then in the field had to be loaded to black-powder pressures when dense, smokeless powders were used. However, there were plenty of the black-powder cartridges on dealers' shelves until well after World War I. Now no American sporting ammo, except for a few blanks, is loaded with the old propellant.

Early high-pressure smokeless powders permitted muzzle velocities of rifle bullets to be increased from about 1,300-1,500 to 1,900-2,400 feet per second in arms made to withstand the additional pressures developed. Plain lead-alloy bullets simply could not stand the gaff of those speeds and pressures. The hot gas melted the base and sides of the bullets, and the bullets skidded in the rifling of the barrel to destroy accuracy. Bullets made completely of harder materials were tried, but they were not heavy enough to maintain their velocity and carry to long distances. It was obvious that lead alloy was the least expensive metal heavy enough for making practical bullets. The lead had to be covered with a protecting material, so early bullets which proved most successful for use with smokeless powder were jacketed with .002- to .003-inch-thick envelopes of soft steel or of cupro-nickel, the latter being most popular. Cupro-nickel is an alloy of copper and nickel, about the same as the metal from which our five-cent pieces are stamped. It is sometimes called German silver. Our early .30-40 Krag and .30-06 Springfield military bullet jackets, as well as jackets for many sporting bullets, were made of this material until after World War I.

Cupro-nickel was not entirely satisfactory as bullet-jacket material. Besides being rather expensive, it often left a heavy, lumpy metal fouling in the rifle bore which was very difficult to remove. It was found that a material called gilding metal was much more suitable for bullet jackets. Gilding metal is a copper alloy containing five to ten per cent of zinc.

Metal-jacketed bullets are of two general types, full-metal cased and expanding. Military bullets, by Hague Convention decree, must be of non-expanding construction, so they are full-metal cased. Heavy thick-skinned

African game, such as elephant and rhino, and the dangerous Cape buffalo almost always require deep penetration and take a lot of smacking down, so heavy, full-metal jacketed bullets—or "solids," as the boys in the know call them—are the medicine prescribed. Practically all bullets for American game are of the expanding variety. The exception is where a hunter wants to shoot through small game, such as wild turkey, for a quick kill without destroying meat. Here the small, hard bullet at medium velocity drills only a small hole.

Expanding bullets are made in many forms and were designed for specific purposes. It is impossible to have one bullet that will expend all, or almost all of its energy on small game of the varmint class, and still penetrate larger and heavier game for the humane, quick kill.

Twenty-two-caliber centerfire cartridges especially for small varmint or pest shooting, such as the older .22 Hornet, on through the Bee, Zipper, Swift and the .222s, all have soft-point or hollow-point bullets constructed to expand quickly on small, inedible game. Some—the .220 Swift bullet, for instance, which leaves the muzzle at more than 4,000 feet per second—expand so quickly that they often literally explode to blow the game to pieces. Such cartridges are super-accurate for making hits on small targets within their individual range limitations of about 150 yards for the Hornet and Bee, maybe 200 for the Zipper, 200 to 250 yards for the .222s, and 250 to 300 yards for the Swift. Remember, I'm talking about good rifles, well tuned by an expert.

We also have some fine dual-purpose calibers which, when used with the lighter-weight bullets designed for pest and varmint shooting, give excellent results. They include the .243 Winchester with eighty-grain bullet at 3,500-feet-per-second muzzle velocity; the 6 mm Remington with eighty-grain bullet at 3,500 fps; the .250 Savage with eighty-seven-grain bullet at 3,030 fps.; the .257 Roberts with eighty-seven-grain bullet at 3,200 fps; the .270 Winchester and .280 Remington, both with light-weight bullets at under 3,400 fps; the .308 Winchester and .30-06 Springfield with hundred-ten-grain bullets at about 3,400 fps. A hunter with any one of the first four caliber rifles is all set for deer when shooting heavier bullets. Cartridges for the last four calibers are available with bullets suitable for practically any American game, except big, dangerous bears.

Jacketed bullets in suitable calibers for big game have been quite a headache for the ammunition-producing companies in past years. Most early sporting bullets were soft point, with exposed lead up to about a third of the bullet length. The first of these bullets were loaded in cartridges such as the .30-30 and .30-40. The idea was for the bullet to expand to about twice its original diameter soon after penetrating the skin of the animal to cause a much larger wound than with a full-jacket bullet and kill quickly. Sometimes, especially if it hit a bone soon after penetrating, the bullet broke up and the core left the jacket and split into pieces. In most instances, no matter what happened to these bullets if they were fairly well placed, they did a good job of killing quickly and humanely on soft-bodied, small-boned animals such as whitetail deer and black bear.

But when a hunter went out after larger and tougher game, such as elk, moose and larger bear, those easily expanding bullets did not work so well. Often they expended their energy near the surface—maybe on large bones—and never reached vital organs. Many a hunter, with a well placed shot, helplessly watched a fine trophy disappear into the brush.

So the ammo makers brought out bullets with heavier jackets and less lead exposed. These harder-to-expand bullets did well on heavy game, but sometimes failed to expand reliably on the softer bodies of deer, and made only small holes without much bleeding. Soon the boys with experience selected the bullet for the game to be hunted, using light and easily expanded bullets on such game as deer and sheep, and heavier and harder bullets for the bigger stuff.

The ammo producers have worked unceasingly with design and experimentation to perfect bullets of big-game calibers that would perform well on any American big game. Progress, necessarily, was fairly slow. After a bullet was designed and tested at the factory, it had to prove itself in the wide-open field laboratory of the American shooter, where final judgment is rendered. A great many kinds of soft-nose, hollow-point, protected-point, copper- and bronze-point, and so on were produced.

Inside view, showing how modern bullets are constructed: Bullet jackets, designed for effective expansion, are formed of sheet gilding metal, and cores are of lead or lead alloy. Left to right: 1. Round-nose soft point; 2. Pointed soft-point; 3. Hollow-point (cavity varies in depth according to purpose of bullet); 4. Remington Bronze Point; 5. Remington soft-point Core-Lokt (also made with open point); 6. Winchester Silvertip. 7. Power Point is Winchester-Western's latest development.

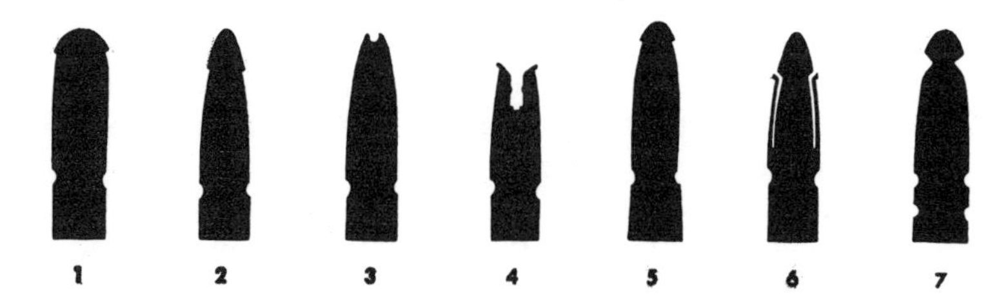

Back in the 1930s the Peters Cartridge Company developed a belted bullet. It was round-nosed and had a shallow, hollow point and a wide, thick band or belt of gilding metal around the outside about a quarter of an inch below the point. If I remember correctly, it was made in 180- and 225-grain weights for the .30-40 and .30-06, and in 225-grain weight for the 300 Magnum, with velocities about the same as those for similar weight bullets. The belted bullet was a great one; the shallow point expanded well on almost any big game, while the belt held the major portion intact to drive into the vitals of the heavier game. The only drawback was that that bullet was very expensive to make. In 1934 Remington Arms Company bought the Peters firm and plans indicated the development of a new big-game bullet—a simplification of the belted bullet that could be produced at a price hunters could afford. Early in 1940 the now thoroughly proved Remington Core-Lokt bullet was announced.

In the meantime, Winchester-Western technicians were also working on the improvement of soft-point bullets. John M. Olin, of Olin Mathieson Chemical Corporation, was attending a sales conference at the Winchester plant in New Haven when he heard of the Remington Core-Lokt bullet. He instructed his ballistics engineers to finish their almost completed experiments, and the now famous Silvertip bullet was born. Production was rushed and cartridges with the new bullet were available in principal big-game calibers for the 1940 hunting season.

The Remington Core-Lokt, known, in Peters production, as the Inner Belted bullet, is made with the jacket greatly thickened around the middle section of the lead-alloy core. This prevents breakdown of the center and base of the bullet when the thinner portion of the jacket, toward the point, expands. The front edge of the jacket of the soft-point Core-Lokt bullet is made with little scallops around its diameter to cause equal expansion and mushrooming on all sides when it penetrates game.

The Winchester-Western Silvertip bullet has the lead-alloy core enclosed in two jackets. The tip is enclosed with a thin, silver-colored metal which extends well into the main jacket to prevent premature expansion while the bullet is penetrating hide and outer muscles, and to prevent the bullet tip from being mutilated by recoil while the cartridge is in the rifle magazine. The main jacket is quite thick at the base and bore-bearing surface on the side, and it tapers in thickness toward the tip.

The Core-Lokt and Silvertip are controlled-expanding bullets and because they are made in most big-game calibers they vary in shape of point, hardness of core, thickness of jacket according to caliber.

The very latest controlled-expanding bullet is made by Winchester-Western. It is being loaded in the .338 Winchester Magnum cartridge. This powerhouse was designed and developed as a powerful intermediate-range cartridge for medium- to large-sized game, such as Kodiak bear, grizzly bear, moose, and general African and Indian game, including lion and tiger. The .338 is loaded in three bullet weights: 200-grain Power-Point with muzzle velocity of 3000 fps, and muzzle energy of 4000 foot pounds, 250-grain Silvertip, which leaves the muzzle at 2700 fps with energy of 4050 foot pounds, and 300-grain Power-Point with 2450 fps and 4000 foot pounds of energy. The Power-Point bullets are soft point, but with a very practical method of controlling expansion. Six notches are crimped into the mouth of the jacket and slightly into the lead core. Upset is more uniform, as the jacket tears or peels back evenly at the notched section at the thinner forward part of the jacket during expansion.

I have examined a number of these bullets that were fired at 100-, 200- and 300-yard velocities into material simulating animal flesh. Mushrooming was excellent at those ranges, with the enlarged forward mass of the bullet measuring more than twice the original diameter in most instances, and with little loss of weight.

For hunting on the American continent, we have a quartet of classes of centerfire game bullets, each category designed for a specific purpose. Light, fast bullets for varmints or pests from chipmunks to coyotes, in calibers from 22 to 30, will break up in small soft bodies or when they strike the ground. Bullets in the second group, also made in various calibers, expand quickly and reliably in small- and medium-sized game, such as whitetail deer, antelope and sheep. In the third class, we have the so-called controlled-expansion, or all-round bullets that give deep penetration on heavy game, such as moose and elk, and still expand enough to be usable on lighter game, such as deer. In the fourth category are the knocker-downers, usually larger than .30-caliber, for dangerous American game such as Kodiak, grizzly and polar bears. These bullets certainly will take moose and elk, and also soft-skinned African game, including lions and tigers.

Besides the complete line of bullets produced by the ammunition companies, there are smaller firms such as Speer, Sierra, Hornady, Nosler, and the Western Tool and Copper Works, which make a great variety of custom bullets for the reloader.

We certainly have plenty of different reliable bullets available, and there is more than one that can be selected for almost any job of shooting. It's just as silly to hope that a bullet designed to take heavy, tough game at close range will work satisfactorily on the small, fleet and eagle-eyed antelope at long range, as it is to suppose than an 80-grain .243 bullet will give clean kills on 1,500-pound brownies. The individual hunter is the guy who knows what he is going to hunt, and it is up to him to choose the right bullet for humane bagging of meat and trophy.

25

Handloading: The Story of Ammunition Development

THE HANDLOADER is a shooter who enjoys loading ammunition for his own use. When working at his loading bench he is occupied in an exacting hobby. Quite a number of elements enter the picture and all are important factors in producing good "homemade" ammunition; each and every step is one of mechanical exactness. In fact, all of the components, and finally the assembled cartridge, are the results of extreme precision.

That is the outstanding reason why handloading cartridges is so fascinating to many shooters.

The handloader first determines the kind of cartridge he is going to put together: that is, in which of his guns it is going to be used, and the purpose of the cartridge. For target practice and plinking, he may cast a quantity of lead-alloy bullets of a design he prefers, or he may use factory-made, full-jacket bullets. For game shooting he will use bullets especially designed for that purpose.

The powder to propel the bullet will be one suitable for the bullet used and for the particular cartridge. The primer will be one designed for the cartridge and load.

Ordinarily, the handloader will use empty cartridge cases that previously have been fired in the rifle or pistol he intends to use with the handloads.

Next, he adjusts his loading tools for the requirements of the cartridge. After double-checking the adjustments, he gets busy with the actual reloading. The whole procedure is one of check and recheck.

Step by step operations in handloading a cartridge are relatively simple. Procedure is about the same, regardless of the tool used, although some tools combine certain operations for speed.

The first thing that must be done is to remove the fired primer from the fired cartridge case. Obviously, this operation is eliminated if new cases are used. Next, the neck of the case is sized to a diameter slightly smaller than that of the bullet. (If the reloaded cartridge is to be used in a gun other than the one in which it previously was fired, the empty case will probably have to be sized full-length. Chambers of guns of the same caliber may vary slightly.)

A live primer is seated into the primer pocket or cavity in the base of the case. The proper charge of powder (either weighed or measured, depending on certain conditions) is poured into the primed cartridge case. The last operation is to seat the bullet to the correct depth into the mouth of the case—and the cartridge is ready to be fired.

Actually, handloading is as old as the oldest gun. Up until the middle of the nineteenth century, practically every shooter was a handloader. In most instances, the powder charge was dumped into the gun from the muzzle and the projectile firmly seated on top of it.

In the case of the flintlock gun, ignition was accomplished by sparks produced by flint and steel. Priming powder in the pan of the mechanism caught fire from the sparks and, in turn, fired the main charge in the breech of the barrel to send the bullet on its way at great speed.

The cap-lock gun was fired by an explosive compound contained in a percussion cap, which flashed a hot flame directly into the powder charge when struck by the gun's hammer.

The earliest cartridge was developed as a convenience for faster shooting of the muzzle-loading gun. These cartridges consisted of nothing more than measured charges of black powder wrapped in pieces of paper or other material. They were crude and fragile, and seem a little absurd when compared to our sturdy modern cartridges which combine the three elements —the primer, the powder charge, and the bullet—packaged in a metallic container called the cartridge case.

In use, the paper, which sometimes was greased to protect the powder from dampness, was torn, and the powder poured into the gun barrel and the ball seated.

Later, someone thought of including the ball in the package. This was another milestone on the road to faster loading and firing of guns. To put it mildly, firearms development was a little on the slow side. The paper cartridge was in use for about three centuries. During that period it was a simple matter for the individual to make his own cartridges.

The last extensive use of that type of ammunition was during our Civil War which started in 1861. Hundreds of thousands of rounds of paper cartridges were produced, issued to troops, and fired during that holocaust.

The usual procedure, when loading, was to bite off a portion of the paper, dump the powder into the gun muzzle and seat the bullet by using a ramrod. Thus, one of the requirements for an infantry recruit was a sound set of teeth.

The first combustible cartridges were similar to the paper cartridge, except that the wrapper was nitrated so that it would completely burn with the powder. This development again increased the shooter's rate of fire, as the whole cartridge could be loaded into the gun without fooling around tearing or biting paper.

Other combustible cartridges were cased with nitrated linen or skin, or with collodion. The construction of some of these rather weird cartridges was quite complicated and beyond the scope of the individual handloader. For instance, one type was made of compressed powder in layers having various degrees of combustibility. The bottom layer burned slowest, with each succeeding layer stepped up to cause greater acceleration of the conical bullet.

Combustible cartridges were ignited by percussion caps placed on a nipple that was a part of the gun, or by the tape primer which was not unlike the rolls of caps used in toy cap pistols. Being easily mutilated, the combustibles usually were packed in wooden containers with a separate hole for each cartridge.

The separate primed variety was a step nearer to our modern cartridge. Those oldtimers were used in breech-loading caplock arms. The cases of this type of cartridge, which held the powder and bullet, were made of various materials, including cardboard, paper and brass, brass and even rubber or gutta-percha.

Edward Maynard's invention probably was the first reloadable brass-cased cartridge. The .50 Maynard (1865) is the best-known version and consists of a brass tube with a perforated brass disc soldered on as a base and extractor rim. Flame from a percussion cap or tape primer passed through the pinhole in the base to ignite the powder. The brass tube of the Maynard cartridge case expanded against the walls of the chamber when fired and made a tight seal that kept gas from escaping to the rear into the shooter's face. Modern cartridges work on this principle.

Development of metallic cartridges from Civil War days to modern—.54 Burnside, .56 Billinghurst, .50 Maynard (each requiring a separate primer to ignite the powder through the pinhole in the base), through pin fire, lip fire, rim fire and the big rimmed Maynard centerfire, with cutaways showing the folded-head case for Berdan primer which has no anvil, folded-head case for Boxer type primer, solid-head case for Boxer primer, including the .458 Winchester Magnum, the .308 Winchester, and .308 bullets.

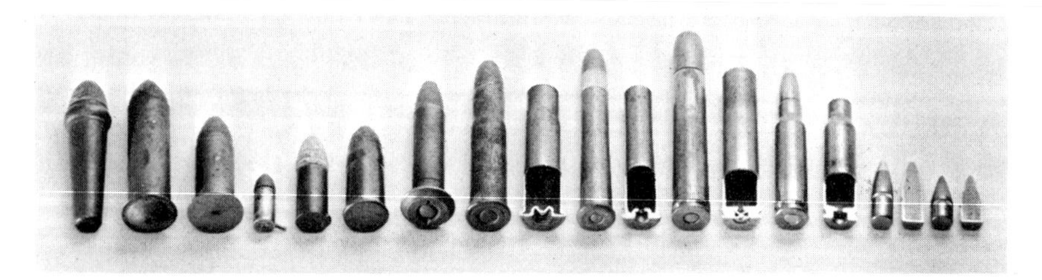

The self-contained cartridge (bullet, powder, and igniter cased as a unit) is the development that has made possible our modern guns, and may well have seen the light of day as a hollow-based bullet containing powder and a fulminate pellet arranged for ignition by a firing pin of the arm.

Gradual evolution finally resulted in the present-day center-fire cartridges, which are reloadable. An immediate stepping-stone to the successful production of such a cartridge was the development (in the 1860s) of a method of drawing or forming brass into the shape necessary for the case.

The cartridge case begins life as a disc of brass. The disc is stretched or drawn to its ultimate form by use of a number of dies and punches. Believe me, this is a complicated art and requires real skill.

By the early 1870s, centerfire cartridge cases were being made sturdy enough to stand up under reloading, and reloading tools began to appear on the market. One of the earliest was a Winchester tool, patented in 1874 and listed in the Winchester catalogue of 1875. This tool, soundly engineered and made of cast-iron, did a good job of reloading rifle ammunition. Of tong type, it is the grandpappy of present day tong loading tools. Modified in 1882, the Winchester tool was made of machined steel and beautifully finished.

In the meantime, practically all of the arms companies were producing reloading tools, and it became common practice for shooters to buy reloading ejuipment when they bought new rifles.

In those days, all cartridges were loaded with black powder and almost anyone with sense enough to remember not to smoke while handloading could produce serviceable ammunition.

My collection of old reloading tools is not extensive, but I have some interesting ones made by Ideal, Marlin, Remington, Savage, Sharps, Winchester, and others. All are beautifully constructed, and each will do an excellent job of reloading the old black-powder cartridges for which they were intended.

The invention of smokeless powder and the beginning of its use in small-arms ammunition in the 1890s put handloading into somewhat of a decline. Shooters knew very little about this new propellant which was much more powerful than black powder. In some instances, three or four times as many cartridges could be loaded with one pound of smokeless powder than with a pound of black powder, for the same ballistics.

Ordinarily, the cases of black-powder cartridges were loaded completely full of black powder. A charge of the more powerful smokeless powder, that would give the same internal pressure and a similar muzzle velocity to the bullet, took up much less space in the cartridge.

It takes no great stretch of the imagination to visualize what happened in some instances. A shooter familiar with black powder would obtain his first canister of smokeless powder, hurry home and load a few rounds of his favorite cartridge. He would follow his usual course of action and fill the case full of powder and seat the bullet on top of it. With the proper charge being a quarter or a third of that amount, the gun and shooter took an awful jolt when the booby trap was fired, sometimes with disastrous results.

Black powder did not immediately die out with the introduction of smokeless powder. My Winchester catalogue of 1913 lists almost 150 different black-powder cartridges.

Handloading coasted along as small groups of experimenters and enthusiasts throughout the country continued to ride their hobby.

The real rebirth in popularity of handloading in the United States took place with the advent of .22-caliber, center-fire varmint cartridges.

The .22 Hornet was the first, and it became very popular. The mainspring in its development was a group of riflemen at Springfield Armory in Springfield, Massachusetts. Utilizing the case of the old .22 Winchester Center-Fire cartridge (which was loaded with a 45-grain lead bullet and given a muzzle velocity of about 1,500 feet per second) a refurbishing job was done that has ended with the factory cartridge that pushes a 45- or 46-grain jacketed bullet from the gun muzzle at 2,690 feet per second. Quite an improvement!

The Hornet started as a wildcat (a cartridge that is not in regular factory production). Before long there were scores of wildcat varmint cartridges being designed and put together by amateur ballisticians throughout the country.

Guns for these hot cartridges often were old falling-block single shots, such as the Winchester High and Low Wall, the Stevens Model 44¼, the Remington Hepburn, the Sharps Borchardt, and so on, that were rebuilt and rebarreled for the wildcats. I have a number of those rehashed jobs and some of them are amazingly accurate.

However, none of the gunsmiths or riflemen who fooled around with those wildcat cartridges and rifles had an accurate or even remotely scientific way of determining the pressures developed when the guns were fired. If the fired cases were difficult to extract from the rifle, or the primers excessively flattened, it was considered that the time had come to reduce the powder load a bit. Fortunately, the strength of those old rifle actions was great and but few were blown up. Actually, the cautious experimenter had very little trouble and some fine cartridges were developed.

High pressures always have been the bugaboo of the handloader since smokeless powder has been available. Each cartridge was designed for a certain working pressure and so was the gun chambered for it. If a handloader exceeds that working pressure with his cartridges he may well be in for some trouble.

During the years, I have received hundreds of letters from readers wanting to know if their .22 rimfire rifles could successfully be rechambered for the .22 Hornet, .218 Bee, .222 or even the .220 Swift. Not realizing that some of the high-intensity cartridges were designed to develop pressures of from 40,000 to 50,000 or more pounds per square inch, and that it takes a very strong rifle to hold them, they just assume that a rifle is a rifle and that barrels may be rebored, or rechambered at will without problems or trouble. Pressures developed by burning smokeless powder evidently are little understood by many shooters.

To get back to handloading of ammunition. The beginner should start by loading nothing but low pressure loads with lead-alloy bullets until he has a good understanding of powder and primers and the technique of handloading. Then he should approach the high-intensity stuff with extreme caution. A sloppy handloader can get into trouble with the hot numbers.

Handloading is a most fascinating hobby for the shooter, and a careful operator is a boon to the shooting game. He not only learns more about his gun or guns, and does more shooting—but he gets others interested in the sport of shooting.

Every shooter, whether or not he is interested in reloading ammunition, should read at least one of the handbooks on handloading ammunition. Then he will know and better understand his gun.

26

Reload those Hulls

"WHAT ARE THE ADVANTAGES a shooter gets from handloading his own ammunition?" That is a slightly loaded and involved question that comes up quite frequently, usually with this addendum: "And will I really save money by handloading cartridges if I do quite a bit of shooting?"

Before we can discuss these questions intelligently, however, there are a few facts we should know.

First, just what is handloaded ammunition? Generally speaking, and without repeating too much from the preceding chapter, it consists of cartridges that have been fabricated by an individual for his own use. In most instances, handloaded ammunition is reloaded ammunition. That is, cartridge cases that have been fired one or more times are used in producing firable cartridges. In reloading the cartridge case, a primer, a powder charge and a bullet are needed. These components are combined into a cartridge with tools made for this purpose, and available in a number of forms. Some are simple in construction and inexpensive, others, which are more complicated in design, cost more but are handier and faster to use.

Back in the days shortly after the Civil War, centerfire cartridges were developed and produced for the market. They were quite primitive when compared to the standardized, dependable and safe factory-loaded product of today. The brass case was by far the most costly of the components that made up the early cartridge (it still is) and it wasn't long before reloading tools were manufactured and shooters began to reload their fired cartridge cases.

Handloading was less complicated then than it is today. Black powder was the only propellent available and the weight of the charge was not critical. For instance, take the .44 W.C.F. cartridge (the famous .44-40), the first Winchester centerfire cartridge. It was developed for the Winchester Model 1873 sporting rifle and carbine. The .44 indicated the caliber—actually between .42 and .43 caliber—and the 40 indicated the black-powder charge in grains. Sometimes as little as thirty grains were used. In reloading, the fired primer was removed and a new one seated in the case, the powder measured and put into the case, the 200-grain, lubricated lead bullet seated on top of the powder, and the mouth of the case crimped around the bullet. Then the cartridge was ready to shoot.

Incidentally, shortly after Winchester introduced the Model '73 rifle, the Colt's Patent Fire Arms Manufacturing Company announced the Single Action Army revolver with chambering for the new .44-40 cartridge. This simplified the ammunition problem for the frontiersman. He could have a rifle or carbine and a belt gun that would take the same cartridge and needed but one set of loading tools to maintain his ammo supply. Today, we have a parallel. The sportsman can have the Ruger carbine or the Winchester Model 94 and a holster revolver, both chambered for the powerful .44 Magnum cartridge.

A set of early reloading tools, which did the complete job of assembling the cartridge, consisted of the loader; a bullet mold, sometimes a part of the loader, and a powder-charge measurer or dipper, some adjustable for

Steps in drawing and forming modern bullets and cartridge cases.

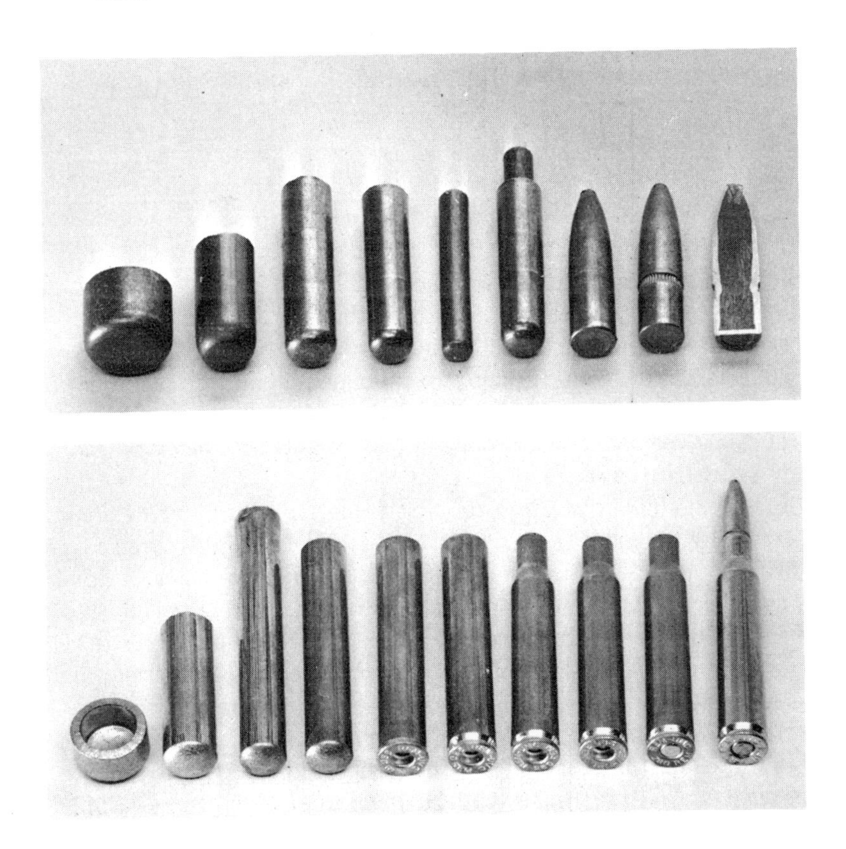

various charges. The nonadjustable hinged-lever or tong-type tool was capable only of loading one particular weight of bullet. A little later, adjustable type tools were popular because they were more versatile.

Now we have a variety of H and C type presses, as well as turret press loaders for progressive and fast operation. These modern tools are precisely made for interchangeability of dies for different calibers and some are arranged for shot-shell dies. Lyman also still manufactures a low-cost, but greatly improved, tong-type tool, the No. 310. It is not so fast in operation as some of the more elaborate tools made by Lyman and others, but a first-class job of reloading can be done with it.

Why does a shooter handload ammunition? Let's look at the situation from the standpoint of the shooter who wants to get the most in accuracy from his individual rifle. Regardless of the fact that American factory ammunition is perfectly made—dependable, safe and accurate—it has to be what might be called standardized. Due to manufacturing problems, certain tolerances must be allowed for in mass-produced firearms and their ammunition. All firearm cartridge chambers and ammunitions are made to within certain determined plus or minus figures for that particular caliber. Thus, the largest loaded cartridge of a certain size or caliber has to fit into the very smallest chamber of any factory rifle or handgun of that caliber, and the smallest cartridge of the caliber must work satisfactorily in the largest chamber made according to the tolerances. All with absolute safety in a normal gun. Also, the combination has to be safe in arctic cold or tropical heat. These tolerances are not much, but they are necessary and they usually are not compatible with the finest accuracy. I say usually, because some rifles, just as they come from the factory and with factory ammunition, will do some very accurate shooting. With such a combination, I have fired, in one instance, a five-shot group at 200 yards that measured but slightly over five-eighths of an inch, .629, to be exact, and this is not a unique instance. I must admit that kind of accuracy certainly is on the unusual side, and groups of about four times that size are really excellent, except for dyed-in-the-wool, competitive, bench-rest shooters and their highly specialized equipment.

Usually, the handloader can develop loads for his rifle or handgun that are especially accurate. He can use cartridge cases that have been expanded by being fired in his rifle for a perfect fit in that particular chamber; he can use selected factory or handmade bullets that are of exactly the right size for the bore of his rifle and he can seat the bullet in the cartridge case for the correct bullet-to-land-of-the-bore relationship. Also, he has a choice of a large number of types and weights of jacketed and lead bullets for various kinds of shooting—say, for big game, varmint, small game, match-target work and for economical plinking and offhand target practice. (In some calibers, factory ammo can be obtained in big-game, varmint and match-target loadings.) Also, the handloader can use superuniform powder charges weighed to a tenth of a grain with an inexpensive powder scale. By experimenting with various loads, he can obtain the very best results his rifle is capable of delivering and can make one rifle do for several purposes.

Handloading ammunition can be economical for the person who wants to do quite a bit of shooting, especially if the time involved is not counted. As I said before, the most costly of the components that make up a cartridge is the brass case. It can be reloaded many times, the actual number depending on the kind of loads prepared. The .30-06 rifle cartridge loaded with the 180-grain jacketed bullet at a muzzle velocity of 2,700 feet per second, suitable for big-game hunting and mid- and long-range target practice, can be handloaded for about half the cost of the factory cartridge, depending on the bullet used and how far components have to be shipped from the retailer to the handloader. Usually, a varmint load will cost less to concoct. Such savings work out with most calibers. The reloader-handgun shooter can save around two bucks per hundred rounds when he buys all components except the cartridge case, more if he molds his own bullets.

Many reloaders who mold their own bullets scrounge around and pick up their bullet metal from old storage batteries, odd pieces of lead and maybe some type metal. Sometimes, this works out all right, sometimes, not so well. Some years ago, I made a very satisfactory plinking load for the .30-06-caliber rifle that consisted of hand-cast, 150-grain bullets of type metal (which I got for free) and ten grains of Unique rifle or pistol powder, all assembled in a reprimed case. As I remember, that load cost me around sixty cents per hundred cartridges.

Actually, I do not believe in taking up handloading strictly as an economy move; it seems to me the other benefits are more important. But I must admit that economy was one of the main reasons I took up the hobby many years ago. I had a .30-40-caliber Krag rifle which was known as an arsenal conversion. The barrel had been cut from thirty inches to twenty-four inches and a Springfield front sight installed. Also, the fore end was cut to sporter length and nicely rounded. I had installed a Pacific receiver sight which mounted in place of the cartridge cut-off assembly. It was a good rifle and I used it for almost all kinds of shooting. I was going to school at the time, had little money and wanted a low-cost load for varmint (crow, woodchuck and prairie dog) shooting. Finally, I settled on the old Lyman #308403 bullet which had been designed by famous Harry M. Pope, the old-time barrel maker and off-hand rifle shot. This bullet was easy to cast and was loaded in the case as it came from the mold without sizing. It was finger-seated in the cartridge case, so all I needed for reloading was some means of decapping and repriming the fired cartridge case and for measuring the powder. I made a tool for knocking out the fired primer by filing the tip of a piece of drill rod to decapping-pin dimensions.

The load for this bullet in the .30-40 case was thirteen or fourteen grains of the now discontinued Du Pont No. 80 powder, so I slightly filed off the mouth of a .38 special cartridge case until it held fourteen grains of the powder, soldered a nail on it to make a dipper and was all set to reload. That was an accurate load for up to 20-yard shooting, but the loaded cartridge had to be handled very carefully due to the fact that the bullet was seated so slightly in the case, it could be knocked out with just about a breath. However, I took a pile of woodchuck and crow with it.

It is a fact that the sportsman who knows his rifle—its zero adjustments and value of sight adjustments, its trajectory at all practical ranges, wind allowances at various ranges, accuracy and any peculiarity of grouping its shots—is the fellow who will be the most effective marksman. To gain this experience will require 500 or 600 rounds fired at target shooting and carefully recorded for reference. A little economy by reloading may be desirable with that kind of shooting. I know a number of shooters who reload for target practice and buy factory ammunition for actual hunting.

What is the attitude of the ammunition manufacturing companies toward the handloader? Offhand, it looks as though reloading would not be so good from the standpoint of sale of factory-loaded cartridges. The effect is the opposite.

The average American sportsman who has a centerfire rifle or handgun buys very little ammunition. The hunter buys maybe two boxes of high-power rifle cartridges a year. He probably fires around twenty shots for sighting in his rifle and uses the other twenty rounds for hunting. The week-end varmint hunter, whose favorite rifle is of .222 or .244 Remington, .243 Winchester or other desirable caliber, may buy as much as 150 cartridges a year.

But handloading makes a fascinating hobby, and the reloader almost always becomes an enthusiast and does a lot more shooting. He learns something about internal and external ballistics and becomes a real gun buff. Almost certainly, each year, he will buy 100 or more rounds of factory cartridges, perhaps 100 primed cases, 1,000 primers, 500 jacketed bullets, perhaps some bullet metal for molding bullets, and five or six pounds of powder. The chances are that in time, he will become interested in other calibers, buy one or more other rifles and handloading components for them. I know quite a number of shooters whose experience has followed this line exactly, and they are very happy fellows. Besides, the more we Americans know about ammunition and shooting, the better off we will be in case of dire emergency. Our ammunition-producing companies understand all this and encourage handloading.

"Is handloading ammunition dangerous in any way?" is the question almost always asked by the uninformed. Frankly, I've never heard of an ac-

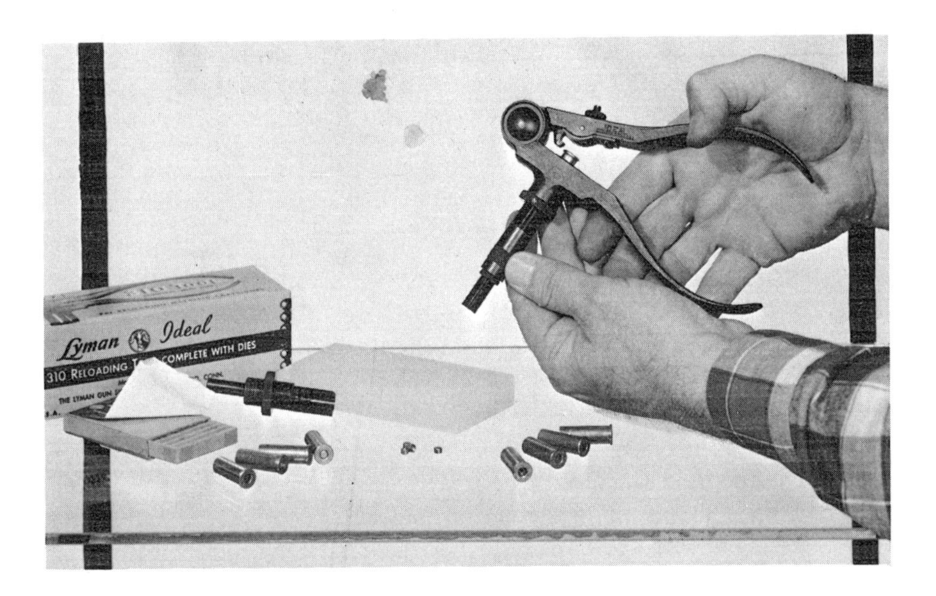

Adjustable hand tools are capable of assembling excellent ammunition, but are slow in operation when compared to bench tools.

cident due to handloading except in unusual cases of gross carelessness or with a couple of individuals who have gone off half-cocked to concoct loads with gigantic powder charges in an effort to make superpowerful cartridges. Anyone who can follow instructions can handload cartridges with safety. But one note of warning: Handloading definitely is not for the person who is habitually careless, or for the individual who has trouble following written instructions, or for the character who thinks he knows more than the ballistics experts. There are a number of excellent instruction manuals or handbooks on reloading. I have listed several at the end of this chapter.

What cartridges can be handloaded by the individual? Only centerfire ammunition, including shot shells. Rimfire cartridges cannot be reloaded.

Let's look briefly at the components used in handloading centerfire ammunition. The American (boxer-type) primer, which furnishes the flame for igniting the powder, consists of a small cup, a small charge of percussion-sensitive priming compound in it, a piece of foil and a small anvil on top of the compound. When the firing pin of the gun strikes the center of the primer, which is seated in a pocket at the base of the cartridge, the priming compound is crushed violently and exploded to start the powder burning to produce the gas that propels the bullet. Most foreign ammunition—except that manufactured in Sweden by Norma for American consumption—is made with the anvil integral with the cartridge case to take the Berdan-type primer, which does not have an anvil. There are four kinds of American primers made for reloading sporting cartridges—the large rifle, the small rifle, the large pistol and the small pistol. The cups of large- and small-pistol primers are made of thinner or softer metal than the rifle primers so as to indent properly under the lighter blows of the handgun mechanisms, and are charged differently from the rifle primers.

The cartridge case is designed and made for proper functioning in arms of its caliber, and if handled properly, usually can be reloaded from twenty-five to fifty times at the pressure for which it was intended. The life depends on the pressure the case has to withstand, the comparative amount of metal and its retention of resiliency. A case is bound to stretch with continued use and become annealed with continual firing so that it loses its original properties. Cases show wear and tear by cracks at the neck, enlarged primer pockets so they will not hold the primer tightly, and by the necks getting thin and perhaps ragged at the mouth. When a case develops any of these defects, it is discarded.

There are a number of smokeless powders available to the handloader in small canisters. Each one is designed for a particular purpose, but unsuited and perhaps dangerous for another use. In handloading, it is imperative to use the right powder for a particular load. Smokeless powder, for transportation purposes, is considered as inflammable and not as an explosive, so under certain restrictions, it can be shipped by express.

Literally hundreds of different bullets are available for the handloader—jacketed types, lead-alloy bullets with gas checks and plain lead-alloy bullets in practically all calibers. Bullets are made by Winchester-Western Division of Olin Corporation, Remington Arms Company, and by a number (at least a couple of dozen) of smaller companies, such as Sierra Bullets, Incorporated, Speer Products Company, Harnady Manufacturing Company, Nosler Partition Bullet Company, R. B. Sisk, Lakeville Arms, Incorporated, Fred N. Barnes, and J. W. Baldwin. Some reloaders prefer to make their own jacketed and swaged lead-alloy bullets, so dies and presses are available for this purpose.

Shooters who really get into the more intricate phases of handloading usually like to try many types of bullets in various calibers and sometimes experiment by changing the size or shape of existing cartridge cases, thus developing what are known as wildcat cartridges.

I have not gone into the mechanics of the many reloading tools on the market. Actually, there are more than six-dozen firms supplying tools and accessories for the handloader. I do not have space to cover all tools that are available. The real old-timers at producing reloading tools are Lyman Gun Sight Corp., Middlefield, Conn. 06455, Pacific Gun Sight Co., Box

4495, Lincoln, Neb. 68504, Belding & Mull, Box 428, Philipsburg, Pa. 16866. RCBS, Inc., Box 1919, Oroville, Cal. 95965, SAECO Rel. Inc., Box 778, Calpinteria, Cal. 93013, Hollywood Reloading, Inc., 6116 Hollywood Blvd., Hollywood, Cal. 90028.

If you never have reloaded cartridges, and want to, the first thing is to obtain one or more of the handbooks to study. The *Lyman Handbook,* 45th Edition; *Hornady Handbook of Cartridge Reloading; Handbook for Shooters and Reloaders,* by P. O. Ackley; *Shooter's Bible Reloader's Guide; Speer Manual for Reloading Ammunition;* and there are many more. They are inexpensive.

How about the cost of reloading tools? It is true that many handloaders have several hundred dollars invested in equipment? My opinion is that the beginner should start with the least outlay of cash possible for tools that will do a good job. The bare necessities for loading cartridges with primers, powder charges and jacketed bullets are a tool, a powder measure and a powder scale. The Lyman No. 310 is the lowest-priced tool available, and die sets for many rifle and pistol cartridges are interchangeable. A tool with dies for one cartridge, an accurate adjustable powder measure and a set of powder scales can be bought for under fifty dollars. And a tool for reloading shot shells in one gauge (12-, 16-, or 20-gauge dies are interchangeable in the same tool) can be bought for about fifty bucks.

Handloading is a fascinating and rewarding part of the shooting sport and it really is fun, especially if you get a kick out of using precision tools.

27

Customize Your Gun Stock!

DO YOU EVER STOP to think, when you pick up a rifle or shotgun, of the thousands of inventors, craftsmen and manufacturers who have had a finger in its development? At least six centuries of effort, involving millions of man hours, have made possible our modern sporting arms. And strange as it may seem, the effective use of any one of these highly developed pieces depends on a part of it that is usually taken as a matter of course. I'm talking about the stock and its design. Accurate shooting is dependent on the form of the stock, and this element of the shoulder gun has received more concentrated and constructive attention during the past fifty or so years than ever before.

Factory-made rifles and shotguns, and most custom-made arms, have stocks that are well standardized—with dimensions that actually are a compromise. This is easy to understand when we consider that standard stocks have to be suitable for every individual, tall or short, heavy or thin, with long or short neck, with square, wide shoulders or narrow, sloping ones, and so on. It stands to reason that such a stock cannot exactly meet all these requirements and perfectly fit all shooters—just as one specific size suit of clothes would certainly not fit every person.

I have heard short, husky fellows complain that all commercial gun stocks are designed for giants, and I have heard tall, lanky shooters maintain that our standard stocks were dimensioned for fat pygmies.

Regardless of such bemoaning, and considering that exact stock fit is more important with a shotgun than with a rifle, it is true that, within reason, almost anyone can adapt himself to our modern sporting shoulder arms and do some good shooting. That is quite a compliment for today's stock designers.

However, the better the stock fit, the better a person can shoot, and as we shall see, very slight changes made on standard stocks may do wonders for shooters who are having pointing and aiming troubles.

The very earliest guns had stocks that were for the birds as far as accurate aiming is concerned. Some were nothing more than sticks of wood tied on for convenience in handling or carrying the pieces. Accuracy was an unknown quantity.

As late as the 1790s, matches at 100 yards between the gun and the long bow were held in England, with accuracy advantage on the side of the arrow.

Actually, some of the flintlock rifles of the eighteenth century, such as examples of the famed Kentucky rifle which have been preserved in good order, give very good accuracy at fairly close range—say, at 100 yards or slightly more. The majority of these arms had very crooked stocks, excessive drop, especially at the heel, with deeply curved, narrow butt plates of the so-called "rifle" type, and very thin combs. History tells us that those low-power, muzzle-loading rifles were used with good success. But a Kentucky-type stock on a modern large-caliber, high-intensity rifle would be murder. The extreme drop at the heel would cause the arm to rotate sharply upwards with the thin comb of the stock giving a machetelike cut at the shooter's cheek. And the thin butt plate certainly would do more than give the shoulder a pleasant massage.

Development of the low-intensity, fixed cartridge about the time of the Civil War made possible practical repeaters, and many of our sporting-magazine rifles of the 1870s and 1880s, and even later, followed the crooked-stock tradition to a certain extent.

Our first successful American high-intensity, bolt action, sporting rifles of .30-caliber were conversions of military arms—namely, the .30-40 Krag and the .30-06 Springfield Model of 1903.

The late Colonel Townsend Whelen, who was the dean of gun writers, used the Krag, as issued, for hunting in the Philippines. His successes led Dr. Paul B. Jenkins, especially noted for his work at the Milwaukee Public Museum, to have a service arm remodeled into the first Krag sporter.

Teddy Roosevelt used a Springfield in Africa, but it was not much of a conversion, being changed only by the addition of sporting sights.

Stewart Edward White, of adventure-story fame, had the first really custom Springfield sporter for his first African trip. The service barrel and action was fitted to a sporting stock of a design which included the ideas of several keen riflemen. Sights consisted of the Lyman No. 34 receiver sight and a blade with bead installed in the regular military front-sight base. Made more than half a century ago, the custom stock of the Stewart Edward White rifle set a pattern and is the forerunner of present-day sporting-rifle stocks.

Exactly what does the modern stock do for the shooter? It gives him a means of holding the gun steadily, permitting quick, accurate aim and good trigger control, and it should keep recoil effect at a minimum.

Sounds simple, but what details of design are important in doing these jobs?

The forearm or fore-end should be shaped for a comfortable grip, not too bulky and not so toothpicklike as to permit the hand to make contact with a hot barrel, but just right for the individual's hand in controlling the arm.

The pistol grip is a means for steadying the butt plate or recoil pad against the shoulder. It should be shaped so that, with a firm grasp, the trigger finger has easy access to the trigger for perfect control in letting off the shot.

Length of pull—the measurement from the trigger directly back to the center of the butt plate—is important for comfortable shooting. The length of pull should be short enough for quick mounting of the gun without hang-up on clothing at the shoulder, and long enough so that the thumb of the trigger-finger hand will not whack the nose with recoil, say an inch or an inch and a-half between nose and thumb with the gun properly mounted and ready to shoot.

Pitch is one element of the stock that is not given much attention by the average shooter, yet if too far off, it can foul up his shooting. It is the angle at which the butt plate is set on the butt stock and it determines the sur-

Paul Doane adjusting a Winchester Model 21 try gun to obtain my exact requirement in length of pull, drop at comb and heel, cast and pitch shotgun measurements.

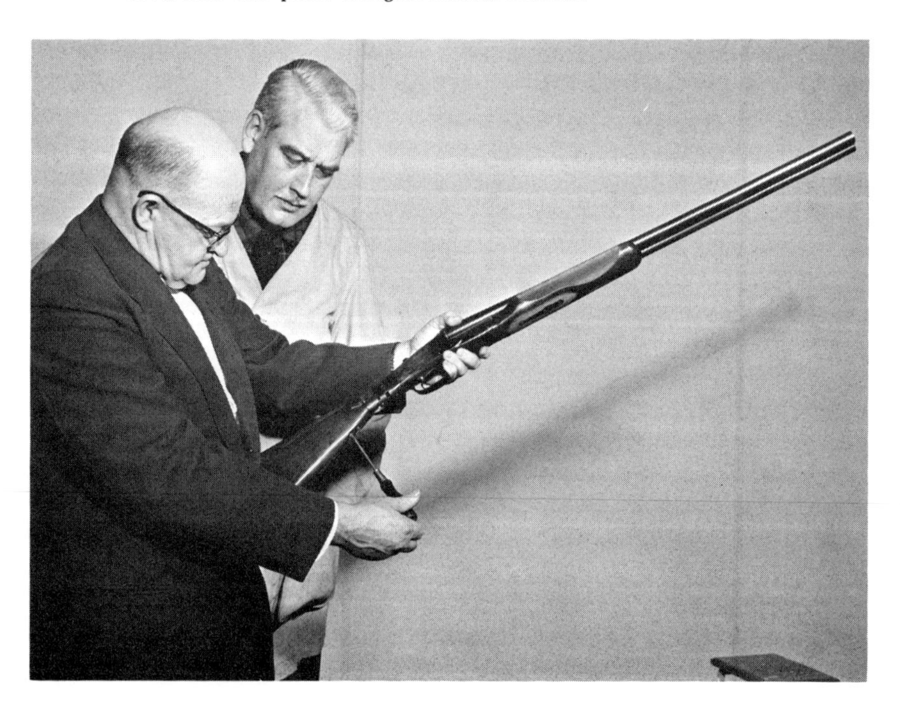

face fit of the butt plate at the shooter's shoulder for no-slip control and even distribution of recoil. Pitch is easily determined by standing the gun upright on its butt plate on a flat surface, such as the floor, and sliding it until the rear of the receiver contacts the wall, which should be at right angles to the floor. The measurement from the gun muzzle to the wall is pitch and it varies with barrel length. If two guns have the same angle of pitch, the one with the longer barrel will have the larger figure representing pitch. If there is too much down pitch, the stock may slip up on the shoulder with a fast shot and cause the shooter to see the breech rather than the sighting plane and result in a low shot with either rifle or shotgun. With too little down-pitch or with up-pitch, the butt may tend to slip down under the arm and the gun point upward for a high shot. A shotgun usually needs less pitch than a rifle and a trap gun less pitch than a field gun. Also, trap-gun stocks average straighter and with longer pull than field-gun stocks because the trap gun is shouldered and pointing when the target is called for and the target is taken on the rising curve.

The butt plate should not be skimpy, but fairly wide to distribute recoil over a larger area of the shoulder. I once had a custom-stocked .30-06-caliber rifle that had a narrow butt plate which came to a point at the toe of the stock. The angle of the plate was practically at zero pitch or straight up and down with the line of sight. It may have had some up-pitch—a sloping rearward from top to bottom. Brother, when anyone shot that rifle, the sharp toe of the butt plate dug in like a land-breaking plow. To say the least, it wasn't pleasant to shoot. Finally I had sense enough to reinstall the butt plate with a little down-pitch. This cured the stabbing tendency, but the butt plate was too narrow for comfortable shooting.

The checkpiece, if any, should be designed to give more support to the side of the face, which helps in steady holding, and its surface should slope slightly so that, with recoil rearward, it tends to slide away from the face and cheek instead of inward.

The most important dimensions of a stock are the drop of the comb below the line of sight (from the line of the rib or sighting plane with a shotgun) and the thickness of the comb, because they determine the position of the eye when the gun is mounted.

It is a fact that a lot of good shooting has been done with rifles having really lousy stocks. Take the Model 1903 Springfield service rifle (known as Style S), for instance. Its butt stock is too crooked, having excessive drop at both comb and heel, and it is too short for almost anyone big enough to get into the Army. Shooters of this rifle soon learn that nose-to-thumb contact can be avoided by riding forward on the stock and cheeking the thumb, in effect, to heighten the comb, or by extending the thumb of the trigger-finger hand along the side of the stock.

It is true that a really good shot can adapt himself to most any stock

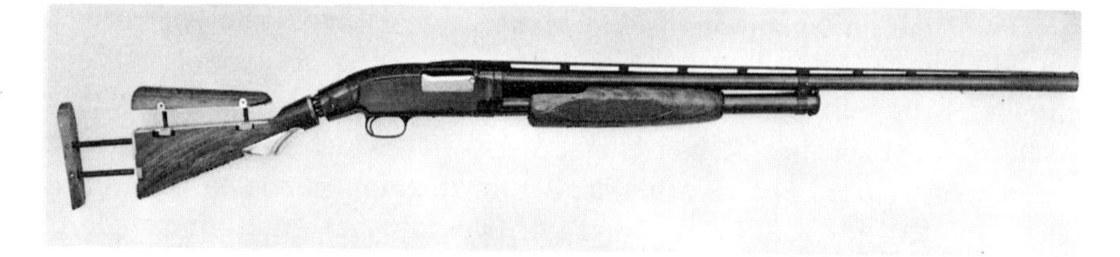

A Winchester Model 12 try gun showing the various adjustable elements for obtaining exact shotgun fit for the individual shooter.

within reason and shoot well. But when the chips are down, you will never see one of these fellows shooting a shoulder arm that does not fit him to his satisfaction.

Let's look at the sporting-rifle stock. For really fast, accurate shooting, the fit of the stock is all-important. Fitting problems vary so much between individuals that no set rule will cover all conditions, but basic fundamentals apply in all instances. When the rifle is quickly mounted, the eye should line up with the sights without any fooling around adjusting the cheek on the comb of the stock. It's as simple as that.

Many big-game hunters practice deliberate shooting, with plenty of time for adjusting the cheek at the comb of the stock, until they can place shots well at almost any reasonable range. But quite often they forget about the probability of having to make one fast shot do a payoff job, or go home empty-handed.

Some years ago, I was part of an experiment having to do with making very quick shots on moving targets. Members of our local gun club were all excellent target shooters. We fired four-position rifle and three-stage pistol matches several times a week in organized leagues. One of our better paper punchers was having trouble with his sporter in making connections on whitetail deer. Several seasons in succession, it happened that he had chances at running animals. He either missed or didn't get off a shot.

Finally, on our outdoor range, we put up, at twenty-five yards, a regular silhouette target, which is about five feet high by eighteen inches wide. Next, we hooked on a small piece of cardboard behind the receiver sight of our subject's .30-06 sporter so that the sights and barrel could not be seen by his right or sighting eye. Then we had him fire five shots at the center of the target, sort of shotgun fashion, by quickly shouldering the rifle while seeing the target only with his left eye, and lowering the rifle between shots.

Four of the bullets printed on the target at the upper left-hand corner, with the fifth evidently missing the paper near that point. We spotted the bullet holes to make sure of their location, and had him fire five shots without the cardboard, and lowering the rifle between shots as before. They were closely grouped in the target's center, but the shots were not made nearly as fast as with the cardboard, and it was obvious that time was lost in adjusting his cheek on the stock so that he could see the sight-target picture.

The shots fired with the cardboard in place, although fairly well grouped, were about eighteen inches high and about six or seven inches to the left. At twenty-five yards that certainly was off quite a lot, but at the time, I was amazed that he hit the target at all. His stock was a little too straight and too thick at the comb where his cheek rested.

In subsequent trials, with the cardboard in place, and by consistently cheeking the rifle more firmly, his groups were lowered and better centered on the target. After due consideration, this chap carefully, and in small doses (with shooting between stages), removed wood at the comb to reduce its altitude and thickness, and ended up with a perfectly fitting stock.

This experiment eventually was tried by most of the members of our club and the majority made slight alterations in the stocks of their sporters. Also, the experiment was responsible for the installation of a running-deer target for practice in fast off-hand shooting at moving targets. Believe me, this kind of practice pays off in the field!

Stock fit is more important with the shotgun because the shotgun is pointed and not aimed. In fact, there usually is no time for actual aiming as with the rifle.

I am what very well could be called oversize, tipping the scale at around 265 pounds and piled six feet, eight inches high—tall, but not skinny. I have always used shotguns with factory or standard dimensions, except for the installation of a slip-on or permanent recoil pad to lengthen the pull.

Being curious about exactly what dimensions I require on a shotgun stock, I visited Paul Doane at Winchester-Western and asked him to check me out with a try-gun, which is equipped with a stock that is adjustable for all critical measurements. Paul has measured thousands of shooters for stocks and knows exactly what he is doing. It turned out that, for a field gun, my measurements are: Pull, 15 inches (14 inches); drop at comb, 1⅞ inches (1½ inches); drop at heel, 2⅝ inches (2½ inches); cast-off, $\frac{3}{16}$ inches (zero); pitch with twenty-eight-inch barrel, 2½ inches (2½ inches). Standard dimensions for most factory field guns are shown in parentheses. Except for pull, it may seem that dimensions for me are quite close to standard. But with the try-gun adjusted to my measurements (indicating that I need a gun with slightly less straight stock than standard), it was a revelation how fast and smoothly it came up to shoulder and pointed exactly where I was looking. Ordinarily, with a standard-dimension gun, being right-handed, I tend to shoot to the left and high. A left-hand shooter would shoot high and to the right.

Paul also measured me for a trap gun. Here I need a straighter stock than with the field gun, but less straight than is standard for trap guns.

Try-guns are few and far between, so without one, how can you determine the important, correct drop at the comb measurement for you? Use any shotgun that is handy. It is better if it has the correct length of pull, as mentioned earlier. Most shotgun stocks slope slightly from comb to heel and are tapered a bit. Place your cheek against the side of the stock so your cheekbone fits snugly on the comb. Now, by moving your head forward or backward, see if you can find a spot on the stock where your line of sight goes out over the exact center of the breech and along the center of the rib or barrel to the front sight. Remember that you should see the surface of the rib or barrel. When you find the spot where your eye has the proper alignment, have a pal mark it on the stock with a piece of soft crayon. Then lay a yardstick—be sure it is a straight one—along the rib. In case of a gun without rib, tie a string around the front-sight bead and, keeping it tight and straight, bring it back in line over the center of the breech and in a continuous straight line to the rear end of the butt stock. Then measure the distance between the bottom edge of the yardstick (or the string) and the top of the comb where it was marked. That is the right drop at the comb for the spot where your cheekbone touches it in normal mounting of the gun. It is the most important measurement of your gunstock.

Just about as important is the thickness of the comb at that vital spot. If your eye is not exactly in alignment with the center of the rib or barrel, the comb's thickness should be altered.

Once you have established the correct measurements, have the comb adjusted so that it has the same dimensions, both for drop and thickness, at least an inch and a-half forward and back of the point where you normally cheek the stock. This will give you the same alignment when you shoot with heavy or light clothing.

Here's a quick way of checking for correct comb dimensions. Close your eyes and mount the gun to your shoulder. Be sure that it comes up smoothly and rests comfortably in shooting position, with neither the toe or heel catching in your clothing as you mount it. When you are sure of a comfortable shooting position—shooting arm elbow level with your shoulder and cheek firmly against the stock—open your eyes. If the rib and front sight are hidden from view, the stock has too much drop and you will shoot low; if you see well above the breech, the stock is too straight—that is, there is not enough drop and you will shoot high. If your line of sight goes straight out over the center of the breech so that you see the rib to the front sight, and if the pitch feels comfortable, you are in business.

28

Oddball Gun Collecting

I KNOW A FELLOW who collects cleaning rods and ramrods of all kinds from the earliest days of the gun up until after the turn of the century. Another chap centers his interest on lock plates and cocks of flintlock and caplock muskets, rifles and pistols. These buffs not only are gun collectors, they are extreme specialists. Many are in this category. They get a kick out of collecting out-of-common gun items.

There are all sorts of collectors. Some go after historic data and archeological tidbits. Some collect books, or coins, or stamps. There are people who collect locks, cameras, telescopes, clocks and watches, furniture, glassware, match boxes, cigar bands and so on. But the gun buffs are a breed apart. They make up a large group with a really dedicated interest. A dyed-in-the-wool enthusiast will collect anything even remotely pertaining to the firearms field, and will sometimes lay an unbelievable amount on the line when riding his hobby.

The arms field is a big one for collectors. Broadly, it is divided into two main schools, guns and ammunition, each with many branches. Collectors, as a group, have brought to light the vast amounts of information on the history of arms and armor that we have at our fingertips today. Throughout the country, many organizations have been formed for the mutual benefit of members, and a sizeable number of previously unknown facts on the subject are constantly being unearthed.

I was gnawed by the gun bug at the age of six or seven and, in a way, began trying to accumulate firearms. My first "collector's item" was my grandfather's Civil War Colt cap-and-ball revolver—which now hangs on my gun room wall—although I must say that it is in poor condition from my early years of abuse.

By the time I had obtained a half-dozen guns, my funds were gone and I was in debt for advance moneys representing several years of lawn mowing and other chores. So, I moved to collecting items that were easier to pick up. My mother called it the pack rat instinct. I had collections of everything from horned toads to bird feathers and eggs, including an assortment of different type nails.

My most successful round of no-cost collecting was with string. The idea came from a blue-ribbon-winning exhibit at the State Fair, which was said to be the largest ball of string in the world. It really was big, measuring several feet in diameter. It was made up of many kinds of string and twine. I became a string collector, devoted to getting as many different kinds of string as possible. It was fun. I didn't learn much, but I had a lot of string.

There are parallels in the gun-collecting field, where buffs have gone in for low-cost items. For instance, with the expiration of certain Colt and Smith & Wesson patents during the ten or so years following the Civil War, it was possible and legal for any manufacturer or gunsmith to make metallic cartridge revolvers. From the early 1870s until about the time of World War I, thousands were produced, with at least a couple of hundred brand names. Most of them were made as cheaply as possible for a mass market. Original prices ranged from about fifty cents to five or six dollars, with fancy, engraved models running as high as nine dollars.

Thirty years ago, these guns were a drug on the used-gun market. They offered a vast field for collecting and study with but little outlay of money. Practically nothing was known about who made them, as most were marked with brand names only. A few collectors became interested in finding as many different kinds as they could locate and classifying them. Now examples of this particular class of revolvers are known as "Suicide Specials," and a book with that title has been written by collector Donald B. Webster, Jr., published by The Stackpole Company, Harrisburg, Pennsylvania.

Briefly, Suicide Specials are single-action cartridge revolvers with solid frames, spur-type triggers, and cylinders which are freed for removal by taking out the center pin, sometimes called base pin or cylinder pin. These revolvers mostly are of .22- and .32-caliber, sometimes .38 or .41, and are usually stamped with a sales or trade name, with no mention of the maker. The Suicide Special certainly offers a fertile field for an interested collector, and going prices still are low enough to permit the accumulation of a representative group without plunking down too much cash.

Sometimes a collector will go off on a specialized tangent. Usually he began by picking up most any kind of gun in most any condition. Then, with experience, he became discriminating and made an all-out effort to find examples in better to mint condition as replacements for his junkers. Such a collector may reach the point where he is interested only in absolutely mint-condition arms or extremely rare ones. Prices are very high for certain old guns in new condition.

Some fellows will specialize in a particular type or kind of arm. The collectors of military weapons, for example, may be divided into such specific categories as collectors of rifles or handguns, weapons of a particular

Gun enthusiasts will collect anything pertaining to the hobby. Shown is a "Suicide Special," with examples selling for as low as 60¢ about 80 years ago; a vest pocket derringer, with some models selling for as low as 52¢ in the 1880s.

period, or weapons of a particular ignition system, weapons used in specific wars, and so on. There are chaps interested only in autoloading or single-shot handguns, or revolvers. And some collect arms of a brand name, such as Colt, Smith & Wesson, Winchester, or others.

There is a large clan specializing in single-shot cartridge rifles of sporting type, with many pinpointing their efforts on an individual make, such as Sharps, Ballard, Stevens, Maynard, Farrow, Bullard, Frank Wesson, Peabody and Peabody Martini, Whitney and Phoenix, Remington, Winchester, and others. Some of these single-shots also were made in military form, which widens the field.

The Ballard has perhaps received more attention in print than the other single-shots and is consequently the most famous. Examples in any condition are difficult to find. Incidentally, collector James J. Grant has written a couple of informative books on the subject: *Single Shot Rifles* and *More Single Shot Rifles,* published by William Morrow and Company.

One of our really exclusive branches of collecting is to specialize in factory-made, cut-away examples of various arms. Very few of these genuine factory-made oddities have been produced throughout the years, and their scarcity makes them tempting items. Cut-aways were made by slicing away portions of the receiver and perhaps portions of the barrel so that the gun could be used for demonstrating visually how the internal parts of the particular model worked. A fascinating cut-away example is the Winchester Model 1895 (model discontinued in 1931) in .30-40-caliber. This rifle, one of the hundreds of historically significant arms on display in the Winchester Gun Museum, New Haven, Connecticut, is one of the finest cut-aways I have examined. With some modern cut-aways, the removed portions are replaced by transparent plastic to keep the parts in place and to prevent dirt and grime from getting into the action.

In all facets of firearms collecting, ammunition offers the most extensive field for study and accumulation of examples. A representative group, even including some of the historically important cartridges, can be assembled with but a slight outlay of cash. Certain rare cartridges, however, have brought the high price of $100 or $200 or more, in good condition. A prime example is the .70-150-650 Winchester Express, usually called the Winchester Elephant cartridge. In case you are not familiar with cartridge nomenclature, the .70 is the caliber in one-hundredths of an inch, the 150 represents the charge of black powder in grains, and the 650 is the weight of the lead bullet in grains. The bullet of this cartridge is of expanding type, with capped hollow copper tube in the hollow point, as was customary with some of the early express bullets.

This cartridge was first loaded in 1888—there was no question that it was with an eye for the African trade—and the rifle for it undoubtedly was built on the Winchester Model 1887 lever-operated repeating shotgun action. No rifle for this mammoth and very rare cartridge is known to exist. Actually, very little is known about the cartridge itself. The .70-150-650 Elephant cartridge is found in only a few collections and one example recently sold for $500.

In case you want to keep your eyes open, here are some very rare ones: The .58-caliber Gallager and Gladdings inside pinfire, patented in 1859. A little blister, seen in the center of the case, is at the end of a crosswise wire firing pin, which when hit by the striker of the gun, exploded fulminate at the opposite side of the case to ignite the black powder charge and send the Minié-type bullet on its way. Bakewell cartridge with square case and bullet, patented in 1863. A percussion cap on the nipple at the base fired the cartridge. Very little, except that it is very rare, is known about this one. A triangular revolver cartridge based on the idea that more cartridges of that shape could be employed in a cylinder of a given size as compared to the customary cartridge with circular cross section. The bullet, as the Bakewell above, has a slight twist to fit the twist of the bore through which it was intended to be fired. This triangular cartridge of about .31-caliber was designed and patented in 1872 by Otto Schneelock and was probably used in Smith & Wesson revolvers converted by him. A wartime nine-millimeter German experimental job, machined of steel and said to have been made at the Walther plant at Zella Mehlis, Thuringia, Germany. This is a jet type, caseless and self-contained, made in an effort to eliminate the extraction and ejection problem of fired cartridge cases. Powder was a high-burning solid kind, and when ignited through the nipple at the base, the gas blasted through eight perforations in a small disc within the lower section, to be diverted through six small holes in the outside lower section.

The early rimless rimfire of .44-caliber was made under the Dupee patent of 1872 by Winchester Repeating Arms Company. A second, also rimless and made under the same patent, is .45-caliber and centerfire, with Millbank primer. Both are very rare. Maynard cartridges of .40- and .64-caliber, made under the patent of 1867. The unusual feature of their construction is the large-diameter centerfire primer which fits over the entire base of each cartridge. The primer is made of a large copper cup and a copper disc which fits inside it. In the center of the disc is a small blister about $\frac{3}{32}$ of an inch in diameter, which contains the priming compound and acts as the anvil. Centered in the blister is a small crosscut through the metal as a flash hole. It worked like the Boxer-type primers found in American centerfire ammunition today. The one-inch Gatling Gun rimfire cartridge. Though this cartridge was used in a light field piece instead of a small arm, it is included as being the largest rimfire cartridge. The previously mentioned .70-150-650 Winchester Express elephant cartridge. The British .577 Pistol, the largest handgun cartridge ever regularly produced, said to have been used in the Webley revolver. The big single-shot and multi-barrel Howdah Pistols—which got their name because they were used as sidearms in a *howdah* on the back of an elephant in the Indian game fields—were chambered for this round. During the period approximately from 1870 to the late 1880s, British officers stationed in Egypt and India sometimes carried Howdah handguns to replace the smaller .450-caliber issue revolvers. One look at the .577 Pistol cartridge leaves no doubt about its stopping power! The cartridge was discontinued in about 1920. Very rare .22-caliber experimental U. S. Navy cartridge made in 1895 (not to be confused with the .236 USN six-millimeter rimless cartridge used in the Lee Straight Pull U. S. Navy Model 1895 rifle in the Spanish-American War). The steel-jacketed bullet of the .22-caliber cartridge weighs 120 grains, measures .224-inch in diameter, is 1.375 inches long, and seems to have a cupro-nickel wash on its surface. Since the development of smokeless powder, our armed forces have experimented with smaller than .30 calibers. Before World War II, our Garand M1 semiautomatic rifle (.30-06-caliber) was designed for the .276 Pedersen cartridge, which was scheduled to be our service cartridge. However, world conditions got hot, and General Douglas MacArthur, Chief of Staff at the time, decided that it was no time to be changing our small-arms caliber, so he directed that the Garand be adapted for the .30-06 cartridge.

Early reloading tools and bullet molds are often collected in conjunction with old cartridges and guns and especially appeal to those who like to shoot the old models.

Cartridge boards were made by various ammunition producers, for dealers, as a means of displaying the line of ammunition. Some boards were elaborately designed and fancifully framed and, of the number made, few have survived the years. A cartridge board represents the super-ultimate to an advanced cartridge collector, and most of the existing examples are out of circulation in the hands of cartridge buffs. When one gets into the open market, it brings a high price.

Old gun and ammunition catalogues are of great value as reference books to the gun and cartridge collector and some members of the fraternity specialize in them. Ordinary examples of old catalogues may sell for from $5 to maybe $15. For instance, I recently paid $5 for a catalogue of the Newton Arms Company, Fifteenth Edition, which contains quite a bit of info about Newton rifles and cartridges. Really rare catalogues are considered priceless by their owners and are difficult to find.

Old gun-company calendars and posters make fine decorations for a collector's den or gun room and are in great demand, although scarce. For 1960, Winchester-Western distributed an exact reproduction of the colorful Winchester Repeating Arms Company calendar for 1899. Already, it is a collector's item, avidly sought after.

Some fellows collect patent paper, working drawings and even inspectors' gauges for early guns. Others go in for letters written by famous men in the field and for cancelled checks of early gun makers. Still others collect swords and bayonets in combination with military arms, and some concentrate on edged weapons with guns permanently attached to them.

As I said before, the real dyed-in-the-wool gun buff will collect anything pertaining to arms and ammunition and their development. More power to them.

29

Why Not Shoot Your Antique Guns?

MANY GUN COLLECTORS are missing half the fun of their chosen hobby. They just collect, and forget that guns were made for shooting. A great many of these old guns are capable of fine accuracy if properly loaded, and it is interesting to experiment with them.

Before attempting to shoot an old arm it is of utmost importance to determine that the piece will safely handle a charge of the type of powder that it was manufactured to take.

All firearms made before the early 1890's were designed to use black powder, so when we mention powder we definitely mean black powder. The smokeless variety, without exception, is dangerous for use in old guns, and if used will, in most instances, blow up the arm with disastrous results to the shooter.

First, all old—or new, for that matter—firearms should be carefully examined to see if they are loaded. If a muzzle-loader is found to be loaded the charge should immediately be drawn. It shouldn't be shot out, for there's no telling with what it is loaded, or the condition of certain parts of the piece.

In case of a caplock arm which has a cap on the nipple, take it to a safe place where no harm will be done in the event of an accidental discharge and carefully remove the cap. The bullet may then—and not before—be safely removed by the use of a worm, or screw, secured to the end of a rod. Next, the probably hardened powder is removed. Flintlocks are unloaded in similar manner except there is no percussion cap to worry about.

When examining a flintlock rifle or pistol with the idea of shooting it, be sure to see that the breech plug (the plug that is screwed into the rear end of the barrel) is in good and tight. In some instances, the threads at this point are so rusted that the plug really is loose, but held in place by rust all ready to fly out when the piece is fired. Naturally, it would be dangerous to shoot an arm in such condition. Check the flash-hole to see that it has not corroded to such an extent that it is dangerously oversize. Also check to see that the barrel is securely fastened to the stock. I once saw the barrel fly completely out of the stock of an old muzzle-loader when it was fired.

We are mainly concerned with caplock arms, as they are much more plentiful and generally in better shooting condition than flintlocks. With these guns, be sure that the breech plug, and the drum and nipple are in good condition. If the threads of the drum or nipple are rusted or if the flash hole of the nipple is enlarged, new ones should be installed.

The caplock revolver is much more complicated than most other members of the charcoal-burning family, so it should be carefully checked in all details. With the hammer of such a handgun at full cock, a chamber of the cylinder should line up exactly with the bore of the barrel. The cylinder should be firmly locked in this position so that it will not turn the least bit. If one or both of these conditions exist, the arm is unsafe to shoot until repaired.

The threads of the nipples, sometimes called cones, and the nipple seats in the cylinder should be looked over to see that they haven't rusted.

Kentucky flintlock rifle with all accessories necessary for shooting—bullet mold, priming or pan powder horn, horn measure for correct main powder charge, and the powder horn.

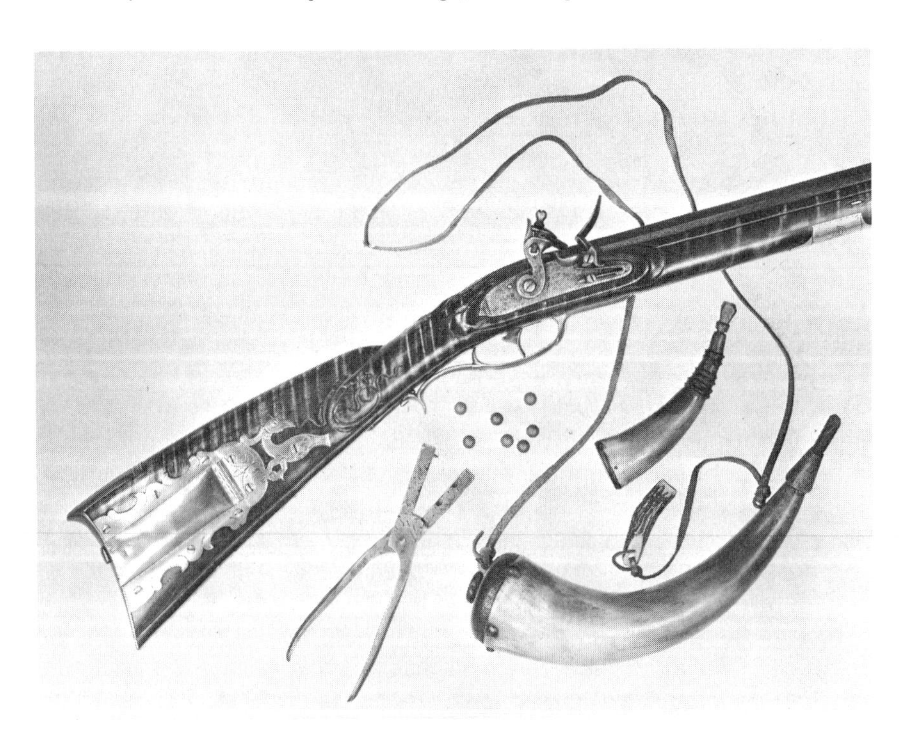

If the clearance between the cylinder and barrel is much more than a hairline, a lot of fire will flash out when the gun is fired. This is dangerous to bystanders and increases the likelihood of more than one chamber firing at the same time, a far from pleasant experience and quite hazardous under certain conditions. Loose-fitting percussion caps—that is, caps that are too large for the nipple—are sometimes responsible for double or multiple firing of the revolver. After definitely determining that an old gun is in condition for safe firing, the proper bullet and powder charge should be established.

For rifles and single-shot pistols using round or conical balls, a snug or push fit in the bore should be obtained by the use of one thickness of greased or saliva-moistened patching material. In certain target rifles, paper patches are used; bed-ticking is good for the large bores, and shirt linen—broadcloth is fine—for smaller calibers.

Conical balls (bullets) with grease grooves and hollow bases should be of push fit without patching material.

The old-timers determined the powder charge for their round-ball rifles by placing a ball in the palm of the hand and pouring out enough powder to completely cover it. Then they made a measure that would hold that amount of powder.

Inasmuch as each gun is a law unto itself, the exact powder charge and grain size should be determined by experiment. Black powder in FG (largest grain size), FFG and FFFG may be purchased from most dealers

Lucky collectors who own such valuable antique guns as this rare Colt Whitneyville-Walker Dragoon revolver hesitate to shoot them because of wear and tear. Actually, there is little or no damage involved in shooting a sound antique gun unless it is in mint condition, in which case its value may decrease with shooting.

who cater to the pig lead and charcoal fan. A large bore gun will work better with large grain powder. FFG is a good all-around size.

Some shooters get more fun out of cap-and-ball revolvers than any other type of firearm—and they are easy to load. The charges are measured into the chambers and the pure lead bullets, round or conical, seated onto the powder by use of the rammer, which is hinged under the barrel.

An indication of the powder charge to use is obtained from an old direction sheet that was originally distributed with Colt cap-and-ball revolvers. The Colt .44 caliber New Model Army Pistol took a charge of twenty-five grains of black powder. The .36-caliber Navy, twenty grains, the 36-caliber Pocket Model fifteen grains, and the .31-caliber Pocket Pistol used thirteen and a half grains, avoirdupois.

Generally, the round ball is as accurate as the conical bullet in cap-and-ball revolvers.

In the early days, unlubricated pure lead bullets were used. But if the gun isn't cleaned after a few shots, accuracy falls off, due to black-powder fouling, which builds up and hardens. To overcome this, a small quantity of cap grease is placed on top of the bullet after it is seated in the chamber. Using this method, I have fired cap-and-ball revolvers all day long without powder caking.

Yes, it's a lot of fun to shoot the old ones, and provided that reasonable care is used and only muzzle-loading guns in generally good condition are tried out, there's no reason for not shooting them.

You'll be surprised how well some of them will shoot!

INDEX